UNSOLVED!
CLASSIC TRUE MURDER CASES

Selected, with an Introduction, by
RICHARD GLYN JONES

PETER BEDRICK BOOKS
New York

First American edition published in 1987 by
Peter Bedrick Books
125 East 23 Street
New York, NY 10010

This selection, Introduction and commentary
© Xanadu Publications Ltd, London

Published by agreement with Xanadu publications Ltd,
London

Library of Congress Cataloging-in-Publication Data

Unsolved! classic true murder cases

  1. Murder. I. Jones, Richard Glyn
  HV6515.U57   1987   364.1'523   86-28836
  ISBN   0-87226-047-X

Contents

Introduction

To fascinate, the mere fact of a murder being unsolved is not enough. After all, hundreds of crimes are committed without even a suspect to show, and thousands of people just vanish never to be seen or heard of again. Nowadays, they do not even make the headlines. No, to fascinate there has to be something more, something to catch the imagination: an unexplained clue, an ambiguity of evidence, a courtroom drama, perhaps with a life hanging in the balance, or simply the sheer thrill of terror.

The cases in this book have all these things in abundance. They are all murders, and every one is a classic of its kind, starting with perhaps the greatest unidentified murderer of them all: Jack the Ripper. Since that appalling series of crimes in 1888, the name of the Ripper has become almost legendary, with a host of books and articles written about him advancing wildly differing theories as to his identity (one of them proposes a Jill the Ripper!), and the case has also inspired movies, novels, plays and even an opera, Alban Berg's *Lulu*. We have been fortunate to be allowed to reprint here for the first time a series of articles by leading Ripperologist Colin Wilson, in which he tells the story of his arrival in London back in 1951 and of his personal quest for the Whitechapel murderer. A worthy opening to our gruesome collection, although Mr Wilson is happy to leave the question of the Ripper's identity as open as ever; which is wise, since however ingenious the theory—and some of them are incredibly complicated—there just isn't the clinching evidence to link the crimes to any one of the suspects proposed so far.

In other unsolved cases there is almost too much evidence.

7

William Herbert Wallace may or may not have killed his wife on that evening in 1932, but once you have read Dorothy L. Sayers' account of the case you will never forget the telephone box, the defective lock, the roaring fire, the non-existent street—and above all you will not forget the mysterious Qualtrough. This is England's classic 'Did He or Didn't He?', and although the debate still rages there has never been a clearer or more sharply analyzed account of the crime than Miss Sayers'. Raymond Chandler once considered writing an analysis of the Wallace case, which he called 'the nonpareil of all murder mysteries', but in the end he did not because, again in his words, 'it has been done to a turn by Dorothy Sayers'. Her piece offers the additional attraction of seeing a mystery writer playing the part of the detective, and Miss Sayers' powerful mind must have been at full stretch when she tried to disentangle that most complex occurrence.

America offers a case equally rich in clues and equally ambiguous (and even more vicious) in the Borden murders. Did Lizzie take an axe and give her mother forty whacks? Again, there is an abundance of detail, again it is maddeningly incomplete, and again many books and articles have been written using the same evidence to 'prove' Lizzie's innocence or guilt, depending on which side the author takes. Edmund Pearson, perhaps America's finest crime-writer, has been accused of bias in his account of this celebrated case (we shall be talking about that later on), but there is no doubt that his piece is easily the best of its kind: *the* place to open any discussion about the redoubtable Lizzie Borden.

One of the most interesting things about the type of detailed description that we find in Sayers' and Pearson's pieces is the startlingly vivid evocation of previous times; in seeking to understand the crimes we gain a sharply focussed view of life in Fall River in the 1880s, or suburban Liverpool in the 1930s. Social histories and novels can do the same thing in a more generalized way, but murder, by forcing us to concentrate upon the tiny things—the gas jets, the wood-burning stove, the maid's daily routine, the local chess-club—can bring a whole era to life in a uniquely powerful manner. This is particularly so in the next of our 'great' murders, the poisoning of Charles

Bravo in his own bed, for which we move back even further in time. Once again, details are plentiful and almost completely ambiguous in interpretation, but here we have added complications in terms of *motive*. At the heart of this crime is the classic triangle of husband, wife and wife's former lover, made stranger by the advanced age of the lover and the intrusive presence of the sinister Mrs Cox, the wife's companion—in bed as well as about the house. Elizabeth Jenkins' account of the Bravo case is sympathetic, very thorough, and it recreates wonderfully the odd personalities in the Priory, and their even more curious lifestyle. Especially for this book, Miss Jenkins has contributed some fascinating further thoughts to her original view of this problem, which suggests another possible solution to this most tantalizing affair.

The Wallace, Borden and Bravo crimes are perhaps the three most notable unsolved cases in the long history of murder, and accordingly they are examined in some depth in the pages that follow. The shorter accounts included are no less fascinating, but in these there tends to be less detail to consider, less information to speculate upon. In the murder of Joseph Ellwell, for instance, the bizarre circumstances of the killing make for interesting reading (and the story is superbly related by the excellent Alexander Woollcott) but the total absence of anyone who could remotely be considered a suspect leaves nothing much to say beyond a statement of the basic facts. What Woollcott says is really all that there is to be said—and the same sort of considerations apply in the cases of Starr Faithfull, Bela Kiss, and The Minister and the Choir Singer (otherwise known as the Hall-Mills affair), though the last of these benefits enormously from James Thurber's drily humorous re-telling, and Willie Stevens is a character that no-one is subsequently likely to forget. The confusion that surrounds the murder of Sir Harry Oakes in Nassau poses the opposite problem; there is almost too much information here, and the astonishingly inept investigation leaves an enormously wide field for speculation. Distinguished critic and crime-novelist Julian Symons has performed a miracle of clarity and compression in his version of the case.

Beyond the immediate shock of gruesome events and strange

circumstances, what ultimately gives these unsolved crimes their fascination is the human personality itself. In testing our wits against those of William Wallace, Lizzie Borden, Florence Bravo or, indeed, Jack the Ripper himself, we are really looking into the depths of our own psyche. How would *we* have behaved in their position? Could we, by any tortured stretch of our imagination, have done what they are assumed to have done? What we see may not be pleasant but, somewhere in our nature, it is there, and it should not be ignored.

—R.G.J.

SOURCES AND ACKNOWLEDGEMENTS

'My Search for Jack the Ripper' by Colin Wilson (first published as a series in the *Evening Standard*, London, 1960). Reproduced by permission of the author and David Bolt Associates.

'A Sort of Genius' by James Thurber, from *My World and Welcome To It*. (published by Harcourt Brace Jovanovich). Copyright © 1942 James Thurber. Copyright © 1970 Helen W-Thurber and Rosemary A. Thurber.

'The Murder of Julia Wallace' by Dorothy L. Sayers, from *Anatomy of Murder*, (first published by Macmillans, New York, 1937). Reproduced by permission of the publisher and the author.

'The Elwell Case' by Alexander Woollcott, from *Long, Long Ago*, renewed copyright © 1968 by Joseph P. Hennessey. Reprinted by permission of Viking Penguin Inc.

'The Balham Mystery' by Elizabeth Jenkins, from *Six Criminal Woman*. Copyright © 1949 by Elizabeth Jenkins. Reprinted by kind permission of Curtis Brown Ltd on behalf of the author.

'Afterword to the Balham Mystery' by Elizabeth Jenkins. Copyright © 1987 by the author.

'Starr Faithfull, Beautiful Wanton' by Sydney Horler, from *Malefactors' Row* (first published by Robert Hale, London, 1940).

'The Borden Case' by Edmund Pearson, from *Masterpieces in Murder* (first published New York, 1924).

'Death of a Millionaire' by Julian Symons, from *A Reasonable Doubt* (1960). Reproduced by permission of Curtis Brown Ltd, London.

COLIN WILSON

My Search for Jack the Ripper

COLIN WILSON

My Search for Jack the Ripper

When I was about eight, someone lent my father a great red volume called *The Fifty Most Amazing Crimes of the Last 100 Years*—I'm not sure why, for I've never yet caught my father reading a book. I was strictly forbidden to read it, in case it gave me nightmares. So I seized on it every time I was left alone in the house, and read it from cover to cover.

I have a copy of it beside me as I write. At the top of every article there is a sketch of the criminal. Landru looks villanous and intellectual; Smith, who drowned his wives in the bath, is an unattractive nondescript. But there is no drawing of Jack the Ripper—only a large black question mark. That question mark started me on my search for Jack the Ripper. It is not logical, of course, but the mind of a child is romantic and not logical. Why should the Ripper be more interesting than Landru, just because he was never caught? No-one has yet discovered how Landru destroyed every trace of his victim's bodies, and, in its way, this mystery is far more interesting than guessing at the identity of Jack the Ripper. And yet it is the Ripper who exercises a fascination beyond that of any other mass murderer.

Most of them are boring little men, like Christie and Haigh—shifty, weak and unimpressive. Many of them have had long criminal records—petty theft, swindling, burglary or confidence trickery—like Heath, Kurten and Dr Marcel Petiot Murder has not yet produced its Caesar, its Napoleon. Murderers are a dull lot.

Perhaps the Ripper was a sneak-thief, with many prison sentences behind him; perhaps it was only Wormwood Scrubs, and not death, that put an end to his amazing career. We shall never be certain. And that is enough to make the Ripper almost

13

unique in the annals of mass murder. We know almost nothing about him.

How many murders did he commit? Even that is the subject of debate. All that we do know is that at least five murders of unparalleled brutality were committed in the latter part of the year 1888. Four of them took place in the Whitechapel district of London, at night; the victims were all prostitutes, although none of them was what we would call 'professionals'. All London panicked. There were meetings in the streets; bands of citizens formed themselves into vigilante groups to patrol Whitechapel at night; thousands of men were questioned, and released; men carrying black bags were attacked by mobs; the Commissioner of Police resigned. And finally, after a lull of more than a month, the Ripper committed yet another crime, this time indoors. The pieces of the victim—a girl in her early twenties—were left spread around the room like bits of a jigsaw puzzle. The panic reached new proportions; there were so many blue uniforms in Whitechapel that the place resembled a police barracks. And then nothing more happened. The murders stopped.

In the following year, 1889, there were two more murders of prostitutes in the Whitechapel area, but without the same appalling mutilations; we shall never know whether the same man was responsible for these.

When I came to London in 1951, Whitechapel exercised a deep and powerful fascination over me, but it was no longer the Whitechapel that Jack the Ripper had wandered around. Whitechapel is still a tough district, but by no means as tough as it had been in 1888. Then, sailors from foreign ships crowded the streets; there were dozens of cheap doss houses where the layabouts could sleep for as little as fourpence a night. And although many 'respectable' married women lived in Whitechapel, a large proportion of the female population was made up of non-professional prostitutes: women without men, women whose men had left them, or simply women whose men had spent their wages on drink.

It was a Whitechapel whose narrow, cobbled alleys were lit by gas lamps that stuck out of the walls; a Whitechapel where human derelicts slept out on the pavements or in entries at night; where murder and robbery were so commonplace that the newspapers didn't even bother to report them. This is the reason why the first two crimes attributed to the Ripper were not mentioned in the newspapers until the inquests.

All this has changed. In 1888, after the Annie Chapman murder, Bernard Shaw wrote a letter to the press in which he suggested that the murderer was a social reformer who wanted to draw attention to social conditions in the East End. He was probably wrong, but German high-explosives have done what Shaw failed to do, and changed the face of Whitechapel. When I first visited the district, bombs had left great empty spaces, and many of the houses were windowless and filled with rubble. After dark, tramps slept on the floors of these ruins. Huge blocks of council flats had sprung up in Hanbury Street, only a hundred yards from the spot where Annie Chapman was murdered, in a yard behind a barber's shop. The council school at the end of Old Montague Street stood black and empty, with political slogans chalked on its walls; now the school has disappeared, with only the black walls of the playground still standing.

The Whitechapel of the Ripper is disappearing day by day. In five years it will be non-existent.

Who was the first victim of the Ripper? It might have been Emma Smith, of George Street, Spitalfield, who was stabbed to death in Osborn Street.

Osborn Street is a sinister little thoroughfare that runs between Old Montague Street and the Whitechapel Road. Emma Smith lived for twenty-four hours after the attack, and stated positively that she had been assaulted and robbed by four men, one of whom had stabbed her with an iron spike in the abdomen. It was a brutal and stupid murder, and its victim was a pathetic, drunken prostitute of forty-five, who had never had more than a few shillings in her purse. She was staggering home drunk at four in the morning when the attack took place. (There were no licensing hours in those days, and many pubs stayed open all night.) An hour later, she was admitted to hospital, her head bruised, her right ear almost torn off. Her death was due to peritonitis.

At the time of the murders, many journalists stated that this
was the Ripper's first crime. It seems unlikely, but the murder
is worth mentioning for the insight it gives into the Whitechapel
of the 1880's. A man or woman might be found like this almost
any morning, robbed and battered; it was too commonplace to
be reported in the daily press.

Many criminologists believe that the murder of Martha
Turner was quite definitely the first Ripper crime. This took
place on August Bank Holiday, 1888.

Martha Turner was a prostitute who lived in George Yard
Buildings, Commercial Street. In the early hours of the morning, she was found on one of the outside landings of the
lodging-house; the post mortem revealed that she had been
stabbed thirty-nine times with some weapon like a bayonet,
and the coroner stated that the wounds had been inflicted by a
left-handed man. Martha Turner had been seen talking to a
guardsman on the evening before the murder, and since the
injuries resembled bayonet wounds, the police started to look
for a left-handed soldier. All the guards in the Tower of London
were paraded, but no arrest was made. Within a few weeks, the
murder had been forgotten. How could anyone guess that a
super-criminal was starting on a series of the most sensational
murders of all time?

No-one knows the precise location of George Yard Buildings
where Martha Turner, probably the Ripper's first victim, was
stabbed to death, but we know the district. If you take a tube to
Aldgate East station on a Sunday morning, you will see
Whitechapel looking something like the Whitechapel of 1888.
Wander up Middlesex Street—known as 'Petticoat Lane'—
and you will find it hard to breathe among the crowds jammed
around the market stalls. To your right and left there are still
cobbled streets that looked exactly the same when Jack the
Ripper walked through them in that 'Autumn of Terror'. Turn
off to your right, walk fifty yards, and you will find yourself in
Commercial Street, the heart and jugular vein of Whitechapel.
Late at night, the police still walk two abreast on these pavements. It is a tough district. And yet if you come here at five
o'clock on a Sunday afternoon, the quiet will surprise you. The

market has closed, and the people of Whitechapel are indoors having their tea, or sleeping off their lunchtime beer.

In 1888, it would have been very different. To begin with, the pubs would still have been open; drunks would have been snoring in the small alleyways off Hanbury Street; but you would have been sensible enough not to explore them, for your chances of being coshed and robbed would have been very high. Probably in no other part of England was so much of the inhabitants' total income spent on beer or spirits—and those were the days when pubs were approximately five times as numerous as they are today. Alcohol was the best chance of forgetfulness, the best way to escape from the dirt and over-crowding and near-starvation.

This may be the reason why Jack the Ripper chose Whitechapel as his hunting-ground. In a sink of human misery, the individual life does not count for much, and the sight of a body prostrate in an alleyway causes no alarm—and, in fact, this is what happened in the case of Mary Anne Nichols, the Ripper's second victim.

In the early hours of the morning of August 31st, 1888, a carter named William Cross was walking along Buck's Row, on his way to work. Buck's Row is another street that has not changed since 1888, although its name is now Durward Street. On one side of the road are small houses, all absolutely uniform, and on the other are blocks of warehouses. Cross noticed something on the other side of the street—a bundle which he took to be a tarpaulin. Then he saw that it was a woman, apparently drunk. She was sprawled in the entrance to an old stable-yard, with her head in the gutter. Another man walked up as he stood there, looking down at her, and the newcomer said: 'Come on, let's get her on her feet.'

They bent down to turn her over, and Cross jumped back, exclaiming: 'Blimey, she's bleeding!'

The other man confirmed this, and commented: 'She's not drunk—she's perishing well dead.'

The two men ran off to find a policeman, and while they were away the body was discovered by another policeman. Within a few minutes, four men were standing around the body. It was about four o'clock in the morning.

Both the policemen were puzzled; they had beats that took them past where the body was now lying, and both of them had been in the street, at either end of Bucks Row, for the past quarter of an hour. Neither had seen anyone. Someone summoned Dr Ralph Llewellyn, who felt the woman's pulse, commented that she had been dead about half an hour, and told the police to take her to the mortuary at the Old Montague Street workhouse. The noise of the discussion attracted several people from the nearby houses. A Mrs Emma Green, whose bedroom was within ten yards of the spot where the body had been found remarked that 'whoever had done it' must have been very quiet, since she had been lying awake for several hours, and had heard no sound.

In the morgue, a young policeman lifted the woman's clothes to gain some idea of the extent of her injuries. What he saw made him vomit. The woman's body had been ripped open from the throat to the stomach. The policeman rushed off to find Dr Llewellyn, who had to give him first aid before he hurried to the morgue.

The first problem was that of identification. This was quickly solved: the woman's name was Mary Anne Nichols, she was forty-two years old, and was known to her friends and acquaintances as Polly. She had been married to a printer's machinist and had born him five children, but they had been separated for seven years; her love of the gin bottle, and the slovenliness that resulted from it, had made him leave her. But as he stood over her body in the mortuary, he was heard to say: 'I forgive you for everything now that I see you like this.'

Since her marriage had broken up, Polly Nichols had sunk steadily lower. She had lived with several men in quick succession and had taken a job as a servant, but she had to steal from her employers to get money for drink, and had then gone to live in Whitechapel. Here she lived as a prostitute, sleeping in nightly doss houses where a bed could be had for fourpence. The main necessity was drink, however, and she would go with a man for the price of a glass of gin—a few pence. A few hours before her death, Polly had arrived at the doss house in Thrawl Street, completely drunk and without money. The lodging-house keeper turned her away. 'Don't

Top: Bucks Row. Bottom: Hanbury Street.

woryy,' she told him, 'I'll soon get the money. Look what a
fine hat I've got.'

An hour later, an acquaintance saw her at the corner of
Osborn Street, where Emma Smith had met her death a few
months earlier. Asked if she was having any luck, Polly replied
that she wasn't, but staggered off up Osborn Street, singing
cheerfully to herself. She probably then turned right into Old
Montague Street and wandered towards Vallance Road at the
end. And somewhere along here, she met a man.

It is still not certain how Jack the Ripper killed Polly Nichols
with so little sound. A bruise on her face indicates that he
clamped his hand over her mouth as he cut her throat, but they
were standing on the three-foot-wide pavement of Bucks Row,
and people were sleeping within a few yards. A policeman
would have been visible at the end of the street, and there were
five others within call. Men were climbing out of bed, getting
ready to go to work, and others were returning home from
Smithfield meat market or from jobs in the docks.

But the luck was with Jack the Ripper; he murdered Polly
Nichols without being heard, and walked off into the dawn.
Ultimately, this is one of the most amazing features of the whole
business—the extraordinary luck that never deserted the
Whitechapel sadist. As far as we know.

The nickname 'Jack the Ripper' was not invented until shortly
before the notorious double murder of September 30th, but the
police were intrigued to hear the phrase 'Leather Apron' used
again and again in connection with the killer. Who was he?

No-one seemed to be sure. Some people described him as a
short, villanous-looking cobbler who carried his clicking knife
in the pocket of his leather apron. Others said that he led a gang
that terrorized prostitutes, and demanded a percentage of their
earnings. Yet other were of the opinion that he was a maniac
who enjoyed frightening women, but who was probably harmless.

The police traced three men whose nickname was Leather
Apron. The most likely suspect was a Polish jew named Pizer,
who was arrested on suspicion. His alibi proved to be unshake-
able, and he was released.

The enquiries came to nothing, but one journalist who visited a doss house in Dorset Street reported an interesting conversation. An old prostitute had wandered in to drink a glass of gin in the early hours of the morning, and the journalist asked her if she was not afraid of meeting Leather Apron. The woman replied: 'I hope I do meet him. I'm sick of this life. I'd rather be dead.'

It throws some light on the mental state of some of these women, and explains why Jack the Ripper never seemed to have had any difficulty finding a victim, even at the height of the terror.

A week after the murder of Mary Anne Nichols the murderer found his third victim, and the pattern of the crime was curiously similar to that in the previous case. Mary Nichols had been turned away from a doss house in Thrawl Street and went off to seek a 'customer'. Annie Chapman was turned out of a doss house in Dorset Street by the keeper, a man named Donovan, and, like Mary Nichols, her life was sacrificed for fourpence, the cost of a bed.

If you walk up Commercial Street from Aldgate, you will pass Dorset Street on your left-hand side. Since 1888, its name had been changed to Duval Street. An extension of Spitalfields market now stands on the site of the lodging-house from which Annie Chapman was turned away in the early hours of Saturday, September 8th. When she left number 35, Dorset Street, she had only a few hundred yards to walk to her death. Halfway down Hanbury Street stands a barber's shop, number 29, which was still a barber's shop when I came to London; I occasionally went there for a haircut. In front of this shop, she met a man who allowed himself to be accosted. As it happened, 29 Hanbury Street was a convenient meeting-place for a prostitute and a prospective client, for a passage runs by the side of the house, with a door at each end. These doors were never kept closed. And at the far end of the passage was a back-yard—a yard that looked exactly as it did 72 years before, when the Ripper entered it with Annie Chapman.

They tiptoed down the passageway, and crept into a corner of the yard by the fence. The man moved closer; she was not even aware of the knife he held in his left hand. A moment later she was dead; the first thrust had severed her windpipe. The man allowed her to slide down the fence. He slipped out of his dark overcoat, and bent over the woman.

The sight of the blood roused in him a kind of frenzy, and for five minutes he remained there, crouched over her. Then he wiped the knife on her skirt, and cleaned some of the blood off his shoes. It was already getting light. He pulled on the overcoat, and crossed to the tap that projected from the fence three feet to the left of the body. From his overcoat he pulled a bundle, which he soaked in water and used to wipe his hands, then he dropped it under the tap. It was a leather apron.

As he pulled it out of his pocket, an envelope dropped out too. The man picked this up, tore off its corner, which was marked with the crest of the Sussex Regiment, and dropped it into Annie Chapman's blood. It would be another false trail for the police to follow. Before leaving the yard, another idea struck him. He searched the pockets of the dead woman's jacket, and removed two brass rings, a few pennies and some farthings, then arranged these carefully by her feet.

A few pennies! Annie Chapman had actually possessed just enough money to stay in the lodging-house! Did she know this? Or could it be that my reconstruction is wrong, and the Ripper took the pennies from his own pocket, as a sort of ironical payment for the pleasure she had given him?

An hour went by, and one of the inhabitants of the house, John Davies, came downstairs and looked into the yard. The body was huddled against a fence. He rushed to Spitalfields Market, where he worked as a porter, and brought two of his fellow-workmen back with him. A few minutes later the police arrived, and the divisional surgeon, Mr Philips, was summoned. His first act was to remove the handkerchief tied around the woman's throat; immediately, the head rolled sideways—it was only just attached to the body. By now, the windows of all the surrounding houses were crowded with sightseers, and some of the local householders even charged a small fee for access to their windows.

Finally, the body was removed to the mortuary, where Mr Philips discovered that the injuries were even more extensive

Contemporary report of the murders in Berners Street and Mitre Square.

than they had been in the case of Mary Nichols. In addition to
numerous stab wounds, there were incisions in the woman's
back and abdomen. Moreover, a careful examination of the
body revealed that certain internal organs had been removed
and taken away by the murderer. So too had two of her front
teeth—a curious touch that repeated a feature of the murder of
Mary Nichols.

At the inquest, Dr Philips expressed the opinion that the
murderer must have been a man with some anatomical knowledge and medical skill. And the weapon must have been some
kind of long-bladed knife, at least eight inches long, which
might have been 'an instrument such as a doctor would use for
surgery'.

Of all the Ripper sites, this one is best preserved. When I
knocked on the door, it was opened by Mrs Kathleen Manning,
who, with her husband and daughter, were the sole occupants
of the house; in 1888, sixteen people lived in it! Mrs Manning
knew that one of the Ripper murders had been committed
there, but she knew no details of the crime. But she told me
how, on one occasion, she mentioned casually that Jack the
Ripper had committed a murder there. To her surprise, the
friend disappeared abruptly into the street, and refused to go
back into the house!

Within a hundred yards of this last grim remnant of 1888,
blocks of council flats have replaced the insanitary lodging-
houses and narrow alleyways through which the Ripper escaped.
If the Whitechapel maniac visited his old haunts today, it is
doubtful whether he would be able to find his way around!

Children sing and play today on the spot where the Ripper's
next victim was killed. It was in the back-yard of the International Working Men's Club at 40, Berners Street, where the
Ripper began the most sensational night's work in English
criminal history. The yard is now part of the playground of a
London council school. No-one I talked to in the area even
knew that Jack the Ripper had committed a murder there. But
although the club has disappeared, the upper part of Berners
Street still looked much as it did when the Ripper walked down
it on the night of September 30th, 1888.

The story of that remarkable night begins at 1 a.m., when the steward of the club tried to guide his pony and trap into the back-yard. He had some difficulty, for the pony was obviously unwilling to enter. The cart blocked the gateway, and the man—Louis Delmschutz—dismounted and peered into the darkness, trying to find out what was frightening the pony.

He did not know it, but he was very close to death. A few feet behind him, still holding a knife, was the Whitechapel murderer. But Delmschutz was not aware of this, for he saw the body of a woman lying against the wall, and rushed into the club to raise the alarm.

The man who would soon be known as Jack the Ripper clambered over the wheel of the cart and slipped out into Berners Street. A moment later, he had disappeared into an alleyway.

Delmschutz emerged from the club followed by a crowd of men who babbled in Polish and Russian. Someone struck a light. The body was that of a tall woman, shabbily dressed. Her throat had been cut, and one of her ears was slightly torn. The ripper had been interrupted. The doctor who was called verified that the woman had been killed very recently indeed.

At the moment that the murderer walked out of Berners Street into the Commercial Road, a prostitute named Catherine Eddowes was released from Bishopsgate Police Station, where she had been in charge for drunkenness since 8 o'clock. Five hours in a cell had not sobered her appreciably; she walked down Bishopsgate towards Aldgate, and the man who had just left Berners Street was walking along the commercial road towards his usual haunts. Berners Street was the farthest afield that he had yet ventured; it is on the right as you go down the Commercial Road towards the East India Dock Road—a good half-mile from Commercial Street, the Ripper's usual hunting-ground. Perhaps he was finding the narrow streets of Spitalfields too hot for him; policemen in rubber-soled boots walked through his alleys, and the tradesmen of Whitechapel also prowled around in bands of 'vigilantes' in the hope of catching the murderer. At all events, the Ripper avoided Spitalfields and walked on towards Bishopsgate.

At the corner of Houndsditch he met Catherine Eddowes.

After a brief conversation, the two of them turned off to the right, into Duke Street. Half-way up Duke Street there is a narrow alleyway called St James Passage; in 1888 it had been known as Church Passage. At its far end lies Mitre Square, which looks today almost exactly as it looked in 1888. On its north side stands a warehouse.

The Ripper was standing on the south side of the square, near Church Passage, when PC Watkins walked through the square on his beat; as the policeman walked by, he pressed back into the shadow of a doorway, and, as soon as the steps were out of earshot, he placed a hand over Eddowes' mouth and cut her throat.

Exactly a quarter of an hour later, PC Watkins again walked through Mitre Square, but this time a mutilated body lay in the right-hand corner, near Church Passage. There was no doubt about the identity of the killer, for the body had been stabbed and cut ferociously, and the face had also been mutilated beyond recognition. And two of the woman's internal organs were missing.

The murderer had not given himself much time. The doctor who examined the body agreed that it must have taken at least ten minutes to inflict so many injuries; besides, the removal of the organs revealed some medical skill. And yet the man walked off without fear into Duke Street and right across Whitechapel into Dorset Street, where he found a convenient sink in which to wash his hands. He had torn off a fragment of the woman's apron, and used this to wipe off the blood. Major Smith, of the City Police, actually saw the sink before the bloodstained water had had time to drain away. Possibly some noise frightened the killer there, for he hurried off without finishing the wash, and continued to wipe off the blood as he walked towards Aldgate again. He finally dropped the piece of bloodstained apron in Goulston Street, within a short distance of the scene of the murder.

Although the Ripper did not know it then, Dorset Street was to be the scene of his most horrible murder, six weeks later.

Early the following morning, the Central News Agency received a letter written in red ink, signed 'Jack the Ripper'. It was their second letter bearing this signature. The first had arrived two days before the murder, and promised 'some more work' in the near future. It also promised to clip off the ladies' ears and send them to the police. No-one had taken the first letter seriously—it was assumed to be another practical joke—but this second letter altered the complexion of things. To begin with, it arrived early in the day, before the news of the murders was generally known. Secondly, there *had* been an attempt to cut off the ear of the first victim in Berners Street, and in his second letter the Ripper apologised for not sending it, saying that he had been interrupted!

The murder of Annie Chapman in Hanbury Street had caused a sensation, but it was nothing to the furore that followed the double murder. Hysteria swept the country. Sir Charles Warren, the unpopular Commissioner of Police, was bombarded with furious telegrams demanding his resignation. (He did, in fact, finally resign.) He was also bombarded with letters full of theories about the identity of the murderer and how to catch him.

It is almost impossible to give an adequate idea of the commotion caused by the murders, but the newspapers of the day devoted more space to them than our own journalists give to a royal wedding.

The police arrested about a dozen men a day, but all of them were released after questioning. Sometimes cranks gave themselves up as Jack the Ripper, for after the two letters had been made public the name had caught the popular imagination.

It took the police some time to identify the two women who had been killed that night. The woman who had been killed in Berners Street was finally identified as Elizabeth Stride, a Swedish woman who had taken to drink and prostitution after some emotional tragedy. (One story has it that she saw her children drowned in an accident on a Thames steamer.) The second victim was less easy to trace, because the mutilations to her face made recognition difficult, and there was one stage when she was identified as an Irishwoman named Mary Anne Kelly—an astounding coincidence in view of what was to come. Eventually, the evidence of her clothes established that she was Catherine Eddowes, aged forty-five, and that she had been in police custody only three-quarters of an hour before she was murdered.

There are very few streets in London whose names have been changed because of some evil notoriety associated with the original name. I know of only one in recent years: Rillington Place, the site of the Christie murders. There seems no doubt that Jack the Ripper holds the record for altering street names: Bucks Row, the scene of the murder of Mary Nichols, is now Dunward Street; Dorset Street, the scene of his last murder, has become Duval Street; and I have never been able to discover what became of George Street, where his first murder took place.

In 1888, Dorset Street was a narrow and shabby thorough-fare running parallel with Spitalfields market, in Brushfield Street. On its north side, extending towards the market, was an entry labelled Millers Court. It was in a house in Millers Court that the Whitechapel murderer killed and dismembered his last victim, a twenty-four-year-old prostitute called Mary Jeanette Kelly.

Five weeks had elapsed since the double murder, and London had begun to hope that the Ripper had left town. The police and vigilante groups began to relax a little. Then, on the morning of November 9th, a man knocked on the door of Mary Kelly to ask for the rent. Getting no reply, he went round to the window and peered through the half-open curtains. What he saw was probably the most appalling sight in London's violent criminal history.

The body that lay on the bed had been taken to pieces like a jigsaw puzzle, and the pieces had been scattered around the room, draped over a picture, or piled upon the sideboard. The heart lay on the pillow, beside the head. The hysteria in London reached new heights.

At some time after two o'clock on the morning of November 9th, the Ripper had been solicited by Mary Kelly outside her room in Millers Court. A man named Hutchinson had actually watched the 'pick-up' and described the man as a 'toff', a short, thickset man with a curling moustache, and carrying a parcel of some sort. A short time later, a neighbour heard Mary Kelly

Mary Kelly entering Millers Court with Jack the Ripper.

singing 'Sweet Violets'. At 3.10 the same neighbour heard a cry
of 'Murder!' And for the next two hours there was silence, as
Jack the Ripper dissected the body. Then the Ripper left, and
the great mystery begins.

For how did he walk through London in clothes that must
have been soaked in blood? Why did he burn a pile of clothes in
the grate of Mary Kelly's room? Above all, what happened to
the murderer after November 9th? There is no case in history of
a maniacal killer who simply stopped of his own accord. Why
did he stop?

These questions have puzzled students of crime ever since.
There are theories by the dozen, but no shred of evidence. Is it
possible, at this late date, that someone will prove the identity
of Jack the Ripper? Are there papers somewhere in police files,
or in some mental home, that tell the whole story?

We come, then, to the theories of the case. My own conviction is
that the Ripper was a sadist—that is, a mentally sick person
who found it impossible to gain sexual satisfaction except by
inflicting pain, or producing large quantities of blood. It is just
conceivable that he might have stopped killing of his own
accord, completely satiated by his final crime.

The best-known theory of the Ripper's identity and motives
was propounded by Leonard Matters, who declared—without
producing a shred of evidence—that the Ripper was a certain
Doctor Stanley, a widower who had been passionately fond of
his only son. The son had died of syphilis, contracted from
Mary Kelly, and Doctor Stanley had then devoted his life to a
search for the woman. He questioned all his victims about her,
and murdered them to make sure that they kept silent. Finally,
after he found Mary Kelly, he ceased to stalk the East End.
Matters alleges that Doctor Stanley died in Buenos Aires, and
made a circumstantial deathbed confession.

One of the most popular theories in police circles is that
George Chapman was Jack the Ripper. Chapman was actually
a Pole whose real name was Severin Klossowski and, at the
time of the murders, he was working as a barber in
Whitechapel. In 1889, Chapman went to America, returning to
London in 1892. During the next ten years, Chapman poisoned

three women with whom he cohabited. There was no motive for the murders; he gained nothing by them; it is almost certain that they were purely sadistic. Chapman was executed in 1903, and Chief Inspector Abberline, who had been in charge of the Ripper investigations, stated dogmatically that Chapman was the Ripper.

Certainly, the dates correspond closely enough, and Hargrave Adam, who edited *The Trial of George Chapman*, declared that the 'Ripper murders' took place in Jersey City while Chapman was living there in 1890. But it is hard to believe that the man who dismembered Mary Kelly could have changed his method to antimony poisoning.

One of the most plausible theories of the Ripper's identity was recently put forward by Donald McCormick in his book *The Identity of Jack the Ripper*. McCormick points out that among the papers of Rasputin, the Russian 'monk' who was murdered in 1917, there was a document which claimed that Jack the Ripper was an insane Russian who had been sent to England by the Tsarist police, with the sole aim of embarrassing the English police. McCormick unearthed a great deal of evidence to connect the Ripper murders with Russian immigrants in the East End, and particularly with a barber-surgeon named Pedachenko.

He claims to have seen an issue of a Russian secret police gazette which reports the death of Pedachenko in a Russian mental home, and mentions that he had committed five murders of women in the East End in 1888. If this piece of evidence is still in existence, it is probably the most definite lead we have to the Ripper's identity. According to McCormick's theory, Pedachenko lived in Walworth, and was helped in his murders by two accomplices. His description corresponds closely with that given by the witnesses who claimed to have seen the Ripper: a short, broad-shouldered man, with a large moustache, well-dressed and wearing a gold watch-chain. If it is definitely established that the Ripper was Pedachenko, one of the great mysteries of crime will be at an end.

The East End of Jack theRipper is disappearing fast, but it is still to be found in a few alleyways and narrow entries into old buildings. His murders were a product of these slums and of cheap gin, starving women and fourpence-a-night doss houses. In spite of their 'local colour', it will be as well when they disappear forever.

AFTERWORD

Since Colin Wilson wrote these words in 1960, many of these places have indeed disappeared, although the curious no longer need to hunt for the Ripper murder sites: guided pedestrian tours are regularly held, and they are well attended by Londoners and visitors alike.

But despite much research and many new theories, the identity of the Ripper remains as elusive as ever. In the absence of further evidence, Pedanchenko has fallen from favour as a suspect, but a new candidate was soon afterwards proposed in the person of M.J. Druitt, a young lawyer with a history of mental instability, who may have been in the Whitechapel area at the time of the killings, and who killed himself shortly after the murders ceased. Other potential Rippers include J.K. Stephen, the Duke of Clarence, and—in an extremely complicated theory involving the painter Walter Sickert, freemasonry, more royalty and the Chief of Police—a threefold murderer (for the whole crazy story see Stephen Knight's Jack the Ripper: the Final Solution*).*

The year 1988 is the centenary of Jack the Ripper, and there are rumours of new 'final' solutions to come, including a new book from Colin Wilson himself. There is no doubt that the final word on the Whitechapel murderer will not be written for some considerable time yet.

JAMES THURBER

*A Sort of
Genius*

JAMES THURBER

A Sort of
Genius

On the morning of Saturday the 16th of September, 1922, a boy
named Raymond Schneider and a girl named Pearl Bahmer,
walking down a lonely lane on the outskirts of New Brunswick,
New Jersey, came upon something that made them rush to the
nearest house in Easton Avenue, around the corner, shouting.
In that house an excited woman named Grace Edwards listened to them wide-eyed and then telephoned the police. The
police came on the run and examined the young people's
discovery: the bodies of a man and a woman. They had been
shot to death and the woman's throat was cut. Leaning against
one of the man's shoes was his calling card, not as if it had fallen
there but as if it had been placed there. It bore the name Rev.
Edward W. Hall. He had been the rector of the Protestant
Episcopal Church of St John the Evangelist in New Brunswick.
The woman was identified as Mrs Eleanor R. Mills, wife of the
sexton of that church. Raymond Schneider and Pearl Bahmer
had stumbled upon what was to go down finally in the annals of
our crime as perhaps the country's most remarkable mystery.
Nobody was ever found guilty of the murders. Before the case
was officially closed, a hundred and fifty persons had had their
day in court and on the front pages of the newspapers. The
names of two must already have sprung to your ming: Mrs Jane
Gibson, called by the avid press 'the pig woman', and William
Carpender Stevens, once known to a hundred million people
simply as 'Willie'. The pig woman died eleven years ago, but
Willie Stevens is alive. He still lives in the house that he lived in
fourteen years ago with Mr and Mrs Hall, at 23 Nichol Avenue,
New Brunswick.

It was from that house that the Rev. Mr Hall walked at

The four suspects: Henry de la Bruyere Carpender (top left), Henry
Stevens (top right), Willie Stevens (bottom left) and Mrs Edward
Hall (bottom right).

around 7.30 o'clock on the night of Thursday the 14th of September, 1922, to his peculiar doom. With the activities in that house after Mr Hall's departure the State of New Jersey was to be vitally concerned. No. 23 Nichol Avenue was to share with De Russey's Lane, in which the bodies were found, the morbid interest of a whole nation four years later, when the case was finally brought to trial. What actually happened in De Russey's Lane on the night of September 14th? What actually happened at 23 Nichol Avenue the same night? For the researcher, it is a matter of an involved and voluminous court record, colorful and exciting in places, confused and repetitious in others. Two things, however, stand out as sharply now as they did on the day of their telling: the pig woman's story of the people she saw in De Russey's Lane that night, and Willie Stevens' story of what went on in the house in Nichol Avenue. Willie's story, brought out in cross-examination by a prosecutor whose name you may have forgotten (it was Alexander Simpson), lacked all the gaudy melodrama of the pig woman's tale, but in it, and in the way he told it on the stand, was the real drama of the Hall-Mills trial. When the State failed miserably in its confident purpose of breaking Willie Stevens down, the verdict was already written on the wall. The rest of the trial was anticlimax. The jury that acquitted Willie, and his sister, Mrs Frances Stevens Hall, and his brother, Henry Stevens, was out only five hours.

A detailed recital of all the fantastic events and circumstances of the Hall-Mills case would fill a large volume. If the story is vague in your mind, it is partly because its edges, even under the harsh glare of investigation, remained curiously obscure and fuzzy. Everyone remembers, of course, that the minister was deeply involved with Mrs Mills, who sang in his choir; their affair had been for some time the gossip of their circle. He was forty-one, she was in her early thirties; Mrs Hall was past fifty. On the 14th of September, Mr Hall had dinner at home with his wife, Willie Stevens, and a little niece of Mrs Hall's. After dinner, he said, according to his wife and his brother-in-law, that he was going to call on Mrs Mills. There was something about a payment on a doctor's bill. Mrs Mills had had an operation and the Halls had paid for it (Mrs Hall

had inherited considerable wealth from her parents). He left
the house at about the same time, it came out later, that Mrs
Mills left her house, and the two were found murdered, under a
crab apple tree in De Russey's Lane, on the edge of town, some
forty hours later. Around the bodies were scattered love letters
which the choir singer had written to the minister. No weapons
were found, but there were several cartridge shells from an
automatic pistol.

The investigation that followed—marked, said one New
Jersey lawyer, by 'bungling stupidity'—resulted in the failure
of the Grand Jury to indict anyone. Willie Stevens was questioned for hours, and so was Mrs Hall. The pig woman told her
extraordinary story of what she saw and heard in the lane that
night, but she failed to impress the Grand Jurors. Four years
went by, and the Hall-Mills case was almost forgotten by
people outside of New Brunswick when, in a New Jersey court,
one Arthur Riehl brought suit against his wife, the former
Louise Geist, for annulment of their marriage. Louise Geist had
been, at the time of the murders, a maid in the Hall household.
Riehl said in the course of his testimony that his wife had told
him 'she knew all about the case but had been given $5,000 to
hold her tongue.' This was all that Mr Philip Payne, managing
editor of the *Daily Mirror*, nosing around for a big scandal of
some sort, needed. His newspaper 'played up' the story until
finally, under its goading, Governor Moore of New Jersey
appointed Alexander Simpson special prosecutor with orders
to reopen the case. Mrs Hall and Willie Stevens were arrested
and so was their brother, Henry Stevens, and a cousin, Henry
de la Bruyere Carpender.

At a preliminary hearing in Somerville the pig woman, with
eager stridency, told her story again. About 9 o'clock on the
night of September 14th, she heard a wagon going along
Hamilton Road near the farm on which she raised her pigs.
Thieves had been stealing her corn and she thought maybe they
were at it again. So she saddled her mule, Jenny (soon to
become the most famous quadruped in the country), and set off
in grotesque pursuit. In the glare of an automobile's headlights
in De Russey's Lane, she saw a woman with white hair who was
wearing a tan coat, and a man with a heavy mustache, who

looked like a colored man. These figures she identified as Mrs Hall and Willie Stevens. Tying her mule to a cedar tree, she started toward the scene on foot and heard voices raised in quarrel: 'Somebody said something about letters.' She now saw three persons (later on she increased this to four), and a flashlight held by one of them illumined the face of a man she identified first as Henry Carpender, later as Henry Stevens, and it 'glittered on something' in the man's hand. Suddenly there was a shot, and as she turned and ran for her mule, there were three more shots; a woman's voice screamed, 'Oh, my! Oh, my! Oh, my!' and the voice of another woman moaned, 'Oh, Henry!' The pig woman rode wildly home on her mule, without investigating further. But she had lost one of her moccasins in her flight, and some three hours later, at 1 o'clock, she rode her mule back again to see if she could find it. This time, by the light of the moon, she saw Mrs Hall, she said, kneeling in the lane, weeping. There was no one else there. The pig woman did not see any bodies.

Mrs Jane Gibson became, because of her remarkable story, the chief witness for the State, as Willie Stevens was to become the chief witness for the defense. If he and his sister were not in De Russey's Lane, as the pig woman had shrilly insisted, it remained for them to tell the detailed story of their whereabouts and their actions that night after Mr Hall left the house. The Grand Jury this time indicted all four persons implicated by the pig woman, and the trial began on November 3rd, 1926.

The first persons Alexander Simpson called to the stand were 'surprise witnesses'. They were a Mr and Mrs John S. Dixon, who lived in North Plainfield, New Jersey, about twelve miles from New Brunswick. It soon became apparent that they were to form part of a net that Simpson was preparing to draw around Willie Stevens. They testified that at about 8.30 on the night of the murders Willie had appeared at their house, wearing a loose-fitting suit, a derby, a wing collar with bow tie, and across his vest, a heavy gold chain to which was attached a gold watch. He had said that his sister had let him out there from her automobile and that he was trying to find the Parker Home for the Aged, which was at Bound Brook. He stuttered and he told them that he was an epileptic. They directed him to a trolley car and he went stumbling away. When Mrs Dixon identified Willie as her visitor, she walked over to him and took his right hand and shook it vigorously, as if to wring recognition out of him. Willie stared at her, said nothing. When she returned to the stand, he grinned widely. That was one of many bizarre incidents which marked the progress of the famous murder trial. It deepened the mystery that hung about the strange figure of Willie Stevens. People could hardly wait for him to take the stand.

William Carpender Stevens had sat in court for sixteen days before he was called to the witness chair, on the 23rd of November, 1926. On that day the trial of Albert B. Fall and Edward L. Doheny, defendants in the notorious Teapot Dome scandal, opened in Washington, but the nation had eyes only for a small, crowded courtroom in Somerville, New Jersey. Willie Stevens, after all these weeks, after all these years, was to speak out in public for the first time. As the New York *Times* said, 'He had been pictured as "Crazy Willie", as a town character, as an oddity, as a butt for all manner of jokes. He had been compared inferentially to an animal, and the hint of an alien racial strain in his parentage had been thrown at him.' Moreover, it had been prophesied that Willie would 'blow up' on the stand, that he would be trapped into contradictions by the 'wily' and 'crafty' Alexander Simpson, that he would be tricked finally into blurting out his guilt. No wonder there was no sound in the courtroom except the heavy tread of Willie Stevens' feet as he walked briskly to the witness stand.

Willie Stevens was an ungainly, rather lumpish man, about five feet ten inches tall. Although he looked flabby, this was only because of his loose-fitting colthes and the way he wore them; despite his fifty-four years, he was a man of great physical strength. He had a large head and a face that would be hard to forget. His head was covered with a thatch of thick, bushy hair, and his heavy black eyebrows seemed always to be arched, giving him an expression of perpetual surprise. This expression was strikingly accentuated by large, prominent eyes which, seen through the thick lenses of the spectacles he always wore, seemed to bulge unnaturally. He had a heavy, drooping, walrus mustache, and his complexion was dark. His glare was sudden and fierce; his smile, which came just as quickly, lighted up his whole face and gave him a wide, beaming look of an enormously pleased child. Born in Aiken, South Carolina, Willie Stevens had been brought to New Brunswick when he was two years old. When his wealthy parents died, a comfortable trust fund was left to Willie. The other children, Frances and Henry, had inherited their money directly. Once, when Mrs Hall was asked if it was not true that Willie was 'regarded as essential to be taken care of in certain things,' she replied, 'In certain aspects.' The quality of Willie's mentality, the extent of his eccentricity, were matters the prosecution strove to establish on several occasions. Dr Laurence Runyon, called by the defense to testify that Willie was not an epileptic and had never stuttered, was cross-examined by Simpson. Said the Doctor, 'He may not be absolutely normal mentally, but he is able to take care of himself perfectly well. He is brighter than the average person, although he has never advanced as far in school learning as some others. He reads books that are above the average and makes a good many people look like fools.' 'A sort of genius, in a way, I suppose?' said Simpson. To which the Doctor quietly replied, 'Yes, that is just what I mean.'

There were all sorts of stories about Willie. One of them was that he had once started a fire in his back yard and then, putting on a fireman's helmet, had doused it gleefully with a pail of water. It was known that for years he had spent most of every day at the firehouse of Engine Company No. 3 in Dennis Street, New Brunswick. He played cards with the firemen, ran errands for them, argued and joked with them, and was a general favorite. Sometimes he went out and bought a steak, or a chicken, and it was prepared and eaten in the firehouse by the firemen and Willie. In the days when the engine company had been a volunteer organization, Willie was an honorary member and always carried, in the firemen's parades, a flag he had bought and presented to the firehouse, an elaborate banner costing sixty or seventy dollars. He had also bought the black-and-white bunting with which the front of the firehouse was draped whenever a member of the company died.

After his arrest, he had whiled away the time in his cell reading books on metallurgy. There was a story that when his

sister-in-law, Mrs Henry Stevens, once twitted him on his
heavy reading, he said, 'Oh, that is merely the bread and butter
of my literary repast.' The night before the trial opened,
Willie's chief concern was about a new blue suit that had been
ordered for him and that did not fit him to his satisfaction. He
had also lost a collar button, and that worried him; Mrs Henry
Stevens hurried to the jail before the court convened and
brought him another one, and he was happy. At the preliminary hearing weeks before, Simpson had declared with brutal
directness that Willie Stevens did indeed look like a colored
man, as the pig woman had said. At this Willie had half risen
from his chair and bared his teeth, as if about to leap on the
prosecutor. But he had quickly subsided. All through the trial
he had sat quietly, staring. He had been enormously interested
when the pig woman, attended by a doctor and a nurse, was
brought in on a stretcher to give her testimony. This was the
man who now, on trial for his life, climbed into the witness chair
in the courtroom at Somerville.

There was an immense stir. Justice Charles W. Parker
rapped with his gavel. Mrs Hall's face was strained and white;
this was an ordeal she and her family had been dreading for
weeks. Willie's left hand gripped his chair tightly, his right
hand held a yellow pencil with which he had fiddled all during
the trial. He faced the roomful of eyes tensely. His own lawyer,
Senator Clarence E. Case, took the witness first. Willie started
badly by understating his age ten years. He said he was
forty-four. 'Isn't it fifty-four?' asked Case. Willie gave the room
his great, beaming smile. 'Yes,' he chortled, boyishly, as if
amused by his slip. The spectators smiled. It didn't take Willie
long to dispose of the Dixons, the couple who had sworn he
stumbled into their house the night of the murder. He answered
half a dozen questions on this point with strong emphasis,
speaking slowly and clearly: he had never worn a derby, he had
never had a gold watch and chain. Mr Case held up Willie's old
silver watch and chain for the jury to see. When he handed
them back, Willie, with fine nonchalance, compared his watch
with the clock on the courtroom wall, gave his sister a large,
reassuring smile, and turned to his questioner with respectful
attention. He described, with technical accuracy, an old revol-

ver of his (the murders had been done with an automatic pistol, not a revolver, but a weapon of the same caliber as Willie's). He said he used to fire off the gun on the Fourth of July; remembering these old holidays, his eyes lighted up with childish glee. From this mood he veered suddenly into indignation and anger. 'When was the last time you saw the revolver?' was what set him off. 'The last time I saw it was in the courthouse!' Willie almost shouted. 'I think it was in October, 1922, when I was taken and put through a very severe grilling by—I cannot mention every person's name, but I remember Mr Toolan, Mr Lamb, and Detective David, and they did everything but strike me. They cursed me frightfully.' The officers had got him into an automobile 'by a subterfuge', he charged. 'Mr David said he simply wanted me to go out in the country, to ask me a very few questions, that I would not be very long.' It transpired later that on this trip Willie himself had had a question to ask Detective David: would the detective, if they passed De Russey's Lane, be kind enough to point it out to him? Willie had never seen the place, he told the detective, in his life. He said that Mr David showed him where it was.

When Willie got to the night of September 14th, 1922, in his testimony his anger and indignation were gone; he was placid, attentive, and courteous. He explained quietly that he had come home for supper that night, had gone to his room afterward, and 'remained in the house, leaving it at 2.30 in the morning with my sister.' Before he went to bed, he said, he had closed his door to confine to his own room the odor of tobacco smoke from his pipe. 'Who objected to that?' asked Mr Case. Willie gave his sudden, beaming grin. 'Everybody,' he said, and won the first of several general laughs from the courtroom. Then he told the story of what happened at 2.30 in the morning. It is necessary, for a well-rounded picture of Willie Stevens, to give it here at some length. 'I was awakened by my sister knocking at my door,' said Willie, 'and I immediately rose and went to the door and she said, "I want you to come down to the church, as Edward has not come home; I am very much worried"—or words to that effect. I immediately got dressed and accompanied her down to the church. I went through the front door, followed a small path that led directly to the back of

the house past the cellar door. We went directly down Red-
mond Street to Jones Avenue, from Jones Avenue we went to
George Street; turning into George Street we went directly
down to Commercial Avenue. There our movements were
blocked by an immense big freight automobile. We had to wait
there maybe half a minute until it went by, going toward New
York.

'I am not at all sure whether we crossed right there at
Commercial Avenue or went a little further down George Street
and went diagonally across to the church. Then we stopped
there and looked at the church to see whether there were any
lights. There were no lights burning. Then Mrs Hall said, "We
might as well go down and see if it could not be possible that he
was at the Mills' house." We went down there, down George
Street until we came to Carman Street, turned down Carman
Street, and got in front of the Mills' house and stood there two
or three minutes to see if there were any lights in the Mills'
apartment. There were none.' Willie then described, street by
street, the return home, and ended with 'I opened the front
door with my latchkey. If you wish me, I will show it to you. My
sister said, "You might as well go to bed. You can do no more
good." With that I went upstairs to bed.' This was the story
that Alexander Simpson had to shake. But before Willie was
turned over to him, the witness told how he heard that his
brother-in-law had been killed. 'I remember I was in the
parlor,' said Willie, 'reading a copy of the New York *Times*. I
heard someone coming up the steps and I glanced up and I
heard my aunt, Mrs Charles J. Carpender, say, "Well, you
might as well know it—Edward has been shot." ' Willie's voice
was thick with emotion. He was asked what happened then.
'Well,' he said, 'I simply let the paper go—that way' (he let his
left hand fall slowly and limply to his side) 'and I put my head
down, and I cried.' Mr Case asked him if he was present at, or
had anything to do with, the murder of Mr Hall and Mrs Mills.
'Absolutely nothing at all!' boomed Willie, coming out of his
posture of sorrow, belligerently erect. The attorney for the
defense turned, with a confident little bow, to Alexander
Simpson. The special prosecutor sauntered over and stood in
front of the witness. Willie took in his breath sharply.

Alexander Simpson, a lawyer, a state senator, slight, perky, capable of harsh tongue-lashings, given to sarcasm and innuendo, had intimated that he would 'tie Willie Stevens into knots'. Word had gone around that he intended to 'flay' the eccentric fellow. Hence his manner now came as a surprise. He spoke in a gentle, almost inaudible voice, and his attitude was one of solicitous friendliness. Willie, quite unexpectedly, drew first blood. Simpson asked him if he had ever earned his livelihood. 'For about four or five years,' said Willie, 'I was employed by Mr Siebold, a contractor.' Not having anticipated an affirmative reply, Simpson paused. Willie leaned forward and said, politely, 'Do you wish his address?' He did this in good faith, but the spectators took it for what the *Times* called a 'sally', because Simpson had been in the habit of letting loose a swarm of investigators on anyone whose name was brought into the case. 'No, thank you,' muttered Simpson, above a roar of laughter. The prosecutor now set about picking at Willie's story of the night of September 14th: he tried to find out why the witness and his sister had not knocked on the Mills' door to see if Mr Hall were there. Unfortunately for the steady drumming of questions, Willie soon broke the prosecutor up with another laugh. Simpson had occasion to mention a New Brunswick boarding house called The Bayard, and he pronounced 'Bay' as it is spelled. With easy politeness, Willie corrected him. '*Bi*yard', said Willie. 'Biyard?' repeated Simpson. Willie smiled, as at an apt pupil. Simpson bowed slightly. The spectators laughed again.

Presently the witness made a slip, and Simpson pounced on it like a swooping falcon. Asked if he had not, at the scene of the murder, stood 'in the light of an automobile while a woman on a mule went by', Willie replied, 'I never remember that occurrence.' Let us take up the court record from there. 'Q.—You would remember if it occurred, wouldn't you? A.—I certainly would, but I don't remember of ever being in an automobile and the light from the automobile shone on a woman on a mule. Q.—Do you say you were not there, or you don't remember? A.—I say positively I was not there. Q.—Why did you say you don't *remember*? A.—Does not that cover the same thing? Q.— No, it don't, because you might be there and not remember it.

A.—Well, I will withdraw that, if I may, and say I was not there positively.' Willie assumed an air of judicial authority as he 'withdrew' his previous answer, and he spoke his positive denial with sharp decision. Mr Simpson abruptly tried a new tack. 'You have had a great deal of experience in life, Mr Stevens,' he said, 'and have read a great deal, they say, and know a lot about human affairs. Don't you think it sounds rather fishy when you say you got up in the middle of the night to go and look for Dr Hall and went to the house and never even knocked on the door—with your experience of human affairs and people that you met and all that sort of thing—don't that seem rather fishy to you?' There was a loud bickering of attorneys before Willie could say anything to this. Finally Judge Parker turned to the witness and said, 'Can you answer that, Mr Stevens?' 'The only way I can answer it, Your Honor,' said Willie, scornfully, 'is that I don't see that it is at all "fishy".' The prosecutor jumped to something else: 'Dr Hall's church was not your church, was it?' hs asked. 'He was not a *Doctor*, sir,' said Willie, once more the instructor. 'He was the Reverend *Mister* Hall.' Simpson paused, nettled. 'I am glad you corrected me on that,' he said. The courtroom laughed again.

The prosecutor now demanded that Willie repeat his story of what happened at 2.30 a.m. He hoped to establish, he intimated, that the witness had learned it 'by rote'. Willie calmly went over the whole thing again, in complete detail, but no one of his sentences was the same as it had been. The prosecutor asked him to tell it a third time. The defense objected vehemently. Simpson vehemently objected to the defense's objection. The Court: 'We will let him tell it once more.' At this point Willie said, 'May I say a word?' 'Certainly,' said Simpson. 'Say all you want.' Weighing his words carefully, speaking with slow emphasis, Willie said, 'All I have to say is I was never taught, as you insinuate, by any person whatsoever. That is my best recollection from the time I started out with my sister to this present minute.' Simpson did not insist further on a third recital. He wanted to know now how Willie could establish the truth of his statement that he was in his room from 8 or 9 o'clock until his sister knocked on the door at 2.30 a.m. 'Why,' said Willie, 'if a person sees me go upstairs and does not see me come downstairs, isn't that a conclusion that I was in my room?' The court record shows that Mr Simpson replied, 'Absolutely.' 'Well,' said Willie expansively, 'that is all there was to it.' Nobody but the pig woman had testified to seeing Willie after he went up to his room that night. Barbara Tough, a servant who had been off during the day, testified that she got back to the Hall home about 10 o'clock and noticed that Willie's door was closed (Willie had testified that it wouldn't stay closed unless he locked it). Louise Geist, of the annulment suit, had testified that she had not seen Willie that night after dinner. It was Willie's story against the pig woman's. That day in court he overshadowed her. When he stepped down from the witness chair, his shoulders were back and he was smiling broadly. Headlines in the *Times* the next day said, 'Willie Stevens Remains Calm Under Cross-Examination. Witness a Great Surprise.' There was a touch of admiration, almost of partisanship, in most of the reporters' stories. The final verdict could be read between the lines. The trial dragged on for another ten days, but on the 3rd of December, Willie Stevens was a free man.

He was glad to get home. He stood on the porch of 23 Nichol Avenue, beaming at the house. Reporters had followed him there. He turned to them and said solemnly, 'It is one hundred and four days since I've been here. And I want to get in.' They let him go. But two days later, on a Sunday, they came back and Mrs Hall received them in the drawing room. They could hear Willie in an adjoining room, talking spiritedly. He was, it came out, discussing metallurgy with the Rev. J. Mervin Pettit, who had succeeded Mr Hall as rector of the Church of St John the Evangelist.

Willie Stevens, going on seventy, no longer visits the firehouse of No. 3 Engine Company. His old friends have caught only glimpses of him in the past few years, for he has been in feeble health, and spends most of his time in his room, going for a short ride now and then in his chauffeur-driven car. The passerby, glancing casually into the car, would not recognize the famous figure of the middle 1920's. Willie has lost a great deal of weight, and the familiar beaming light no longer comes easily to his eyes.

After Willie had been acquitted and sent home, he tried to pick up the old routine of life where he had left it, but people turned to stare after him in the street, and boys were forever at his heels, shouting, 'Look out, Willie, Simpson is after you!' The younger children were fond of him and did not tease him, and once in a while Willie could be seen playing with them, as boisterously and whimsically as ever. The firemen say that if he encountered a ragged child he would find out where it lived, and then give one of his friends the money to buy new clothes for it. But Willie's adventures in the streets of the town became fewer and farther apart. Sometimes months would elapse between his visits to the firehouse. When he did show up in his old haunts, he complained of headaches, and while he was still in his fifties, he spent a month in bed with a heart ailment. After that, he stayed close to home, and the firemen rarely saw him. If you should drop by the firehouse, and your interest in Willie seems friendly, they will tell you some fond stories about him.

One winter Willie took a Cook's tour to Hawaii. When he came back, he told the firemen he had joined an organization which, for five dollars, gave its subscribers a closer view of the volcanoes than the ordinary tourist could get. Willie was crazy about the volcanoes. His trip, however, was spoiled, it came out, because someone recognized and pointed him out as the famous Willie Stevens of the Hall-Mills case. He had the Cook's agent cancel a month's reservation at a hotel and rearrange his schedule so that he could leave on the next ship. He is infuriated by any reference to the murders or to the trial. Some years ago a newspaper printed a paragraph about a man out West who was 'a perfect double for Willie Stevens'. Someone in the firehouse showed it to Willie and he tore the paper to shreds in a rage.

Willie still spends a great deal of time reading 'heavy books'—on engineering, on entomology, on botany. Those who have seen his famous room at 23 Nichol Avenue—he has a friend in to visit him once in a while—say that it is filled with books. He has no use for detective stories or the Western and adventure magazines his friends the firemen read. When he is not reading scientific tomes, he dips into the classics or what he calls the 'worth-while poets'. He used to astound the firemen with his wide range of knowledge. There was a day a salesman of shaving materials dropped in at the enginehouse. Finding that Willie had visited St Augustine, Florida, he mentioned an old Spanish chapel there. Willie described it and gave its history, replete with dates, and greatly impressed the caller. Another time someone mentioned a certain kind of insect which he said was found in this country. 'You mean they used to be,' said Willie. 'That type of insect has been extinct in this country for forty years.' It turned out that it had been, too. On still another occasion Willie fell to discussing flowers with some visitor at the firehouse and reeled off a Latin designation— *crassinae carduaceae*, or something of the sort. Then he turned, grinning, to the listening firemen. 'Zinnias to you,' he said.

Willie Stevens' income from the trust fund established for him is said to be around forty dollars a week. His expenditures are few, now that he is no longer able to go on long trips. The firemen like especially to tell about the time that Willie went to Wyoming, and attended a rodeo. He told the ticket-seller he wanted to sit in a box and the man gave him a single ticket. Willie explained that he wanted the whole box to himself, and he planked down a ten-dollar bill for it. Then he went in and sat in the box all alone. 'I had a hell of a time!' he told the firemen gleefully when he came back home.

De Russey's Lane, which Detective David once pointed out to Willie Stevens, is now, you may have heard, entirely changed. Several years ago it was renamed Franklin Boulevard, and where the Rev. Mr Edward W. Hall and Mrs Eleanor Mills lay murdered there is now a row of neat brick and stucco houses. The famous crab apple tree under which the bodies were found disappeared the first weekend after the murders. It was hacked to pieces, roots and all, by souvenir-hunters.

AFTERWORD

One of the theories about the Hall-Mills case not mentioned by Thurber— perhaps he considered it too ridiculous, although others have taken it seriously enough—is that the murders were committed by the Klu Klux Klan. Apparently the Klan was active and powerful in rural New Jersey at that time, and had a reputation for punishing what it considered to be 'sins against morality' by its own violent actions. Certainly, the affair between the Reverend Edward Hall and Eleanor Mills was no great secret in the neighbourhood, and it is possible that it might have attracted the Klan's attention.

On balance, however, it seems that personal jealousy would have provided a much stronger motive, though whether Mrs Hall's family took matters into its own hands or hired others to take action on their behalf (they could have afforded it) will probably now never be known. All the participants in the case, including Willie Stevens, are now dead, of course, and they died without shedding any further light on the matter.

If the Hall-Mills murders seem destined to be forever labelled 'unsolved', that is certainly not the case in our next murder: that of Julia Wallace in Liverpool in 1931. We have already quoted Raymond Chandler's admiring comments on Dorothy L. Sayers' handling of it; now we skip back across the Atlantic Ocean and settle down to let Miss Sayers guide us through the intricacies of this most fascinating of crimes. To quote another remark of Chandler's: 'The Wallace case is unbeatable; it will always be unbeatable.'

DOROTHY L. SAYERS

The Murder of Julia Wallace

DOROTHY L. SAYERS

The Murder of Julia Wallace

The question is not: Who did this crime? The question is: Did the prisoner do it?—or rather, to put it more accurately: Is it proved to your reasonable satisfaction and beyond all reasonable doubt that the prisoner did it? It is a fallacy to say: 'If the prisoner did not do it, who did?' It is a fallacy to look at it and say: 'It is very difficult to think the prisoner did not do it'; and it may be equally difficult to think the prisoner did do it. . . . Can you say, taking all this evidence as a whole . . . that you are satisfied beyond reasonable doubt that it was the hand of the prisoner, and no other hand that murdered this woman? If you are not so satisfied . . . if it is not established to your reasonable satisfaction as a matter of evidence, as a matter of fact, of legal evidence and legal proof, then it is your duty to find the prisoner not guilty — *Mr Justice Wright's summing-up in the trial of William Herbert Wallace.*

When a crime has been committed, the facts may be examined from three different points of view, very carefully distinguished by the learned Judge whose words I have just quoted. The people ask at once: 'Who did it?' The law never has to ask this question; it waits until the people, through their representatives, the police, have produced a tentative answer by accusing a suspect, and it then asks one question only: 'Did the prisoner do it?'—which is not at all the same thing. The detective novelist, a special sort of person among the people, also asks: 'Who did it?' And his professional bias also prompts him to add, and to press with peculiar interest, that further question of which the law can take no cognisance: 'If the prisoner did not do it, who did?'

The people, guided by instinct and communal experience, are naturally inclined to favour the most simple and obvious explanation of the facts; also it is a relief to their minds if they can believe that the right person has been accused, convicted

53

and put out of the way; they prefer, therefore, on the whole, that the accused person should be convicted. The detective novelist, as a class, hankers after complication and ingenuity, and is disposed to reject the obvious and acquit the accused, if possible; and having done this, the law makes an end of the matter. But the detective novelist is uneasy until he has gone further and found some new and satisfying explanation of the problem.

The case of the Wallace murder shows law and people strangely and interestingly at odds, and provides for the detective novelist an unrivalled field of speculation. William Herbert Wallace was convicted by the people and acquitted by the law; and whether he was guilty or innocent the story is of a sort that (one would think) could only have been put together by the perverted ingenuity of a detective novelist. For if he was guilty, then he was the classic contriver and alibi-monger that adorns the pages of a thousand mystery novels; and if he was innocent, then the real murderer was still more typically the classic villain of fiction. And, since law and people pronounced opposing judgments, any explanation that the novelist can suggest will have the professional merit of flouting opinion and avoiding the obvious.

As in every criminal case that comes to trial, the available facts are only such as were openly produced in court. This restricted material is that upon which people, law and novelist alike have to work. The police, indeed, and the solicitors for the defence, may have had other material at their disposal; but since they did not produce it we may suppose that it was not helpful to them; and the law had to base its decision upon the evidence given at the trial. For the purpose of this article I propose, therefore, to use only the published evidence, so as to place law, people and novelist all in the same position. This is the more easy and suitable since there was, throughout the trial, remarkably little conflict of evidence. With a few trifling exceptions the facts were admitted by both sides; the only difficulty was how to interpret them. It will be seen that there is, from first to last, no single incident which is not susceptible of at least two interpretations, according to whether one considers that the prisoner was, in fact, an innocent man caught in a trap or a guilty man pretending to have been caught in a trap. Nowhere shall we find that 'master-clue' beloved of the detective novelist, which can only lead in one direction. The problem of the Wallace murder had no key-move and ended, in fact, in stalemate.

Nothing could be more respectable, more harmless, more remote from savage violence, than the antecedents of the man who in 1931 was accused of brutally beating out his wife's brains with a poker. Born in 1878, in the Lake District, William Herbert Wallace was apprenticed to the drapery trade. At the age of twenty-three (driven, according to his own statement, by a romantic *Wanderlust*) he sailed for India to take up a post as salesman in Calcutta. Here he fell seriously ill, and, after a period of employment as advertising manager in the less trying climate of Shanghai, was forced for his health's sake to return to England. He obtained a situation in Manchester, where he interested himself in politics and was appointed Liberal Agent for the Ripon Division of the West Riding. While visiting Harrogate, in 1911, he made the acquaintance of his future wife, and on March 24, 1913, he married her. When the war put an end to his political work, he obtained employment as a district agent for the Prudential Assurance Company, and moved with his wife to Liverpool. Here they rented a small, two-storeyed house, No. 29 Wolverton Street, in the suburb of Anfield, and here they lived for sixteen uneventful years, in what seemed to be, in the words of a witness, 'the best relations possible'.

It is, of course, always difficult to be certain how far an appearance of married harmony may not conceal elements of disruption. Unless the parties attract the notice of neighbours or servants by the throwing of crockery, by loud and abusive language, by open infidelities or by open complaints, a great deal of quiet mutual irritation may go on without anybody's being much the wiser. The Wallaces had no children, kept no servant but a charwoman who came in once a week, and saw but few friends; so that, if indeed they had any disagreements, they were better placed than many people for keeping their troubles to themselves. A caustic judge once expressed the opinion that, in the case of a married couple, there was no need

William Herbert Wallace.

to look for the motive for murder, since marriage was a motive in itself; while a cynic once argued upon the same lines to the present writer that, who but the husband *could* want to get rid of the wife? Since nobody else could be shown to have any motive for murdering Mrs Wallace, the murderer *must* be the husband, since after all he *was* her husband, and so had his motive ready made. After his release, Wallace wrote:

> Our days and months and years were filled with complete enjoyment, placid, perhaps, but with all the happiness of quietude and mutual interest and affection. Neither of us cared very much for entertaining other people or for being entertained; we were sufficient in ourselves.

It is in that very self-sufficiency, that intimate companionship extended over days and months and years, that some writers have discovered the hidden motive for the crime: they were too close to one another, the monotony was unendurable, the husband's nerves gave way under the silent strain and he killed his wife because he was bored with her. If there had been open quarrels, that fact would have told against the husband; equally, the fact that there were no such quarrels may be held to tell against him also. Where human nature is concerned, there can never be any certainty; it all depends on the way you look at these things.

And yet it is exceedingly rare, when a husband and wife are at odds, that nobody at all should have any knowledge of their difficulties. One might think that, at some time or other during those sixteen years, the self-control of a hopelessly irritated husband would have given way. It is quite certain that, had there been any evidence at all of domestic trouble, the prosecution would have produced it, for the sheer absence of any comprehensible motive was the weakest point in their case against Wallace. There was, at any rate, no 'eternal triangle'—no other woman and no other man; if there had been any such persons it is almost inconceivable that the researches of the police could have failed to unearth them. Nor could Wallace have had any financial motive for murdering his wife, since, though she was insured for a small sum, his accounts were in perfect order and he had a sufficient balance in the bank. We may weave what fancies we like about the situation; the *fact* remains that no evidence of motive was ever put forward for the murder of Julia Wallace by her husband or anybody else.

What evidence can we, *in fact*, produce about the relations between the Wallaces?

There is, first of all, the undisputed fact that they lived together for nearly eighteen years and had no children. What conclusion we ought to draw from this circumstance we do not know, for nothing was ever said about it. Had their married relations always been normal? We do not know; at any rate, no evidence was brought to the contrary. Did Wallace, perhaps, blame his wife for their childlessness and determine to put her out of the way so that he might marry someone else before it was too late? It is a possibility; he was in no position to get a divorce, and the scandal of an irregular relation with another partner would no doubt have prejudiced him in his employment. We can only say that the prosecution made no suggestion of any such motive. Or did Mrs Wallace perhaps lay the blame on her husband and drive him to murderous fury by taunts and insults? There was a case in the last century—closely parallel in some respects to the Wallace case—in which that situation does seem to have occurred; but here, there is again no evidence. Neither William nor Julia Wallace was of strong physique, and their means, though sufficient, were not ample; they may have been incapable of having children, or they may, for reasons of health or finance, have agreed to remain childless; we do not know—all is conjecture.

In the absence of a family, what were their common interests? Here we can draw upon the evidence of the witnesses, on the evidence of Wallace himself at the time of the trial and after, and on the evidence of Wallace's diaries—of which those portions at any rate which were written before the murder may be supposed to be fairly reliable.

In Wallace, then, we have one of those mild dabblers in science and philosophy common among self-educated men of a speculative turn of mind. A witness for the prosecution described him, aptly enough, as ' a man who is intellectual, and varied in his habit of study, and that sort of thing'. It was, indeed, exactly that sort of thing. He 'looked at all things with the eyes of a naturalist'; he read and noted in his journal the newest theories about atomic physics; he made amateur chemical experiments in a back bedroom, which he had fitted up as a laboratory; he strove to model his behaviour upon the stoic precepts of Marcus Aurelius; he was interested in music, and at the age of fifty 'took up' the violin (in half a dozen lessons from a friend); and he was a keen and skilful chess-player. Witnesses spoke of him as 'a placid man', 'scrupulously honest', 'an absolute gentleman in every respect'; one feels that he was perhaps a little fussy, a little pedantic, a little too fond of improving himself and other people, and something perhaps of an old maid married.

His wife Julia was, in his own words, 'an excellent pianist, no mean artist in water-colour, a fluent French scholar, and of a cultured literary taste'. She was dark and small, not very robust, but apparently capable of doing the greater part of the work of their little six-roomed house. One gathers that they enjoyed country rambles and excursions together (he, the naturalist, and she, the artist); that in the evenings they sometimes went out together to a play or cinema, or enjoyed a musical evening at home (she, the pianist and he, the fiddler) in the front sitting-room that was otherwise only used for 'company'. True, Julia failed to appreciate the 'inner significance and real meaning' of *The Master Builder*, and her husband thought this strange; but she evidently did her best to share his interests.

> When she was with me [he wrote after the trial] her passion for novelty and discovery gave me countless hours of joy in explaining, as far as I could, the great riddles of the universe. . . . As I passed from practical to theoretical science my wife tried hard to keep pace with me in the newer problems of physics. . . . The hours and hours we spent together examining specimens under the microscope.

The perfect wife, surely, and model womanly woman! Only one phrase in the diary may perhaps reveal the more trying side of womanliness:

> Nothing can ever bring her back, and however much I want her, or however much I miss her loving smiles and aimless chatter . . .

Was that aimless chatter perhaps less lovable in reality than in retrospect? But probably the plainest expression of the feeling between them is to be found in Wallace's sober entry for March 25, 1929, nearly two years before the murder:

> Julia reminds me to-day it was fifteen years ago yesterday since we were married. Well, I don't think either of us regrets the step. We seem to have pulled well together, and I think we both get as much pleasure and contentment out of life as most people . . .

One feels, perhaps, that here the pupil of the stoics is controlling the pen more firmly than on some other occasions; but it is scarcely the expression of a man driven to madness by disillusionment and exasperation.

And now, having made ourselves acquainted with the principal characters, we come to the strange plot of the melodrama.

> The only time I left my wife alone in our little home [wrote Wallace in a published article] was to visit the Chess Club at the City Café, to deliver my lectures [on chemistry] at the Technical College, or to attend to my insurance business. On all other occasions my wife was my inseparable companion.

Monday was one of the days on which the Liverpool Central Chess Club held its regular meetings, and accordingly, on the night of Monday, January 19, 1931, Wallace left his inseparable companion at about a quarter-past seven, in order to attend the meeting and take part in a championship competition in which his name was down to play that evening. At about 7.20 the telephone rang in the café and was answered by the waitress, who then called Mr Beattie, the captain of the Chess Club, to come and take the message. The caller, who spoke in 'a strong rather gruff voice', asked whether Mr Wallace was in the club. Mr Beattie said no, he was not, but would be there presently; would the caller ring up again. The caller said, 'No, I am too busy; I have got my girl's twenty-first birthday on, and I want to see Mr Wallace on a matter of business; it is something in the nature of his business.' Mr Beattie then offered to take a message, and the caller said he wanted Wallace to come and see him the following evening at 7.30, giving his name as 'R.M. Qualtrough', and his address as 25 Menlove Gardens East, Mossley Hill'.

Half an hour or so later, that is, at about a quarter to eight, Mr Beattie saw that Wallace had come into the café and started a game of chess with a man called McCartney. 'Oh, Wallace,' said Mr Beattie, 'I have a message for you.' 'Oh, who from?' said Wallace. 'From a man named Qualtrough,' replied Mr

Beattie. 'Qualtrough, Qualtrough,' repeated Wallace. 'Who is Qualtrough?' Mr Beattie said, 'Well, if you don't know, I don't,' and gave the message. Wallace again said, 'I don't know the chap. Where is Menlove Gardens East?' Mr Beattie did not know, nor did another member of the club whom they consulted, but they all agreed that it was probably to be found in the same district as Menlove Avenue. Having noted down the name and address in his diary, Wallace went on to finish and win his game of chess. Nothing further seems to have been said about the mysterious message until Wallace was going home, accompanied by two other members of the club. He then asked, 'Qualtrough? Have you heard of that name before?' His friend said he had only heard of one person of that name, and they then discussed the best way of getting to Menlove Gardens. Wallace said he was not sure whether he would go at all, but if he did, he would take the tram to Menlove Avenue. So ended the first act of the tragedy.

Now, whatever else is uncertain about the Wallace case, one thing is abundantly clear: that, whoever sent the telephone message from 'Qualtrough', it was not a genuine message but the first deliberate step towards the commission of a crime. At the trial, Wallace was accused of having sent the message himself, by way of establishing an alibi for the Tuesday evening; he himself maintained that it was sent by an enemy, so as to lure him away from home. Any argument directed to prove or disprove the genuiness of the message is beside the point: there never was an R. M. Qualtrough; there never was a Menlove Gardens East; there never was any genuine insurance business to be transacted. Whoever sent the message was the murderer; all we have to inqure is, was 'Qualtrough' Wallace, or was he somebody else?

The first interesting fact is that the message was sent from a telephone kiosk about four hundred yards from Wallace's own house, and sent at exactly the time that Wallace was due to pass that kiosk on his way to the Central Café. Counsel for the prosecution made great play with this fact.

Assuming he [Wallace] left the house on his three minutes journey at 7.15, he could easily have been in the box by 7.18; but by a singular coincidence the man who wanted him, Qualtrough, was in that telephone box at the identical time at which Mr Wallace might have been there, and, by another singular coincidence, was trying to ring up Mr Wallace. . . . It was a box that he [Wallace] has used. . . . The man in the box telephoned through to the Central Café. Nobody but Wallace knew that Wallace was going to be at the café; no one. . . . The man rings up, and . . . assuming that it was the prisoner . . . no doubt disguising his voice. . . . He is asked if he will ring up later. . . . He says 'No.' . . . If it was Wallace, obviously he would say he could not ring up later, because he would not be there. If the man had important business, and he wanted to speak to a man he did not know, do you not think he would then want to ring up later? And remember, when he was ringing up he was four hundred yards only from the house of Mr Wallace, and it is perfectly clear that he did not call there, and he did not leave any note there. What he did do, was to telephone up to a place where he could not know he [Wallace] was going to be—it is common ground that the man who rang up . . . was planning the murder. . . . You would have thought he would be certain to see that his message . . . would get home. . . . He does nothing of the sort. . . . He never inquires afterwards whether Wallace came there and got his message, but he leaves the whole thing in the air.

Now this argument is curiously contradictory. At one point, counsel asks, 'If the man had important business, would he not have done so-and-so?' But in the next breath he admits that the man had no important business, except crime; therefore it is clear that whatever his actions might be, they could not be such as one would expect of an innocent man making a business appointment. The question that counsel was really trying to ask was not: 'Can we now believe the message genuine?' but: 'Could Wallace at that time have innocently believed the message genuine?' But let us examine the whole business of the telephone call carefully, point by point; for it is the very centre of the problem.

First of all: Is it true that nobody but Wallace could possibly have known that he was going to the City Café on January 19th? It is not true. Wallace was scheduled to play a championship game that night, and the list of fixtures was openly displayed in the café where anybody might see it. The meetings of the chess club always began at about the same time—roughly 7.45. Wallace was a fairly regular attendant, and we know that he was definitely expected on the Monday, because Mr Beattie said as much to 'Qualtrough'. Therefore, any frequenter of the café might reasonably have looked to find him there.

Secondly: Where was the famous telephone kiosk, and what was it like? The Wallaces' house was one of a row, all having their front doors upon Wolverton Street and their back doors upon a lane running roughly parallel to the street. At a point some four hundred yards from No. 29 street and lane converged, and at this strategic point stood the kiosk—a dim little erection, lit only by the reflected rays of a street-lamp. Whether Wallace left his house by the front or the back door, he, was bound to pass the kiosk on the way to the Central Café. Equally, anybody who wanted to know whether he was going to the Central Café that night had only to stand at the corner of the two streets and see whether he passed the kiosk. Thus counsel's 'coincidence' turns out to be no coincidence at all, for if 'Qualtrough' was not Wallace, then he must have been watching in or near the kiosk to make sure that Wallace went to the café, and, having made sure, he telephoned.

Is there anything that might indicate whether 'Qualtrough' was Wallace or somebody else? There is the curious evidence of the girl at the telephone exchange. She was spoken to by the caller, who said: 'Operator, I have pressed button A, but have not had my correspondent yet.' She then connected him and thought no more about it. Now, counsel drew attention to the fact that Wallace often spoke from that call-box; he should, therefore, have known how to use it. But the whole point of button A's existence is that you should *not* press button A *until* you have heard your 'correspondent' speak. Either, then, 'Qualtrough' was unfamiliar with a public call-box, or he was too much agitated to remember the procedure. Whoever he was, he may well have been agitated: but the more usual mistake with button A is to forget to press it at all. The point is a trifling one; but, such as it is, it tells, perhaps, slightly in Wallace's favour.

Now comes the question why 'Qualtrough' rang up when he did. If he was Wallace, then 7.18 was obviously the only time at which he could ring up. If not, then why did he not wait till Wallace had reached the café, or deliver a note or message at the house? There can be only one answer to this: that his face, voice and handwriting were known to the Wallaces and that he did not dare to risk recognition. Still less could he ring again

later in the evening. The voice might have been disguised; Mr
Beattie said that at the time it did not seem to him to be
anything but a natural one, and that it 'would be a great stretch
of imagination' to say that it was anything like Wallace's. But
supposing it was not Wallace, how could 'Qualtrough' venture,
in his own voice or a disguised one, on a prolonged conversation
with Wallace? He would have had to answer every kind of
inconvenient question: details about himself, details about
'Menlove Gardens East', details about the mysterious 'business', and he would have had to be an uncommonly skilful liar
to get through without letting Wallace smell a rat. The tale of
the birthday party was a little fishy; but the vague message sent
through Mr Beattie had its merits, for it held out a bait of
indeterminate size and splendour.

> Seeing the name and the daughter coming of age had been suggested
> [said Wallace in court] I considered it might result in a policy of
> something like £100 endowment, or something of that nature. I did not
> expect it would be less than that.

To a man in Wallace's position, that would have been
business worth getting. Besides, if the name was not to be found
in the directory, or the address was discovered to be non-
existent, how easy to suppose that Mr Beattie had heard
wrongly or noted the details carelessly.

All through this case one has to remember that Wallace lived
in a small way and worked for very small profits. Nobody is
more pertinacious than your small insurance agent. He will go
miles to secure a few shillings. He would not be disconcerted by
failing to find 'R. M. Qualtrough' in a list of householders; the
man might be a lodger, a domestic servant, a newcomer to the
district. Wallace said afterwards that he had not thought to
look up the address in the directory; but in any case, new streets
and houses were being run up all over the place at a great rate,
and it might have been one of those. It was nearly as certain as
death and taxation that Wallace would never rest content till he
had investigated the whole matter personally and on the spot.

And finally, did 'Qualtrough' take no steps to ascertain that
his message had 'gone home'? We cannot say that. He had only
to follow Wallace to the café. Whoever he was, he must have
been a habitué of the place to have known of Wallace's engage-

ment to play there that night. It is possible that he actually arrived in time to hear the message delivered. Once we admit that he must have known Wallace and the café, all the rest follows. Any explanation that fits Wallace as the murderer also fits any murderer we may like to postulate.

The stage being now set, the curtain goes up on Act II. It is preceded by a curious little interlude. At 3.30 on the following afternoon, James Edward Rothwell, a police constable, was bicycling along a street called Maiden Lane, and saw Wallace walking on the pavement.

> He was dressed in a tweed suit and a light fawn raincoat. His face was haggard and drawn, and he seemed very distressed. He was dabbing his eye with his coat-sleeve, and he appeared to me as if he had been crying.

It was suggested to P.C. Rothwell that Wallace's eyes might have been merely watering from the cold, but the constable stuck to his opinion. On the other hand, we have the evidence of three women upon whom Wallace called between 3.30 and 5.45 to collect their insurance, that he seemed 'calm' and 'just as usual', that he cracked jokes with one and enjoyed a cup of tea with another. Whether the constable or the ladies were the better qualified to detect signs of emotion in an insurance agent is a question. Women are said to be observant by nature, and policemen should be observant by profession. The one certain fact is that, on that morning and afternoon of Tuesday, January 29th, Wallace transacted all his business in his ordinary accurate manner.

He stopped collecting, by his own account, at a few minutes to six and then went home for his tea. And it is now that we come to the one serious conflict of evidence in the whole case. Some time between 6.30 and 6.45 the milk-boy called with the milk; Mrs Wallace took it in, and that is the last occasion on which she was seen alive by any disinterested person. The milk-boy, Alan Croxton Close, was 14 years old, and in his evidence he said he knew he delivered the milk at 6.30, because when he passed Holy Trinity Church it was 6.25, and it took him five minutes to get from there to 29 Wolverton Street.

On the other hand, Allison Wildman, aged 16, who was delivering a newspaper at No. 27, next door, said she got there at 6.43, and that when she had delivered her paper and gone,

Close was still standing at the door of No. 29. She, too, relied on Holy Trinity Church clock. Moreover, she was seen by some boys leaving Wolverton Street some minutes after 6.40. Further doubt was thrown on Close's evidence by a number of other little boys who maintained that on the day after the murder he had told them, 'I saw Mrs Wallace at a quarter to seven'; and it was rather suggested that young Close had altered his opinion to fit the police case against Wallace. It is a close thing—a matter of five or eight minutes—the kind of point on which nobody but the characters in a detective novel can reasonably be expected to be accurate; its importance (just as in a detective story) lies in the fact that, if Mrs Wallace was alive at 6.45 it was almost impossible that Wallace could have murdered her; for at 7.10 at the very latest he was changing trams at the junction of Smithdown Road and Lodge Lane, a good twenty minutes' ride from his home. To commit the murder between 6.30 and 6.50 would have been pretty quick work; to commit it between 6.45 and 6.50 would have been something like a conjuring trick.

Wallace stated that he left the house that evening by the back door. This, he explained, was his usual custom in the early part of the evening.

> If I was going out after six, and I knew I was going to be out an hour or two, I might go out by the back door and ask my wife to come down and bolt it after me, and on my return come in by the front door, because I would have my key.

This seems reasonable; we get the picture of the front door with its patent lock and the backyard door with its builder's lock and iron bolts, which (and this must be borne in mind) the householder would *expect* to find bolted against him on his return. Mrs Wallace, on this occasion, accompanied her husband—or so he said—by way of the back as far as the backyard gate and there he left her, with instructions to bolt the door after him.

Now, if 'Qualtrough' was lurking about the telephone kiosk at ten minutes to seven on that dark January night, what might he have seen? In the light of the adjacent street-lamp he would have seen Wallace's slight figure, dressed, not in the fawn raincoat (for the weather had cleared), but in an overcoat, come briskly up from the back lane towards the tramway stop.

That would have been his cue that the coast was clear at No. 29, and that his dupe was out of the way for a good hour at least. Now would be his moment for going to the house. If, by any chance, Mrs Wallace had somebody with her, he could still make some excuse and withdraw; but if she was alone, the path to crime lay open.

Nobody (except the not impossible 'Qualtrough') seems to have seen Wallace at this stage of his journey. He is next heard of some time between 7.6 and 7.10, at the tram-junction at Smithdown Road, asking the conductor, one Thomas Charles Phillips, whether the tram went from there to Menlove Gardens East. Phillips replied, 'No, you can get on No. 5, 5A, 5W or a No. 7 car.' There was nothing in this to suggest to Wallace that Menlove Gardens East might not exist, so he got on, observing that he was a stranger in the district and had important business at Menlove Gardens East. Later, while paying his fare, he reminded the conductor that he wanted to be put off at Menlove Gardens East, and a little later mentioned his destination for the third time and was told to change at Penny Lane. When they got there, Phillips shouted 'Menlove Gardens, change here,' and saw his fussy passenger sprinting to catch the No. 7 car, which went to Calderstone. The time was then 7.15.

On the Calderstone car, Wallace again anxiously asked the conductor to put him off at Menlove Gardens East. Accordingly, he was put off at Menlove Gardens West, the conductor saying to him, 'You will probably find Menlove Gardens East in that direction.' Wallace replied, 'Thank you; I am a complete stranger round here.'

Now, it was said afterwards that these persistent inquiries and repeated asserverations that he was a stranger in the district and had important business there, were unnatural, and showed that Wallace was eager to impress his personality upon the tram-conductors in order to establish his alibi. This may be so—though, if fussy inquiries and irrelevant personal confidences are a proof of criminal intent, then the proportion of criminals engaged daily in establishing alibis on public vehicles must be a shockingly high one.

It is interesting that he did not succeed in impressing himself

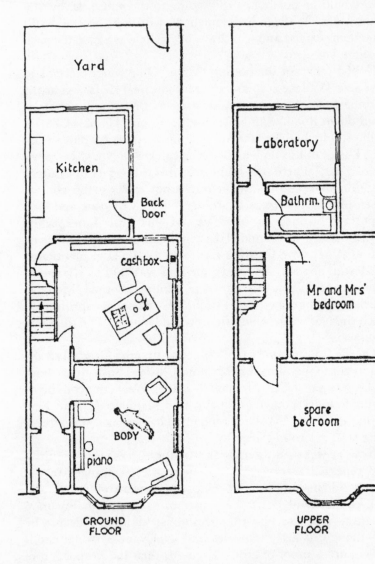

Plan of the Wallace house.

upon the conductor of the first tram—the one nearest home. The early part of the alibi is obviously the most important; did he, being guilty, think it dangerous to attract attention to himself at that stage in the proceedings? Or did he, being innocent, make no inquiry, merely because he knew the way as far as Smithdown Road? We may note at this point that Wallace appears never to have tried to establish an alibi in the strict sense of the word. He never suggested, for instance, that he was already out of the house by the time the milk-boy came. A villain in a book would, one feels, not have neglected this important point; but the argument cuts both ways, since a definite statement about times may be challenged; a mere vagueness leaves the onus of proof upon the prosecution.

Next comes the evidence of Sydney Herbert Green, a clerk, who found Wallace wandering about Menlove Gardens West and looking in vain for Menlove Gardens East. Green informed him that there was no such place. Wallace then said he would try 25 Menlove Gardens West. This he did, asking the wife of the occupier whether anybody called 'Qualtrough' lived there. She said no, and he went away.

Then came a complication which was very damaging for Wallace, for whem he had inspected Menlove Gardens North and South he roamed along Menlove Avenue and then found himself (by his own account unexpectedly) in a road which he did know. Between Menlove Avenue and Allerton Road runs Green Lane, and in Green Lane lived a Mr Crew, who was a superintendent of the Prudential Assurance Company and whom Wallace had visited on five occasions to take violin lessons. This, said the prosecution, proved that Wallace was lying when he said he did not know the district. Mr Crewe said in cross-examination that the violin lessons had been given two years ago and always on winter evenings after dark. There are, of course, some people who, after passing half a dozen times along a tram-route by night are familiar with every crossing and turning to left and right of the route, and who never visit a house without making themselves acquainted with all the surrounding streets. Others (of whom the present writer is one) allow themselves to be carted incuriously from point to point, remaining in the end as ignorant of the general topography of

the district as when they started. Wallace, if one may trust to
his evidence, was of the latter sort. 'How used you to go to
Woolton Woods with your wife?'—'I probably inquired of
some driver of a car, which car would take us there and got on
that car.' A statement which, if untrue, was well invented to
square with his known behaviour on the night of the crime. As
for knowing the lay-out of Menlove Gardens, Mr Crewe, who
had lived just round the corner for three and a half years, said
definitely in evidence that, previously to the trial, he himself
had not had any idea whether there was a Menlove Gardens
East or not.

At any rate, suggested counsel, when Wallace found himself
in Green Lane, why did he not call at Mr Crewe's house and ask
his assistance in finding 'Qualtrough's' address? Wallace replied that he did; he knocked at the door but could get no
answer. Mr Crew was, in fact, out that night; so that the
statement was not capable of disproof.

Having failed here, Wallace met a policeman and again
inquired for Menlove Gardens East. The constable said, cate-
gorically, that there was no such place: there was Menlove
Gardens, North, South and West, and Menlove Avenue, but no
Menlove Gardens East. He suggested that Wallace should try
25 Menlove Avenue (which he pointed out); Wallace thanked
him and then asked where he could find a directory. The
constable said he could see one at the newsagent's in Allerton
Road, or at the police station or post office. Wallace then
explained, 'I am an insurance agent looking for a Mr Qualtrough who rang up the club and left a message for me with my
colleague to ring up [? visit] Mr Qualtrough at 25 Menlove
Gardens East.' Whether this outburst of confidence was a
necessary part of alibi-faking, or was merely the ordinary
citizen's apologetic anxiety to justify his existence in the eyes of
the police, is again a matter of interpretation. Wallace then
said, 'It is not 8 o'clock yet?' and the constable agreed that it
was only a quarter to. The alibi again? or only a reasonable
desire to know whether the newspaper shop would still be
open? However that may be, it is in the shop that we next find
Wallace at 8.10, searching the directory for Menlove Gardens
East. In the meantime, he had apparently been looking for the

post office, but could not find it. He hunted the directory for some time, and then said, 'Do you know what I am looking for?' The manageress said (not unnaturally) that she did not, he then told her that he was looking for 25 Menlove Gardens East. She then assured him that there was no such place. Curiously enough, he does not seem to have mentioned the name of Qualtrough in the shop; he said that he looked for the name in the book and could not find it; and by this time he was probably convinced that, whoever Qualtrough was, he was not a householder.

It was now about 8.20, and according to Wallace himself, he was beginning to get a little alarmed. If he was innocent, this was perhaps not unnatural. There did seem to be something rather queer about 'Qualtrough', and he could not but remember that there had been one or two recent burglaries in the neighbourhood of Wolverton Street, and that it was a well-known trick of burglars to lure away householders with bogus telephone messages. Further, this was a Tuesday night—the night when, as a rule, he had a good deal of the insurance money in the house. So, giving up the vain search for Qualtrough, he walked to the nearest tram-stop to begin the journey home.

In the meantime, Mr John Sharpe Johnston, an engineer, who lived next door to the Wallaces at 31 Wolverton Street, was getting ready to go out with his wife for the evening. The two families had been neighbours for the last ten years, and knew one another, in Mrs Johnston's own words, 'as neighbours'. There seems to have been no very great intimacy. In all those years Mrs Johnston had been into No. 29 'about three times', and then only into the front sitting-room. On all three occasions Wallace had been absent, so that Mrs Johnston had never seen the Wallaces together in their own home; nor, evidently, had the two women been accustomed to run in and out of each other's back kitchens in the informal way that neighbours sometimes fall into. Mr Johnston had, indeed, seen the Wallaces together from time to time, and thought them 'a very loving couple, very affectionate'; but he cannot have known them very well, for he had never heard Mrs Wallace's Christian name—or, if he had, not often enough to remember what it was. Of one thing, however, the Johnstons were quite certain: they had never heard any quarrelling going on next door, though, since the houses shared a party-wall, they would have been likely to hear anything exciting that there was to be heard.

A little before 8.45 on the Tuesday evening, the Johnstons heard somebody knocking, as it might be with a fist or palm of the hand, at the Wallaces' back door. This was nothing unusual, so they paid no particular attention to it. On going out, by way of the back door, into the entry that runs parallel to Wolverton Street, they met Wallace, just coming down at an ordinary walking pace from the Breck Road end of the entry towards his own back door. To Mrs Johnston's polite 'Good evening, Mr Wallace,' he replied only with the question. 'Have you heard anything unusual tonight?' Mrs Johnston said, in some surprise, 'No—why? What has happened?' To which Wallace replied: 'I have been round to the front door and also to the back, and they are both fastened against me.'

It is at this point that the detective-story writer becomes exasperated with the published accounts of the case. To him the exact mechanism of locks and bolts is meat and drink, and in writing his books he makes his witnesses offer precise information on the subject, illustrating his points, if necessary, with neat diagrams. Now, in the Wallace case, we are concerned with no less than three doors and their fastenings, all of which are of the utmost importance; yet, of these, one lock only seems to have been brought into court, and of that there is no published description, while the witnesses are maddening vague in their evidence, so that it is often difficult to say whether by 'lock' they mean a mortice-lock or a safety-lock, or even the mechanism of the door *handle*; whether by 'bolt' they mean an iron bolt, or the catch of a safety-lock; and even whether by 'back door' they mean the kitchen door or the yard door leading to the entry. By careful piecing together of the various statements, we may, however, come to the following conclusions.

1. The front door was the one by which Wallace was accustomed to let himself in with his own key on returning home at night. From the data furnished in evidence, it seems likely that

the lock was an automatic lock, though not of the 'Yale' type; but it is clear that no key can have been left in it on the inside, as this would prevent its being opened by another key from without. It may even have been a small mortice-lock, which Wallace would lock after him, removing and carrying away the key. This door also had a bolt, which is not described. It may have been a safety-catch or a small and easily sliding bolt immediately beneath the lock-plate. If it was a stiff, heavy or double bolt, then one suggestion that was made becomes quite incredible, as will be seen. It is really extraordinary that so few details should have been reported about this bolt.

2. The back *kitchen* door seems to have had a handle, a bolt or bolts, and possibly also a lock. The mechanism of the handle seems to have been stiff and faulty.

3. The back *yard* door had apparently a latch and a bolt. It is not perfectly clear from the evidence whether it was this door or the back kitchen door which Wallace expected his wife to have bolted after him when he left; he apparently contradicted himself a little about this, but no energetic effort seems to have been made to clear the matter up.

In any case, when Wallace told the Johnstons that both doors were fastened against him, they were 'all standing in the entry before the door into the entry had been opened'. As to what followed, let us look first at Mr Johnston's evidence as given at the trial:

What did you say to him then?—I suggested that he tried the door again, as if it was the back door, and if he could not open it, I would get the key of my back door and try.

[By a process of deduction, we may see what Mr Johnston had in his mind. Here was no question of a Yale lock, for which another person's key would be useless; and it would be equally useless to try to open an ordinary lock from outside if the key had been left in the lock *inside*. Therefore, he must have thought that Mrs Wallace had gone out by the back and taken the key with her.]

When you said, 'Try again' and you would see, what did he do?—He went up to the door.

[Apparently the back door of the house; see later.]

Did Mr Wallace say anything when he went in, or when he went up the yard?—When he got to the door, he called out, 'It opens now.'

[Mrs Johnston's evidence here interestingly supplements her husband's. She remembered that Wallace, as he crossed the yard, looked back over his shoulder and said: 'She (meaning his wife) will not have gone out; she has such a bad cold.' Here we have then, Wallace answering, and rebutting, Mr Johnston's unspoken assumption in the matter of the key.]

Were you able to hear, from where you were, whether he tried with his key or anything?—No, he did not seem to try the key; he seemed to turn the knob in the usual way.—And said, 'It opens now?'—Yes.

Mr Justice Wright: Could you see?—Yes; I could see him at the door, my lord.

To supplement this, we have Wallace's own statement made at the police station.

I . . . then pulled out my key and went to open the front door and found it secure and could not open it with my key. I then went round to the back. The door leading from the entry to the back yard was closed, but not bolted. I went to the back door of the house and I was unable to get in. I do not know if the door was bolted or not; it sticks sometimes, but I think the door was bolted, though I am not sure. . . . I tried my key in the front door again and found the lock did not work properly.

Putting these two statements together, it is clear that Wallace meant it to be understood that he had tried first the front door, then the back door *of the house*, and then the front door again, and that he was coming round to the back for the second time when he met the Johnstons in the entry. It is perhaps a little surprising to find Mr Johnston asserting that their conversation took place 'before the door into the entry had been opened'. Did Wallace, then, carefully shut it behind him after his first fruitless attempt on the back door of the house? Unless the door had a spring, and shut to of itself, he must have done; and this does not look very much like agitation of mind. A similar unnecessary carefulness proved the downfall, under cross-examination, of Fox the matricide. Curiously enough, nothing seems to have been made of this point by the prosecution.

Now, with regard to the back door of the house: nobody, except Mr Johnston when he offered the help of his own key, seems to have suggested that it was locked at any time. Wallace said he thought at first that it was bolted, and subsequently came to the conclusion that the handle was merely stiff. At any rate, he eventually got in without using any key. And at this point we may take the evidence given subsequently by a locksmith.

> Witness produced another lock which he said was from the back kitchen door and found to be rusty. When the knob was turned, with difficulty, the spring bolt remained inside the lock and the knob returned to its former position.

The mention of the 'knob' seems to show definitely that the reference is not to the lock, but to the latching mechanism operated by the door handle. This evidence gives support to the theory that Wallace, when he first tried the door, was misled by its stiffness into supposing it to be bolted when, as a matter of fact, the latch had merely stuck.

We shall have to come back later to this question about the locks. We will take up the story at the point where Wallace opened the door, as described by Mr Johnston, and went in, leaving his neighbours in the yard. They do not seem to have noticed any light in the back kitchen (Wallace said that there was a gas-jet, reduced to a very feeble glimmer, over the sink); upstairs, however, the windows of the 'middle bedroom' where the Wallaces slept, and of the 'back room' which Wallace used as a workshop, were dimly lit, as though the gas had been left on, but turned down low.

After Wallace entered the house the Johnstons heard him call out twice, and shortly afterwards they saw first the light in the middle bedroom turned up full and then a match struck in 'the small room at the top of the stairs'. In 'about a minute and a half' Wallace came hurrying out, saying to them: 'Come and see; she has been killed.' His manner, observed Mr Johnston, who was a witness commendably free from any tendency to exaggerate language, 'seemed a bit excited'. Mrs Johnston said he spoke 'in a distressed tone, his words were very hurried you know'—by which, as she explained, she meant 'agitated'.

At this news they all went into the house. Wallace led them through the back kitchen and the main kitchen, where he had already lit the gas, and into the front sitting-room, where a dreadful sight awaited them. The body of Mrs Wallace lay stretched upon the hearth-rug, her feet near the gas-fire and her head towards the door. Her skull had been brutally battered in with such force as to scatter her brains about the floor, and her blood was splashed all around—on the carpet, on the arm-chair by the fireplace, on the violin-case lying on the seat of the chair, and on the wall behind. Mrs Johnston cried out, 'Oh, you poor darling!' and felt the dead woman's hand. It is not recorded what either of the two men said; but Mr Johnston reported that Wallace appeared, all the time, 'as though he was suffering from a shock. He was quiet, walking round; he did not shout, or anything like that.'

There was plenty of light to see the grisly state of things, because, when Wallace had first gone into the house he had lit the gas in the sitting-room. He was cross-examined over and over again about his movements, and nothing could be clearer, or one might think, more natural, than the account he gave. He said that, after passing through the back kitchen, he opened the door into the main kitchen, which was where he would have expected to find his wife, if she was still sitting up. It was dark, and he lit the gas (which was sensible of him if he wanted to see where he was going), and then, matchbox in hand, he went straight upstairs to see if his wife was in the bedroom, calling to her as he went. Here he turned up the light, and, finding the room empty, searched the other rooms on that floor with the aid of his matches, and then came down again to try the front sitting-room—the last place where she might be expected to be, but the only other room in the house.

> The door was closed to, and I pushed it a little open, and then I struck a match in quite the ordinary way, that I probably did every night I went into the room in the dark. I held it up, and as I held it up I could see my wife was lying there on the floor.
> You told the officer that you thought she was in a fit?—That was my first impression, but it only lasted possibly a fraction of a second, because I stooped down, with the same match, and I could see there was evidence of signs of a disturbance and blood, and I saw that she had been hit.
> Did you light the light?—Yes, I did.
> Which light?—The one on the right-hand side near the window.
> Why did you light that one?—It is the one we always use.

Now, the questions asked by the prosecution about this were directed to two points. First: Why, unless he knew beforehand that he was going to find a body on the floor, did he strike a match on the sitting-room threshold at all? He could have seen his way into the room quite well by reflected light from the kitchen. And secondly: Why did he walk round the body to light the farther of the two gas-jets, instead of the one nearest to him?

Now these, one would say, were the sort of questions that could only occur to a man who had never in his life had anything to do with gas. It is absolutely automatic with anyone who lives in a house with gas-lighting, to strike the match *at the threshold*, if he thinks he may have occasion to light the gas; so much so, that the present writer, for some time after making the changeover from gas to electricity, could seldom enter a room at night without first striking a match in the doorway or, at least, making a tentative gesture towards the pocket that held the matchbox. Equally automatic would be the action of lighting the accustomed gas-jet; since a jet that is seldom used may easily turn out to have a clogged burner or a broken mantle, and the realization of this, though quite subconscious, is enough to inhibit entirely any recourse to that jet in an emergency.

Having lit the gas, felt his wife's hand and looked at her injuries, Wallace, as he said, saw that she was quite dead, and at once rushed out and called his friends. It is difficult to see what else he could have done; and all this part of the story seems perfectly consistent with his innocence.

Seeing that poor Mrs Wallace was past all help, they all three went back into the kitchen, and there Wallace drew their attention to the lid of a cabinet, which appeared to have been wrenched off and was lying on the floor. Then he reached up to a shelf and took down a cash-box. Mr Johnston asked whether anything was missing. Wallace said he thought about £4 had gone, though he could not be certain until he looked through his books.

This business of the cash-box is rather mysterious. It was presumably examined for finger-prints, but no evidence about this seems to have been given.[1] Wallace's prints would have

[1] The point was put to Detective-Sergeant Bailey in cross-examination, but he replied vaguely, and the matter was apparently never cleared up.

Julia Wallace.

been on it in any case, since he handled it to take it down; if there were others, we hear nothing of them. It was said, 'Why, if an outside murderer had stolen the money, should he have so carefully replaced the box on the shelf?' It might, with equal force, have been asked why, if Wallace wanted to pretend that the murderer had been there, did *he* put it back? Common sense would have suggested that he should produce the appearance of as much disorder as possible. Like almost everything else in this extraordinary case the question cuts two ways. Then, how did it happen that there had been so little money in the box? Wallace's accounts were gone into very carefully at the trial, and everything he then said was found to be correct. On an ordinary Tuesday he would have had about £30 or £40 of the company's in his possession, ready for paying in on the Wednesday, which was the regular accounting day; on one Tuesday in each month he might have as much as £80 or £100, or even more. On this particular Tuesday, however, he had less than usual, first, because he had been laid up with influenza on the Saturday and had not made his round; secondly, because out of the £14 or so he had collected on the Monday and Tuesday (his other regular collecting-days) he had paid away about £10 10s. 0d., in sick benefit; thus leaving about £4. Let us see which way this evidence tells.

1. Supposing that there was an outside murderer, why did he not come on the Monday night, when he knew that Wallace was safely occupied with his chess-match?—Answer: Because his intention was to steal the insurance money, and what he wanted was to get Wallace out of the way on the *Tuesday* night, when a bigger sum would have been collected.

2. If the intention was to steal, why did not the thief select some night when both Wallace and his wife were out of the house?—Answer: Because (as Wallace said in evidence) when they were both out of the house they always took any of the company's money with them for greater safety.

3. But how could an outside murderer have known this?—Answer: If there was an outside murderer, he was obviously somebody well acquainted with Wallace and his habits, as is clear from other considerations mentioned earlier.

4. If Wallace himself was the murderer, would he not also

select the Tuesday night, in order to suggest that the murderer
was a thief in search of the insurance money?—Certainly he
would.

5. In that case, since he *did* know and was probably the only
person who *could* know that there would be less money that
week than usual, why did he not postpone the crime a day when
he could stage a really impressive robbery?—This question is
difficult to answer; unless, of course, Wallace had some idea
that he might be called upon to make good the loss; in which
case his failure to collect on the Saturday might all be part of the
plan.

It should be said at once that there was never any suggestion
that Wallace himself committed the crime for money: his
accounts were all in order; there was only the £4 of insurance
money; no private liabilities were disclosed; his wife was insured for the trifling sum of £20, and, though she had £90 in the
savings-bank, Wallace's own bank balance was £152—ample
for any emergency.

After looking at the cash-box Mr Johnston suggested that
Wallace should go and see if anything had been taken from
upstairs. Wallace went up and came down almost at once,
saying: 'There is £5 in a jar they have not taken.'

Mr Johnston then went out for the police, and Mrs Johnston
went back with Wallace into the blood-bespattered sitting-
room. Here, he stooped over his wife, and said, 'They have
finished her; look at the brains.' Mrs Johnston, not unnaturally, seems to have preferred not to look at any such thing;
instead, she gazed round the room and said, 'What ever have
they used?'

Wallace made no suggestion about this; he got up and came
round to the other side of the body and then said, 'Why, what
ever was she doing with her mackintosh, and my mackintosh?'

Mrs Johnston then saw that there was a mackintosh lying, as
she expressed it, 'roughed up' and almost hidden under the
body. (Later, a policeman with a gift for description said it was
'as though it had been put in this position round the shoulder,
and tucked in by the side, as though the body was a living
person and you were trying to make it comfortable.') Mrs
Johnston was not quite sure whether Wallace had said 'her' or

'a' mackintosh; she was, however, quite positive that he ended his sentence by identifying the mackintosh as his own. Abandoning the problem of how the garment came there, the two of them then went into the kitchen. The fire was nearly out—'just a few live embers'—and Mrs Johnston, 'feeling that she must do something', relit it, with Wallace's assistance. Then, while they waited together in the kitchen, Wallace, who till then had been 'quite collected', twice broke down and sobbed for a moment, with his head in his hands.

Now Mrs Johnston offers us a little more evidence about the front door:

> A little later there was a knock at the door, I understand?—Yes.
>
> Did you try to open the door?—Yes.
>
> Were you able to?—No; it is a different lock to mine, and I think I was agitated, and I drew back and let Mr Wallace open it.
>
> Do you know whether or not the door was bolted?—I do not.
>
> If he [Wallace] says he undid the bolt, you would not contradict him, would you?—I do not know whether he did, but I cannot remember that.

Nothing here is said about the necessity of a key to open the door from the inside: Mrs Johnston merely attributes her failure to agitation and the fact that the lock was of another pattern from her own. Nor does it seem likely that she could have failed to notice the drawing of a heavy bolt or of the double bolt. The door, at any rate, was opened to admit a policeman; and he said that he did not hear any bolt withdrawn.

To this policeman, by name Frederick Robert Williams, Wallace said: 'Something terrible has happened, officer.' The policeman came in, examined the body, and then heard Wallace's account of his efforts to enter the house, at the front, at the back, at the front again—'this time I found the door was bolted'—again at the back—'this time I found it would open.' Both then, and later, at the trial, Wallace asserted quite definitely and positively that the front door was actually bolted when he let P.C. Williams in, and this is one of the most extraordinary points about the case. If Wallace was innocent, then it is difficult to see why the real murderer or anybody else should have bolted the door; if he was guilty, then, by sticking to the tale of the bolted door (which rested on no evidence but his own), he probably did more damage to his own case than by any other thing he said.

Leaving the matter of the bolts for a moment, let us accompany P.C. Williams on his tour of the house. Omitting the questions of examining counsel, his story ran more or less like this:

> In the middle bedroom the gas-jet was lit; accused said he changed in this room before going out and left the light burning. On the mantelpiece I noticed an ornament from which five or six £1 notes were protruding. Accused partly extracted the notes, and said, 'Here is some money which has not been touched.' I requested him to put the ornament and notes back, which he did.

P.C. Williams should have spoken sooner; a smear of blood was subsequently found on one of the notes, but by that time it was impossible to say that it had not got there from Wallace's hands after his examination of the corpse.

> I approached a curtained recess to the right of the fireplace. Accused said, 'My wife's clothes are there, they have not been touched.' I looked in, and apparently they were undisturbed. In the back room which has been converted into a laboratory, accused said, 'Everything seems all right here'. In the bathroom there was a small light; accused said, 'We usually have a light here.'

So far, everything seemed to square with Wallace's story. Next comes a very curious little circumstance, which squares with no imaginable theory of the crime.

> We went into the front bedroom. It was in a state of disorder; the bed-clothes were half on the bed and half on the floor; there were a couple of pillows lying near the fireplace; there was a dressing-table in the room, containing drawers and a mirror, and also a wardrobe; the drawers of the dressing-table were shut and the drawers of the wardrobe were shut.

On the subject of the front bedroom, the published evidence is more vague and unsatisfactory even than it is about the locks. Counsel for the defence seems to have asked the prisoner:

> It is said that the bed in the front bedroom was somehow disarranged, and there were some of your wife's hats on it?—Yes.

[This is all we ever hear about the hats.]

> Do you know anything about that?—I do not think I had been in that room for probably a fortnight before the 20th or the 19th January.

Here the detective-story writer (and, one would think, everybody else) would ask instantly: Did your wife often go into the room? Were there sheets on the bed? If so, were you, or was your wife proposing to sleep there on the night of the 20th? Why? Did you always occupy the same room as your wife, and if not, why not? According to Wallace, his wife's bedroom 'would look down on the yard' (i.e. she slept in the 'middle bedroom'), and, since he himself changed his clothes in that room, the presumption is that he occupied it with her; but the position is never made clear. If the room was merely a spare room, then, one asks: What is the meaning of the disorder? Would an outside thief and murderer overlook the occupied bedroom with its five £1 notes on the mantelpiece, and make straight for the spare room? And why should he there confine himself to ransacking the bed, either omitting to open any drawers and cupboards, or else carefully shutting them all up after him? And if the murderer was Wallace, trying to present a convincing picture of a search for valuables, then why did he stage it, so absurdly, in this room rather than in the other?

It seems highly probable that the disorder in the front room had nothing to do with the murder; there is, however, a curious and interesting parallel in the case of the Gilchrist murder (Edinburgh, 1909). Here, the murderer, after battering his victim to death, made straight, not for the old lady's own bedroom where she kept her jewels in the wardrobe, but for the spare bedroom, where, disregarding various articles of value upon the dressing-table, he broke open a box containing papers. In this case, however, the murderer is known to have been interrupted in the middle of his activities, and it has been suggested that some paper, and no ordinary valuable, was the real object of his search. Our detective novelist might play with two theories in this connection: (1) The rather melodramatic one that the murderer of Julia Wallace was in search of something that he had cause to believe might be found secreted under the spare room mattress; or (2), the idea that Wallace, in staging his murder, deliberately modelled his effects upon the Gilchrist case; this might explain his curious insistence in the matter of the bolted front door, and his subsequent statement that he at first believed the murderer to be still in the house.

Having searched the bedrooms, they went downstairs again. In the kitchen Wallace showed P.C. Williams the cabinet and the cash-box, and also picked up a lady's handbag from a chair, saying that it belonged to his wife. It contained a £1 note and some small change. They were then joined in the sitting-room by Police Sergeant Breslin, in whose presence Williams observed: 'That looks like a mackintosh.' Wallace, who was standing in the doorway, said, 'Yes, it is an old one of mine,' and, glancing out into the hall, added, 'it usually hangs here.' It was not until past 10 o'clock that the mackintosh was closely examined. By that time Superintendent Moore had arrived, and he, after hearing Wallace's story and examining the rooms and doors of the house, again asked Wallace whose the mackintosh was. This time Wallace seemed to hesitate in his answer, and the Superintendent pulled the mackintosh out, saying, 'Take it up and let's have a look at it. It's a gent's mackintosh.' Wallace said, 'If there are two patches on the inside it is mine,' and, finding the patches, continued in the same breath, 'It is mine.' A great deal was made, later, of this brief hesitation; it appears, however, quite natural that, seeing the importance the police were inclined to attach to the mackintosh, Wallace should have thought it well to verify, by proof, his first general impression that the garment was his.

When the mackintosh was pulled out it was found to be heavily spattered with blood on the right side, both inside and out. Also—which was more remarkable—it was very much burnt, and part of Mrs Wallace's skirt was burnt also. Yet the gas-fire before which she lay was not alight when the body was found. Two theories were advanced to account for the burning. One was that the murderer (in that case Wallace) had tried to destroy the mackintosh by burning it at the gas-fire and had accidentally burnt Mrs Wallace's skirt in the process; the other, that the fire had been alight when the murder was committed, that Mrs Wallace had fallen against it and set her skirt alight, and that either she was wearing the mackintosh at the time, or that the murderer had been wearing it and had burnt it in stooping to turn out the gas.

In the same way, two theories were advanced to account for the blood. Mrs Wallace (who had a cold) might have slipped the mackintosh loosely about her shoulders for warmth, let the murderer in at the door, stooped down to light the gas fire and been struck down with the mackintosh still about her; or else, the murderer might himself have put on the mackintosh to protect himself from bloodstains.

One thing seemed fairly clear: unless the murderer had had some sort of protection he must have been heavily spattered and stained with blood. Now, throughout the house, there were no signs of bloodstains (except, of course, in the sitting-room), other than the smear on the £1 note in the bedroom and a small clot on the lavatory pan in the bathroom, which, it was admitted, might have been dropped there by one of the numerous policemen[1] who were roaming about the place all night. There were no damp towels in the bathroom and no appearance that anybody had recently taken a bath. Nor was any blood found on Wallace, nor on any clothes belonging to him.

Next comes the question of the weapon. The charwoman, Sarah Jane Draper, gave evidence that since her last visit on January 7th two objects had disappeared from the house: the kitchen poker and an iron bar that was usually kept in the sitting-room for cleaning under the gas fire. Search was made for these all about the house and yard and in every conceivable place, including the drains, along the tram route between Wolverton Street and Menlove Gardens where they or one of them might have been thrown away; but neither of them was ever found. Nor was any suggestion ever put forward why two weapons should have been used or why either of them should have been removed (unless, indeed, on the general principle of 'making it more difficult'). For consider: whoever did the murder, it was to his advantage to leave the weapon in the house. There are only three reasons for getting rid of a weapon: (1) To conceal the fact that a murder has been committed at all; in this case no attempt was made to pretend that the death was suicide or accident. (2) To prevent identification by finger-prints; in this case finger-prints could easily have been wiped off. (3) To destroy a ready means of identification, as, for instance, where the murderer uses his own pistol or walking-

[1] These included a constable, a police-sergeant, a detective-sergeant, a detective-inspector and a detective-superintendent. Novelists who restrict their commission of inquiry to a 'man from the Yard' and a gifted amateur are letting themselves off too easily. But it is hard work inventing names and characteristics for so many different policemen.

stick; in this case the weapon was identified only with the house
itself, and if the murderer came from outside, the use of a
weapon identified with the house would assist him in throwing
the blame on Wallace, whereas, if Wallace himself was the
murderer, by far the readiest way of fixing suspicion upon
himself was to use a weapon belonging to the house *and remove it*,
since its removal created a strong presumption that no weapon
had been brought from outside. Whichever way one looks at it,
the carrying away of the weapon (still more, two weapons) was
an idiotic and entirely unnecessary error, involving the risk of
discovery. Still, somebody made that error and took that risk,
and since it could benefit nobody it gives us no help in solving
the mystery. It seems likely that the weapon actually used was
the iron bar; the poker, if it was not used to break open the
cabinet, may have been lost on some other occasion, or Mrs
Draper have merely imagined the loss of a poker.

The body itself was examined by various medical witnesses,
who, as usual, differed a good deal about the probable time of
death. Professor MacFall, called by the prosecution, judged,
from the fact that *rigor mortis* was present in the neck and upper
part of the right arm when he saw the corpse at ten o'clock, that
death had taken place 'four hours or more' before his arrival.
Since Mrs Wallace had been seen alive by the milk-boy certainly not *earlier* than 6.30, this witness *must* have been at least half
an hour out in his calculations. Dr Pierce, also a witness for the
prosecution, agreed with him in giving 'about six o'clock' as the
probable time of death. Prosecuting counsel at this point
supplied the world with an admirable example of the folly of not
letting well alone:

> You say about six o'clock. What limit on either side would you give?—I
> would give two hours' limit on either side.
> Mr Justice Wright (*pouncing on this admission of human fallibility*): It might
> have been between four and eight?—Yes, my lord.
> Counsel (*making the best of it*): Would you say that death could not
> possibly have occured after eight o'clock?—I would say definitely it could
> not have occurred after eight o'clock.
> Cross-examining Counsel (*consolidating his advantage, after ascertaining that
> witness had omitted to apply all the tests he might have applied*): When you say you
> think it was six o'clock, it might have been four o'clock in the afternoon or
> might have been eight o'clock?—And there were other factors as well.
> So it follows she might have met her death at any hour within this time
> that night?—Yes.

From all this the detective novelist may well conclude that he ought not to allow his medical men to be too dogmatic in deducing the exact time of death from the appearance of the body. In fact, in the words of Professor Dibble, F.R.C.S., who was called for the defence, 'it is an enormously difficult subject, full of pitfalls'. Nothing, in fact, emerged at the trial except that it was probable, on the whole, that Mrs Wallace was murdered round about the time that Wallace left the house. This is exactly what one would expect. If Wallace did it, the only possible time was between about 6.30 and about 6.50; if anybody else did it, he would no doubt have entered the house as early as possible after Wallace's departure, so as to give himself an ample margin for retreat.

To go back to the night of the murder: Superintendent Moore, who came on the scene at 10.5, carefully examined all the doors and windows of the house, and found no signs that anyone had broken in. Having borrowed Wallace's latchkey and tried it in the front door, he found that, though it would open the door with a little trouble, the lock was defective. Wallace, when told, said, 'It was not like that this morning'— though, actually, it turned out that the lock must have been out of order for some time. Wallace's first account was that the first time he tried the front door lock the key would not turn and that the second time he became convinced that the door was bolted. Superintendent Moore's account was that the key had a tendency to slip round in the lock, and 'that if the key was turned beyond a certain point it would re-lock the door'. At one point Wallace adopted Superintendent Moore's explanation, and was much criticized because this did not agree with his earlier account of the matter.

It seems quite possible that both Wallace's accounts were perfectly honest. When he first arrived at the house the key may have stuck in the defective lock as he said. The second time it may have turned too far, as it did with Superintendent Moore, and re-locked the door. Wallace, in the flustered state of his mind, finding that, though the key turned, the door would not open, may have jumped to the conclusion that the bolt had been shot between his two attempts. As to his saying, 'it was not like that this morning', that may amount to no more than any man's natural reluctance to admit that he can have made a conspicuous ass of himself. It is curious that he did not, apparently, on that night, inform Superintendent Moore that the door had been actually bolted when he opened it to admit P.C. Williams.

Apparently, however, he had told P.C. Williams and he may well have thought this enough. At the trial he said, wearily, that he really could not remember what he *had* said to the Superintendent. After all, when one has had to tell the same story half a dozen times in one night, and innumerable times since then, it may be difficult to remember exactly to which policeman one told what details of it.

We may bring down the curtain upon the third act of the tragedy by quoting two little word-pictures of Wallace's demeanour on that memorable night. Professor MacFall said:

> I was very struck with it, it was abnormal. He was too quiet, too collected, for a person whose wife had been killed in that way that he described. He was not nearly so affected as I was myself. . . . I think he was smoking cigarettes most of the time. Whilst I was in the room, examining the body and the blood, he came in smoking a cigarette, and he leaned over in front of the sideboard and flicked the ash into a bowl upon the sideboard. It struck me at the time as being unnatural.

Detective Inspector Herbert Gold, who arrived on the scene at 10.30, agreed that Wallace was 'cool and calm'.

> When I first went into the house on the night of the murder, he was sitting in the kitchen. In fact, he had the cat on his knee and was stroking the cat, and he did not look to me like a man who had just battered his wife to death.

Wallace's own comment, in an article written after the trial, was:

> For forty years I had drilled myself in iron control and prided myself on never displaying an emotion outwardly in public. I trained myself to be a stoic. My griefs and joys can be as intense as those of any man, but the rule of my life has always been to give them expression only in privacy. Stoicism is so little practised today that when seen it is called callousness.

The Emperor Marcus Aurelius is, it would seem, not the wisest counsellor for those who may have to make their appearance before a British jury.

At about four or five o'clock on the Wednesday morning,

Wallace was allowed to leave the house to sleep—supposing he could sleep—at his sister-in-law's. During twelve hours of the next day he was detained at the police station, making a statement and answering questions about his movements on the Monday and Tuesday evenings. In particular, he was told that the fateful telephone call had been put in from a call-box in the Anfield district near his own home.

The consequence of this was that on January 22nd, happening to meet Mr Beattie, Wallace questioned him very closely about the exact time of the call, adding, most unfortunately for himself: 'I have just left the police; they have cleared me.'

This conversation was reported back to the police, who, of course, pounced on it like tigers. Why should Wallace be so much interested in the time? Why should he announce that he was 'cleared' when nobody, so far, had suggested that he was suspected? As to the first, Wallace replied: 'I had an idea; we all have ideas; it was indiscreet of me.'

Asked at the trial to amplify this cryptic remark, he explained that by this time he had realized he might be suspected and thought that, if he could ascertain from Mr Beattie that the call had been put through at seven, whereas he himself did not leave his house till 7.15, it would be a complete proof of his innocence. Thinking it over, he saw that for him, a suspected person, to be seen talking to a witness in the case, was an indiscretion. Yes; but *why* should he imagine himself suspected? To which Wallace replied that if his conversation with Mr Beattie had been reported he must have been followed and watched, and that this showed clearly that he *was* suspected, a fact which he realized at the time. Looking at it from the purely common-sense point of view, one must confess that Wallace would have been a fool indeed *not* to realize that, in a case where a married woman is murdered, the husband is always the first person to be suspected. It was in fact admitted by the police witnesses at the trial that, between the time of the murder and of the arrest, Wallace had to be given police protection while he was collecting his insurance money because the people in the district were hostile to him. Some further light may be thrown on his statement, 'I had ideas; we all have ideas,' by the fact that on that same January 22nd he mentioned the name of a certain man, known to him and his wife and connected with the Prudential, who was the object of his own suspicions. This person turned out to have an alibi, and nothing, of course, was said about him at the trial; but it is quite likely that he may have had something to do with Wallace's indiscreet 'ideas'. On the same occasion, Wallace mentioned the name of another possible suspect, and, after his death in 1933, papers were found among his belongings in which he named the murderer. Nothing, however, was discovered that definitely pointed to the guilt of anyone else, so on February 2nd Wallace was arrested and charged, and on March 4th, at the conclusion of the police court inquiry, was sent up for trial at Liverpool Assizes.

It is not necessary to go through the trial[1] itself, since most of the important points in the evidence have already been discussed. We may, however, spend a little time in examining the theory of the prosecution as it eventually took shape in court.

The theory was that Wallace, having prepared his alibi the evening before, suggested to his wife after tea that they should have one of their customary violin practices in the front room. While she went to light the gas fire and get the music ready Wallace went upstairs and stripped himself naked, so that his clothes should not be stained with blood. He then slipped on the mackintosh, came down, and, catching his wife just as she was stooping to light the fire, struck her dead with repeated blows from the iron bar, with which he had already armed himself. Then, wiping his bare feet on the hearth rug, and perhaps making a hasty attempt to burn the incriminating mackintosh at the gas fire, he went upstairs, dressed, disarranged the front room and broke open the cabinet in the kitchen and then hurried out to catch his tram and establish his alibi, taking (for some reason or other) the bloodstained weapon with him.

As regards this part of the theory, several criticisms may occur to us. To commit a murder naked is no new idea; the thing was done by Courvoisier, who murdered Lord William

---

[1] April 22, 1931, before Mr Justice Wright; for the Crown, Mr E. G. Hemmerde, K.C., Recorder of Liverpool, and Mr Leslie Walsh; for the defence, Mr Roland Oliver, K.C., and Mr S. Scholefield Allen.

Russell in 1840, and it was suspected in the case of Lizzie Borden, tried for murdering her father and stepmother in Fall River, Massachusetts, in 1892. But the mackintosh complicates the matter. It can scarcely be supposed to have been slipped on in order to take Mrs Wallace more effectively by surprise; even if the poor woman had been given a preliminary warning by the startling apparition of a naked husband on the threshold, the smallness of the room would have enabled him to spring upon her before she could escape or call for assistance. The only conceivable justification for the mackintosh would be a curious prudery. That is not impossible. In the lower middle class there is no doubt many a man who would not—literally to save his life—appear mother-naked before his wife, even if he knew for certain that that astonishing sight was the last sight she was doomed ever to see in the world. Yet it seems strange that a murderer who had shown so much foresight in preparing the alibi should have allowed such a consideration to influence him. As for the suggested attempt to burn the mackintosh, a moment's thought would suggest that the proper place for that was not the gas-fire in the sitting-room, but the coal fire in the kitchen, which, at 6.30, when they had just finished tea, must have been burning cheerfully. It was stated in evidence that the mackintosh was of a material that would burn easily; an hour in the kitchen grate would probably have destroyed all but the buckle and buttons, which might easily have escaped search or identification. It is most unlikely that the burning of the mackintosh was anything but accidental, whoever committed the murder.

The second point is, of course, the witlessness of the disturbance created in the front room and elsewhere. Anybody wishing to suggest that a thief had gone upstairs would have removed the £1 notes from the middle bedroom and flung open the drawers and wardrobe as though in search for money.

The third unsatisfactory point is the time factor. It is astonishing what can be done in twenty minutes, which was the longest time possible that Wallace can have had at his disposal. Still, he must, at any rate, have washed his face, hands and feet, and that so carefully as to leave no smear of blood anywhere in the bathroom, dressed from top to toe, broken open the cabinet

and rifled the cash-box and administered (again without leaving a trace) as much rough cleaning to the iron bar as would
enable him to carry it away without staining anything it
touched. The thorough removal of bloodstains is no very quick
or easy matter, as anybody knows well who has tried to clean up
the mess produced by a cut finger.

The other part of the theory brings us back to the vexed
question of the locked doors. The theory was that Wallace, in
order to get witnesses to his discovery of the body, pretended
that he could not get in, when, in fact, he could have done so.
We may, I think, dismiss any suggestion that he had in fact
entered the house before encountering the Johnstons. What
they heard and saw agreed very well with the estimated time of
his arrival home and his account of his own actions. They heard
him knocking, as he said, at the back door and, a few minutes
later, met him coming down from the end of the entry as
though, in the interval, he had been round to the front. If he was
the murderer he would probably not risk making an actual
entry, which might be observed by someone living in the street,
if he was going to deny it afterwards.

Let us assume that Wallace is guity and is endeavouring to
present a picture of a murder committed by a third party. It is
going to be a ticklish business—more ticklish than it appears at
first sight. The proper handling of bolts and locks has in all
likelihood planted more grey hairs in the heads of detective
novelists and other planners of perfect murders than any other
branch of this amiable study. Let us see how it must have
presented itself to him—remembering that his meeting with the
Johnstons was entirely fortuitous, and could not have entered
into his calculations one way or the other.

First, then, the simplest way to suggest an intruder from
without is, obviously, to follow the excellent example set by the
wicked Elders who accused Susannah. They, it will be remembered, 'opened the garden doors' and subsequently testified
that an apocryphal young man had been in the garden 'and
opened the doors and leaped out'. So, the apocryphal murderer
must be supposed to have left the house by some means or
other, and the most natural thing would be to make it appear
that he escaped either by the front, leaving the door on the

automatic lock, or by the back, leaving the door latched, or—more picturesquely—wide open as though in rapid flight. But alas! Where a murderer could get out Wallace could get in, and this would mean 'discovering' the body without any witness to support him. He must, therefore, find 'both doors locked against him'. But he cannot *really* find them so, for two reasons: (1) because he is not skilled as the murderers of fiction in shooting inside bolts from the outside by means of strings and other gadgets, and (2) because, if he did, then by hypothesis the murderer would be still inside the house when Wallace arrived with his witnesses, and it would be exceedingly difficult to fake the hasty departure of a non-existent murderer after the door was opened. He must, then, only *pretend* to be unable to get in, and *pretend* to suppose that the murderer might be still in the house. As a matter of fact, he did say all along that his first thought was that the murderer was still there, but that he abandoned that theory when they got in and found the house empty. Now, it is at this point that the emergence of the Johnstons from their back door must have upset the plans of a guilty Wallace most horribly. But for them he might have pretended that his knocking at the back door had disturbed the murderer, who must have then opened the kitchen door and fled while Wallace was trying the front for the second time. With the Johnstons there to see and hear anybody escaping, he could not very well put up that story.

Supposing the Johnstons had not come out, could the story have held water? The detective of fiction would say no; and for this reason: A cautious medical witness, inspecting a corpse at 9 o'clock, may find it difficult to say precisely whether the person was killed within two hours either way of 6 o'clock. But he will have no hesitation in saying whether or not death took place within the last quarter of an hour or so. 'I would say definitely,' said Mr Pierce, 'it could not have occurred after 8 o'clock.' That being so, how could the murderer be supposed to have been occupying the time between the murder and Wallace's return? To explain such unaccountable lingering on the scene of the crime, one would have to present the picture of a thorough ransacking of the house from top to bottom; and this, as we know, was not done. But a consideration of this kind would probably not have occurred to Wallace beforehand, or perhaps to anybody except a detective novelist.

But, as things turned out, there the Johnstons were: and now what was Wallace to do about the front door? Was he still to insist that it had been bolted, put it on the bolt (if this had not been already done), and draw the Johnstons' attention to the bolt? This he certainly did not do, and it is odd that it does not seem to have occurred, either to him or to Mrs' Johnston, to verify that matter of the front door bolt while they were waiting for the police. If, on the other hand, Wallace, thinking his story over, had decided to leave the question of the bolt in a decent obscurity, it is odd that he should have persisted at the trial in asserting that it *was* bolted, when, in the meantime, the police themselves had offered him a perfectly good explanation for his inability to make the door open. Perhaps he felt that, having once told P.C. Williams the door was bolted, he had better stick to his story. Perhaps, when all is said and done, it really was bolted and he was telling the truth. The more we examine the question the more complicated it becomes, espeically when we are left in such doubt as to the exact machinery of the lock.

Then again, if Wallace, having come back in the ordinary way and been unable to get in at the front, had gone round to the back and found the door locked, this ought not to have surprised or alarmed him. In the ordinary way it would be locked, since Mrs Wallace would expect him to enter by the front. His story was that he was both surprised and alarmed. Why? Because of the queerness of the telephone call and the fact that he could see no light in the front kitchen. But if the curtains of the front kitchen window were drawn he could not have seen a light in any case, so why the alarm? To this he replied that by looking sideways at the back kitchen window one could have seen the light shining through from the front kitchen. Not if the door between the two kitchens was shut? Well, no. This did not seem satisfactory. If he thought his wife was upstairs, why did he not shout to her instead of knocking gently? Wallace replied simply that he did not think of it. If he had been trying to give the impression that the noise he made had scared the murderer away, one would rather expect him to make as much hullabaloo as possible. On the other hand, too much hullabaloo might have brought out the neighbours. The neighbours did, in point of fact, come out for another reason.

That Wallace's mind was confused, both at the time and after, about the locked doors is evident. He said, for instance, that when he could get in by neither door, he at first thought his wife might have slipped out to the post. This is inconsistent with the statement that he thought a man was in the house, but is not in itself unreasonable, and is supported by his remark to the Johnstons as he crossed the yard. He might, in that case, having tried and failed at the front door and got no answer at the back, have thought that Mrs Wallace had 'slipped out' the back way, locking the back door after her and taking the key. If so, it would naturally be useless to shout at her bedroom window, and he would go round and make another attempt on the front door while waiting for her return. And it was possibly then that he first became really disturbed in his mind. It is not easy to remember the exact sequence of one's actions or thoughts in a moment of agitation. His own phrase, used in the course of cross-examination, probably corresponds with the feelings of the normal person in such a situation: 'I was both uneasy and not uneasy, if you follow me.' One has often felt like that: vaguely worried yet able to present one's self with a number of possible explanations, inconsistent with one another, but all quite credible separately.

And, of course, the fact remains that both those locks *were* defective, and had been so for a long time. Whether Wallace, knowing this, used the circumstance deliberately to throw an atmosphere of confusion about the whole case, or whether he was genuinely mistaken in supposing both or either of the doors to be fastened, it seems not impossible to say. It is pretty certain that he did not himself deliberately damage either of the locks in advance in order to support his story.

Now let us take the other side of the question. Suppose Wallace was innocent, how did the murderer get in? The answer was suggested by the defence. He presented himself at the front door and was let in by Mrs Wallace, saying that he wanted to leave a note for Wallace or wait for his return. She had thrown Wallace's mackintosh over her shoulders before opening the front door (we know she had a slight cold at the time). She took the murderer into the front parlour (the usual place for receiving guests and strangers) and was there struck down. Her skirt caught fire. The murderer extinguished the flames with the bloodstained mackintosh, turned out fire and gas-light, bolted both doors in order to have notice of Wallace's return (?), washed his hands in the back kitchen (?), refled the cash-box and cabinet, and departed, leaving the back door latched (and the front door still bolted?) and carrying the iron bar with him (!)

There are, of course, difficulties about this too. We know that there were several people, including the two men suspected by Wallace, whom Mrs Wallace would readily have let in if they had called. She would also, if Wallace had told her (as he said he did) about the message from 'Qualtrough', have let in anyone giving that name. Whoever the caller was, he was probably known to Mrs Wallace, so that she had to be murdered lest she should identify him later. Would not the intending murderer in that case have brought his own weapon with him? We do not know that he did not. We have no evidence that the iron bar was the weapon used. We know only that it disappeared. An outside murderer might, seeing it handy, have used it in preference to his own or, more subtly, having used his own, he might have removed the iron bar for the express purpose of incriminating Wallace. In fact, the only thoroughly satisfactory reason anybody could possibly have for taking it away would be that it was clean and, therefore, if left behind, could *not* incriminate Wallace. But one cannot expect (outside a detective novel) a thoroughly satisfactory reason for any person's actions.

An explanation of the iron bar's disappearance is offered by Miss Winifred Duke in her novel, *Skin for Skin*, which presents a reconstruction of the crime on the hypothesis that Wallace was the murderer. She makes him conceal the bar in his umbrella and drop it down a drain at the far end of his tram journey, in the neighbourhood of Menlove Gardens. The only reply that can be made to this is that the police said they had searched 'everywhere', and they can scarcely have omitted to search the Menlove Gardens district. Wallace could scarcely have carried it very far afield, for his time-table leaves no room for such an excursion. If the bar had been found in the neighbourhood, it would have certainly incriminated Wallace. Since it was never found it incriminates nobody, and such witness as it bears is slightly in Wallace's favour. Its chief function is to darken counsel. Indeed, the iron bar has bothered everybody who has attempted to deal critically with the case.

Our alternative theory does indeed leave us with the blood-stained murderer obliged to clean himself and escape. But whereas Wallace had twenty minutes only in which to do everything and then travel by tram, the 'other man' had getting on for two hours and might then remove himself inconspicuously on foot (possibly to a bicycle, or a car parked somewhere handy). He had more time for cleaning, and he need not appear so scrupulously clean.

Further, we are not obliged to suppose that the outside murderer went upstairs at all. The £1 notes would then be left unappropriated because he never went near them, and the bathroom clean and dry because he did not wash himself there. As for the front bedroom, the likeliest explanation of all is that the murderer never went there and had nothing to do with it. His ring at the door may have disturbed Mrs Wallace when she was engaged in turning over the bedding for some domestic purpose of her own. Perhaps she had piled the bed-clothes and pillows on the foot of the bed, and they fell off, as they usually do in such circumstances. The appearance of the room, as described, is more suggestive of some such household accident than of a search by a thief.

The trial itself occupied four days. Wallace himself made a very good witness—too good, perhaps, for a jury. He was, as ever, 'cool and collected', and there is no kind of prisoner a jury dislikes so much, except, indeed, a hot and agitated one. But he impressed the judge. 'When reference is made to discrepancies in his statement,' said Mr Justice Wright summing up, 'I cannot help thinking it is wonderful how his statements are as lucid and consistent as they have been.' Counsel for the prosecution, though as usual conspicuously fair in the general treatment of the case, perhaps helped a little to confuse the issues by arguing, from time to time, as though the defence was that 'Qualtrough's' call was a genuine business inquiry, which it could not on any hypothesis have been; while Mr Roland Oliver, in endeavouring to cast contempt upon the theory of the prosecution, asked the prisoner, absurdly enough, 'Were you accustomed to play the violin naked in a mackintosh?' which again confused the issue. The defence also attacked the police vigorously for not having called the newspaper girl and the little boys who supported her testimony, going so far as to accuse them of deliberately suppressing evidence in order to give colour to their case. This may have prejudiced the jury, who commonly do not care to hear the police attacked, though the judge, while deprecating the attack, said he thought the police had committed an error of judgment. There was probably also a certain amount of prejudice arising from the evidence that had already come out in the magistrate's court, and from the general tendency to suspect married persons of murdering one another. But the chief difficulty in the way of the defence was the difficulty with which we started out: that the common man, however well he knows that his duty is to ask, 'Did this man do it?' will insist on asking instead, 'Who could have done it, if not this man?' It is perfectly evident, in the judge's summing-up, that he was aware of this difficulty. He summed up dead in the prisoner's favour, and again and again repeated his caution that the verdict must be given according to the evidence.

> Members of the jury, you, I believe, are living more or less in this neighbourhood: I come here as a stranger . . . you must approach this matter without any preconceived notions at all. Your business here is to listen to the evidence, and to consider the evidence and nothing else. A man cannot be convicted of any crime, least of all murder, merely on probabilities . . . if you have other possibilities, a jury would not, and I believe ought not to, come to the conclusion that the charge is established. . . . The question is not: Who did this crime? The question is: Did the prisoner do it? . . . It is not a question of determining who or what sort of person other than the prisoner did the crime or could have done the crime; it is a question whether it is brought home to the prisoner, and whether it is brought home by the evidence. If every matter relied on as circumstantial is equally or substantially consistent both with the guilt or innocence of the prisoner, the multiplication of those instances may not take you any further in coming to a conclusion of guilt. . . . In conclusion I will only remind you what the question you have to determine is. The question is: Can you have any doubt that the prisoner did it? You may think: 'Well, some one did it.' . . . Can you say it was absolutely impossible

Menlove Gardens North – an important part of Wallace's alibi.

that there was no such person [as an unknown murderer]? . . . Can you say . . . that you are satisfied beyond reasonable doubt that it was the hand of the prisoner, and no other hand, that murdered this woman? If you are not so satisfied, if it is not proved, whatever your feelings may be . . . then it is your duty to find the prisoner not guilty.

The jury, after an hour's retirement, found the prisoner guilty.

The prisoner, being asked if he had anything to say, briefly replied: 'I am not guilty. I don't want to say anything else.'

In passing sentence, the judge, whose summing-up had been a most brilliant exposition of the inconclusive nature of the evidence, pointedly omitted the customary expression of agreement with the verdict.

It is said that, when the verdict was announced, a gasp of surprise went round the court. On the general public, if not on the jury, the summing-up had produced a deep impression.

Nor, whatever rumours may have been going about beforehand in the neighbourhood of Wolverton Street, was the main body of Liverpudlians at all happy about the conviction. Their extreme uneasiness led to one result which was logical enough, no doubt, but highly unusual in this Christian country: a special Service of Intercession was held in Liverpool Cathedral that God might guide the Court of Criminal Appeal to a right decision when the case of Wallace came before it.

The answer to prayer might be considered spectacular. On May 19th, the Lords of Appeal, after a two days' hearing quashed the conviction on the ground that the evidence was insufficient to support the verdict; this being the first time in English legal history that a conviction for murder had been set aside on those grounds. The phrasing of the judgment is exceedingly cautious, but, in the words of the learned barrister to whom we owe the best and fullest study of this extraordinary case:

> The fact that the Court of Criminal Appeal decided to quash the conviction shows how strong must have been the views of the judges that the verdict was not merely against the weight of evidence, but that it was unreasonable.

Judges in this country are, indeed, exceedingly jealous of any interference with the powers and privileges of a jury, and will in general always uphold its verdict unless they see very strong reason to the contrary.

The judgments of God, unlike those of earthly judges, are, however, inscrutable. Any writer of fiction rash enough to embellish his *dénouement* with an incident so unlikely as a public appeal to Divine Justice must interpret the answer according to his own theological fancy. If he believes that the All-Just and All-Merciful declared for the innocent through the mouths of the Lords of Appeal, the facts will support that theory; but if he believes that the world is ruled by an ingenious sadist, eager to wring the last ounce of suffering out of an offending creature, he may point out that Wallace was preserved only to suffer two years of complicated mental torture and to die at length by a far crueller death than the hangman's rope. Like every other piece of testimony in the Wallace case, the evidence may be interpreted both ways.

The Prudential Assurance Company, who had behaved throughout in a very friendly way to Wallace, expressed their full belief in his innocence by at once taking him back and giving him a new job in their employment. It was, however, impossible for him to continue with his work as a collector on account of the suspicion which still clung about him. He was, in fact, obliged to leave Liverpool and retire to a cottage in Cheshire. The diary which he kept for a year after his release contains many references to the rebuffs he received from his former acquaintances, together with expressions of his love for his wife which have every appearance of being genuine. He seems to have spent his spare time pottering about his garden and equipping his home with little ingenious household gadgets, and trying every means to fight off the appalling loneliness of spirit which threatened to overcome him. 'What I fear most is the long nights.' 'I seem to miss her more and more, and cannot drive the thought of her cruel end out of my mind.' 'There are now several daffodils in bloom, and lots of tulips coming along. How delighted dear Julia would have been, and I can only too sadly picture how lovingly she would have tended the garden.'

On September 14, 1931, occurs a remarkable passage:

Just as I was going to dinner —— stopped me, and said he wanted to talk to me for a few minutes. It was a desperately awkward position. Eventually I decided not to hear what he had to say. I told him I would talk to him some day and give him something to think about. He must realize that I suspect him of the terrible crime. I fear I let him see clearly what I thought, and it may unfortunately put him on his guard. I wonder if it is any good putting a private detective on to his track in the hope of something coming to light. I am more than half persuaded to try it.

Other allusions to the same person are made from time to time. Are we to believe them sincere? Or must we suppose that all this was part of some strange elaborate scheme for bamboozling the world through the medium of a private diary, which there was no reason to suppose that anyone was likely to see but Wallace himself? That he should have made this kind of accusation (as he did) in newspaper articles proves nothing; but the diary (which is far more restrained and convincing in style than the statements published over his signature) is another matter. One can only say that, if he was a guilty man, he kept up the pretence of innocence to himself with an extraordinary assiduity and appearance of sincerity.

On February 26, 1933, Wallace died of cancer of the kidneys. It is, of course, well known that disease affecting those organs produces very remarkable and deleterious changes in a person's character; but whether the trouble had already begun in 1931, and if so, whether it could have resulted in so strange a madness, with such a combination of cunning and bestial ferocity as the murderer of Julia Wallace displayed, is a matter for physicians to judge. So far as can be seen, Wallace showed no signs of mental or spiritual deterioration either before or after the crume.

It is interesting to compare the case of Wallace with that of the unfortunate clergyman, the Rev. J. S. Watson, who in 1869 murdered his wife under rather similar circumstances. Here, again, it was the case of a childless couple who had married for love and lived peaceably together for many years. The husband, a man of mild behaviour and considerable literary ability, suddenly seized the opportunity one afternoon, when the servant was out of the house, to batter his wife to death with exactly the same uncontrolled brutality as was used on Mrs Wallace. But here the resemblance ends. Poor Mr Watson had for some time shown symptoms of melancholia and disturbance of mind; the wife was known to drink; there had been quarrels; and the husband, though at first he denied his guilt, soon after made an attempt at suicide and confessed the crime; nor, though he at first made some blundering efforts to cover up his tracks, did Watson contrive anything remotely approaching the elaborate ingenuity of the 'Qualtrough' alibi. The superficial resemblances only serve to emphasize the fundamental disparity between the two cases.

Though a man apparently well-balanced may give way to a sudden murderous frenzy, and may even combine that frenzy with a surprising amount of coolness and cunning, it is rare for him to show *no* premonitory or subsequent symptoms of mental disturbance. This was one of the psychological difficulties in the way of the prosecution against Wallace. Dr MacFall gave it as his opinion that the brutality of the murder was a sign of frenzy. He was asked:

> So, if this is the work of a maniac, and Wallace is a sane man, he did not do it?—He may be sane now.

> If he has been sane all his life, and is sane now, it would be some momentary frenzy?—The mind is very peculiar.

> The fact that a man has been sane fifty-two years, and has been sane while in custody for the last three months, would rather tend to prove that he has always been sane?—Not necessarily. . . . We know very little about the private lives of persons or their thoughts.

The mind is indeed peculiar and the thoughts of the heart hidden. It is hopeless to explain the murder of Julia Wallace as the result of a momentary frenzy, whether Wallace was the criminal or another. The crime was carefully prepared in cold blood; the extraordinary ferocity of the actual assault was probably due less to frenzied savagery than to sudden alarm at the actual moment of the murder. It has, over and over again, come as a shocking surprise to murderers that their victims took so long to die and make such a mess about it; they have struck repeated blows, to make sure, confessing afterwards, 'I thought she would never die'; 'Who could have thought that the old man had so much blood in him?'

Before leaving the case for the consideration of those who may like to make of it a 'tale for a chimney-corner', two small points ought perhaps to be mentioned. One is the statement

made by a young woman at the trial that on the night of the
murder she saw Wallace at about 8.40 at night 'talking to a
man' at the bottom of the entry to Richmond Park, near Breck
Road. She did not know Wallace at all well, and he himself
denied the whole episode. In all probability she was quite
mistaken, nor could anything very much be made out of the
story either by the prosecution or the defence; it is mentioned
here only for completeness and for the sake of any suggestion it
may offer for the novelist's ingenuity to work upon. The only
practical step that was taken about it seems to have been that
the police made an especially careful search of the waste ground
in and about Richmond Park in the hope of finding the iron bar;
but without success.

The second point concerns the choice of the name 'Qualtrough'. This name is extremely common in the Isle of Man,
and should also, therefore, be pretty familiar to Liverpudlians.
It might therefore seem a suspicious circumstance that Wallace
should have professed never to have heard it before, but that it
was apparently unknown also to Mr Beattie, and that among
Wallace's other acquaintances at the chess club only one said
he had 'heard it once before'. Now, if one is preparing to give a
false name, one will, as a rule, give a name that is exceedingly
common, such as Brown or Smith, or one that is subconsciously
already in one's mind for some reason or another. Since, to
Manxmen, the name 'Qualtrough' is apparently as familiar as
'Smith' to an Englishman, it might seem reasonable to look for
a murderer who either came from Man, or frequently went
there for reasons of business or pleasure. On the other hand, if it
could be shown that Wallace (either through the books of the
Prudential or in some other connexion) had recently had the
name brought to his notice, then that fact would strengthen
suspicion against him, particularly in view of his categorical
statement that he had never heard it before. It is a little curious
that if the name was exceedingly well known in that part of
Liverpool, no one should have drawn attention to the fact in
evidence. The detective writer ought not, I think, to neglect
that line of investigation.

There, then, the story remains, a mystery as insoluble as
when the Court of Appeal decided that there was no evidence

upon which to come to a conclusion. 'We are not,' said the Lord Chief Justice, 'concerned here with suspicion, however grave, or with theories, however ingenious.' But the detective novelist does, and must, concern himself with ingenious theories, and here is a case ready made for him, in which scarcely any 'theory, however ingenious' could very well come amiss. It is interesting that the story should already have been handled twice by writers of fiction, and both times from the point of view that Wallace may have been guilty. Mr George Goodchild and Mr C. E. Bechhofer Roberts in *The Jury Disagree* have used the case only as a basis on which to erect a story which includes fresh incidents and complications not forming part of the actual evidence, and have given it a 'key-incident' solution in the recognized 'detective' manner. Miss Winifred Duke, in *Skin for Skin*, has followed the facts with scrupulous exactness, concerning herself almost exclusively with the psychological problem of how Wallace might have come to do it (if he did do it) and what effect it had upon him.

With both novels, the criminal's motive may be summed-up in the cynical words of *Marriage à la Mode*:

> Palamede: O, now I have found it! you dislike her for no other reason but that she's your wife.
> Rhodophil: And is not that enough?

It remains for some other writer, who does not find it 'enough', or who is convinced by his study of the case that Wallace was telling the truth, or who merely prefers the more out-of-the-way solution to the more obvious one, to tell the story again, identifying 'Qualtrough' with that to us unknown man whom Wallace himself named as the murderer.

AFTERWORD

A personal note: when I was twelve, my family moved to the Merseyside village of Bromborough. I had just built myself a canoe, and the couple living in the bungalow opposite our house kindly offered to let me keep it in their loft. I was astonished and not a little thrilled when the local boys told me not to set foot in the bungalow because a murderer *had once lived there. The older villagers remembered him well. They at least had no doubt that he had 'done away with' his wife and, I gathered, had taken every opportunity to make their views clear to him.*

More than twenty years after Wallace's death, in the village to which he had retired he was still a sort of bogeyman.

For someone who was acquitted it seems a harsh fate, and most modern criminologists would uphold that final verdict—indeed, they have gone to great pains to try and establish once and for all Wallace's innocence. Not long ago there was an unofficial re-trial in Liverpool, where the evidence was reconsidered and, I gather, the 'real' murderer was identified: a man known to both Wallace and his wife, but still alive and who therefore could not be named publicly. For obvious reasons, this cannot be explored further at this moment, but it is highly probable that some day soon the Wallace case will be—well, perhaps not solved, but certainly re-opened.

Sightseers often visit the Menlove complex of streets in Liverpool, but not to try and find Menlove Gardens East or anything else to do with William Herbert Wallace. They are looking for Penny Lane, which is just around the corner, or Strawberry Fields, or Menlove Avenue, where Auntie Mimi looked after the young John Lennon, another victim.

ALEXANDER WOOLLCOTT

The Elwell Case

ALEXANDER WOOLLCOTT

The Elwell Case

In a sense which would have delighted Sherlock Holmes, the Elwell murder was marked by a set of extremely prominent teeth. You may remember the mystery in which Holmes called the attention of the Scotland Yard inspector to the curious incident of the dog in the nighttime.

'But,' said the obliging inspector, 'the dog did nothing in the nighttime.'

'That,' said Holmes, 'was the curious incident.'

In the murder of Joseph B. Elwell, his false teeth provided a similarly curious incident. In fact they were so conspicuous by their absence that they became important evidence in the case.

When Elwell's housekeeper, arriving for work as usual on the morning of June 11, 1920, found her kind employer dying in the reception room with a bullet wound in his forehead, the gleaming teeth which had illumined many a seductive smile in his career as a philanderer, were not where she had always seen them. They were upstairs in the glass of water beside his bed.

Upstairs also was the entire collection of toupees which had long helped to maintain the illusion that he was still a dashing young blade. Forty wigs there were in that hidden collection, yet not one of them was on his head when his fate came roaring at him out of the muzzle of a .45 automatic on that June morning twenty-three years ago.

Before that day's sun was high in the heavens, detectives and reporters were delightedly swarming over the Elwell house, which, since his housekeeper, valet and chauffeur all slept out, was exceptionally convenient for hanky-panky.

In particular the reporters relished the boudoir delicately furnished for a guest, the monogrammed pajamas left behind

Joseph Elwell on one of his racehorses.

there by one greatly embarrassed visitor, and the long telephone directory—obviously compiled with loving care—of fair
ladies, each of whom was promptly called upon for an alibi.

But if one thing is certain about Joseph Elwell's death, it is
that he would have shot himself rather than let one of these
ladies see him as the bald and toothless old sport he really was.

The press yearned to assume that that bullet was fired by a
woman scorned, but although there is no doubt that Elwell was
a ladies' man, the one who killed him was certainly no lady.

This case caused the greater stir at the time because not since
a Pittsburgh defective named Harry Thaw shot and killed the
great Stanford White had the victim of a murder been a man
already so widely known. For this Joseph B. Elwell was the Ely
Culbertson of the bridge world shortly after the turn of the
century.

In the days when contract was undreamed of and the
courtesy of the time said that one might not even lead at all until
one's partner had replied, 'Pray do,' to the question, 'Partner,
may I play?' all earnest addicts studied *Elwell on Bridge.*

Elwell left the writing of these textbooks to his wife, and he
also left his wife.

After their separation, he moved on up in the sporting world,
with houses of his own at Palm Beach, Saratoga Springs, and
Long Beach and, for a final touch of magnificence, a racing
stable in Kentucky.

It was, however, in his New York house at 244 West 70th
Street that he was killed, and only the night before he had been
dining at the Ritz and attending the Midnight Frolic of the
Ziegfeld Roof in company with men and women whose names
and faces were already familiar in what later was to be known
as Café Society.

All the evidence tends to suggest that he went home alone
and remained alone at least until after the first visit of the
postman next morning, for he had come downstairs barefoot
and in his wrinkled pajamas, and was reading a letter out of the
morning mail when he was shot.

Now the postman dropped that mail at 7.10 and the murderer had departed before the arrival of the housekeeper one hour
later. It is difficult to escape the conclusion that the murderer

was someone Elwell himself admitted, maybe someone he had sent for and was expecting, perhaps someone bringing a report from the early morning workout at a racing stable, certainly someone in whose presence he would not mind sitting with his wig off and his teeth out, reading a letter.

But why not a burglar trapped in the house and shooting his way out? Or why not an enemy—Elwell had more than one man's share of enemies—who, having gained access the day before, had been biding his time ever since? To each of these questions there are many answers, but one conclusive answer fits them both. It is difficult to imagine why an unexpected person would (or how any unexpected person could) have come around the calmly seated Elwell (whose chair, with its back to the wall, faced the fireplace), stood squarely in front of him and shot him between the eyes.

No, Elwell must have known Mr X was there. He merely did not know that Mr X was going to kill him.

One other point. The upward course of the bullet led the police to suspect that Mr X shot from the pocket or from the hip. Of course there is always the possibility that he may have been a midget, a belated suggestion which will either amuse or annoy him if he happens to read this memoir of his successful but anonymous achievement. Whoever he was, or wherever he is, he also has it on his conscience that he brought into this world one of the most irritating detectives in the whole library of criminous fiction.

It was the nice police problem presented by the Elwell murder which prompted a previously obscure pundit named Willard Huntington Wright to try his hand at his first of many detective stories. Under the pen name of S. S. Van Dine he turned Elwell's obituary into *The Benson Murder Case*, introducing for the first time that laboriously nonchalant, cultured, and tedious detective, Philo Vance.

ELIZABETH JENKINS

The Balham
Mystery

ELIZABETH JENKINS

The Balham Mystery

Some lives suggest irresistibly the theory of reincarnation; actions which their possessors commit appear to us no worse or more momentous than the identical actions committed by scores of others with complete impunity, yet in these lives their consequences are so profound, so ruinous, it seems impossible to believe that the cruel punishment was earned by the single act. We feel that some awful pattern of cause and effect is being woven on a plane that is beyond our immediate vision; that the retribution has been set in motion by the single act, but that it was earned elsewhere and at another time; that what we see in front of us is a short length of a chain whose beginning and end are hidden from us in this existence.

Such feelings are hard to withstand when one thinks about the Balham Mystery, with its victim, its criminal who was never named and the broken lives left in its wake.

The Campbells were a wealthy merchant family, with a country house, Buscot Park, in Berkshire, and a town house in Lowndes Square. They had several children, of whom the most interesting was their daughter Florence. This was an unusually attractive girl, radiant and gentle, but with a somewhat erratic strain of self-will. She was of a small, pretty, rounded figure, with large and widely set blue eyes, and a mass of hair that is variously described as red-gold and bright chestnut. There was no difficulty in marrying off such a charming creature, and in 1864, when she was nineteen, she was married to Captain Ricardo, a wealthy young guards officer of twenty-three.

Captain Ricardo undoubtedly had a great deal of money, but there his eligibility as a husband might be said to have begun and ended. The fact that he had married a beautiful girl of nineteen did not deter him from keeping a mistress, and the amount he drank seemed deplorable even to a hard-drinking age. Nor was he a man who could be left to drink himself under the table while a wife quietly pursued an independent existence; the unhappy bride was subjected to all the harassing torments of reconciliations, promises, relapses and promises again. Such an introduction to married life would have broken down most girls, and Florence was particularly unfitted to bear it. Her vitality was high—her glowing appearance and her strong natural faculty for enjoyment proclaimed it—but it was a purely physical characteristic. When she was subjected to any emotional strain she went to pieces, and the experiences of five years as Captain Ricardo's wife had all but reduced her to a nervous wreck. If she had been a plain woman, who had learned to adapt herself to slights and to make the best of what was going, she would have managed better; but she had come from an affectionate home, in all the natural self-confidence of a lovely girl. The shock and bewilderment, the undreamed-of humiliations of her position, had undermined her completely. There was only one consolation which she had found in her married life. It was drink, She had found out that the best way to endure Captain Ricardo's weakness was to share it.

By the time she was twenty-four she had sunk into absolute ill-health. Her mother persuaded her to come away to Malvern to try the hydropathic cure, and Captain Ricardo in one of his fits of reconciliation and promised amendment was to join her there. It was hoped, with singular optimism, that he, too, might find benefit from the water treatment.

Malvern had long been a spa, but it had developed with great rapidity as the Metropolis of the Water Cure, since 1842, when Dr Wilson and Dr Gully had settled there and introduced their system which had become nationally famous. Though Wilson had introduced the idea of hydrotherapy, which he had picked up abroad from a Bavarian peasant named Preissnitz, Gully was so much the abler man of the two that he soon became the leading figure, and in a few years had made Malver famous all over the British Isles. His system consisted in the application of water in every form: packing in wet sheets, sitz baths, douches, compresses, showers whether lateral or horizontal, spinal washings, foot baths, plunge baths and friction with dripping towels. His patients included Tennyson, Carlyle, Charles Reade, Bulwer Lytton, Bishop Wilberforce and 'a host of the favourites of society'. Though his success was sensational, there was no suspicion of quackery about him. He was a thoroughly trained medical man; and though his success was no doubt assisted by his great personal magnetism, the influence this gave him over his patients was a legitimate attribute of the eminent doctor. He was now sixty-two, not tall, but dignified and erect, with handsome, clear-cut features and an expression of warmth and candour.

Florence Ricardo had once been taken to Dr Gully when she was a child of twelve, so that her present visit to Malvern was in a sense the renewal of an old acquaintance. That she succumbed at once to the influence of Dr Gully's personality needs no explanation and hardly an excuse. She was ill because she was miserable and miserable because she was ill. Dr Gully treated her with the profound sympathy and scientific understanding, the warm, impersonal kindness, which only a doctor can bestow. She had never known anything like it. Her experience of men had begun at nineteen when she found herself married to a husband who left the house to go to a mistress and drank himself silly when he stopped at home. Though she was headstrong she was not self-reliant; she would have leaned on a husband if she could. As it was, her husband was weaker than she, and his scandalous ill-treatment of her alternated with fits of grovelling repentance and self-abasement. Dr Gully, who was authoritative, calm and kind, provided exactly the support that her unhappy state cried aloud for; above all, he was an exceptionally able physician, under whose care she got well again. It was no wonder that when her whole nature turned towards him with gratitude and admiration, her emotion overpassed the prescribed boundary and turned into romantic love. The fact that Dr Gully was old enough to be her father was no hindrance to this. Her devastating experience of a young husband made her yearn for the lover who would be also a father.

Matters were in this somewhat equivocal state when fresh outbursts on Captain Ricardo's part decided the Campbells

that their daughter should not be asked to continue this
existence; the outcome of their decision was that Captain
Ricardo consented to a deed of separation by which Florence
was to live apart from him and to receive an allowance of one
thousand two hundred pounds a year. This took place in 1870.
The following year, Captain Ricardo, who had retired to
Cologne with a mistress, died there suddenly, before he had
revoked the will made on his marriage. Thus at twenty-five
Florence was left a widow, with four thousand pounds a year in
her own right.

Her family regarded the event as a release, and yet the
position was far from reassuring. Up till now Florence had been
first under her parents' control, and then under the nominal
control of a husband. She had not caused anybody anxiety,
except by her unhappiness and ill-health, but if she had, her
father or her husband could have exerted considerable pressure
on her by the mere fact that she had no means of support except
what either of them chose to give her. Now it was very different.
As a widow, she was completely her own mistress, with a large
income entirely at her own disposal. There she was, in Malvern, and there was Dr Gully.

Released from the monstrous bondage in which the first
years of her adult life had been passed, her wilful, luxurious
nature now asserted itself. To look at the likeness of her face,
with its large, emotional eyes, its expression of mingled softness
and intensity, is to feel that it is no unkind or unreasonable
judgment that the motive force which brought together her and
Dr Gully came from her. Dr Gully was a very busy man, in a
large and exacting practice; not only had he been grounded in
the high traditions of his profession, but if he had not been a
man whose emotions were under his own control he would
never have achieved his remarkable success. On the other
hand, if a determined siege were to be laid to him, this of all
others was the time of his life when it might be expected to
succeed. He was nearing the end of his professional life.
Though left to himself he would no doubt have continued in
practice for some time longer, he was within sight of the time
when he would have relinquished it in any case. He was
extremely well-to-do (the income from his practice was esti-

mated at ten thousand pounds), and though he was in fact a married man, his son was grown up and his wife, who was in an asylum, had been separated from him for thirty years. If anyone could be excused for regarding himself as a free agent when in actual fact he was not it was surely a man in the position of Dr Gully. On the other side Florence was very young, but she was not inexperienced. However impetuous her approaches had been, he would have been very unlikely to admit them had she been an unmarried girl, but her misfortunes had made her a woman of the world, and she was responsible to nobody but herself. At the same time, she was not only fascinating but she had the charm of youth, and to Dr Gully as a man of over sixty her devotion was not only enchanting, it was flattering to an unusual degree. It was difficult to prove at what date they became lovers, but it was afterwards considered certain that it was while Dr Gully was still in practice at Malvern. A great deal depended on this point, and when it was regarded as having been proved the decision was fatally unfortunate for him.

Florence very early in her widowhood became at variance with her family, who strongly disapproved of her infatuation for Dr Gully, and before long her parents told her that they would have no communication with her until she gave it up. So strong was the convention of the time that Mr and Mrs Campbell took this drastic step of refusing all intercourse with their daughter, although they imagined her infatuation to be indiscreet rather than actually immoral. It was a strange characteristic in a charming young woman that she was almost friendless. Perhaps her capacity to absorb herself in an emotional adventure argued a certain self-centredness that would repel a friend as it would attract a lover. At all events, her separation from her family left her without a social circle, and she accepted the offer of accommodation from her solicitor, Mr Brooks, in his house on Tooting Common. Mr Brooks had three daughters, for whom he employed a daily governess, an unremarkable woman of middle age, a widow named Jane Cannon Cox. The most noticeable feature of Mrs Cox's appearance was her spectacles, which apparently had the effect of quite obscuring the expression of her face. Drawings of her emphasize this so much that it

seems likely the glasses were tinted. Her dark hair, in one of the
less prepossessing fashions of the time, was scraped back from
her temples and so arranged that the top of her head looked
pointed like a bee-hive. The dress of the 'seventies, which
concentrated all the fullness of the drapery at the back, left the
front of the figure, rigidly corseted, tightly outlined from the
shoulder to the knee. The effect on Mrs Cox's somewhat low
and meagre frame was to give her the outline of a black beetle.

Mrs Cox had the efficiency and self-possession of a woman
who has had to make her way against odds. Her husband had
been an engineer in Jamaica, but he had died and left her to
provide for three young sons. She had been assisted by a
wealthy friend, a Mr Joseph Bravo. By his advice she had
invested her small amount of money in a furnished house in
Lancaster Road, Notting Hill, which she let, while she herself
went out as a governess to Mr Brooks's family. Her three boys
were placed at a school in Streatham for the sons of distressed
gentlefolk. Quietness, respectability, usefulness and pleasant-
ness to an employer were not, in Mrs Cox's case, mere unself-
conscious traits of character; they would more properly be
described as weapons, held in an unfaltering grasp, with which
she waged the battle with the world that was to win the
livelihood of her children and herself. She was not in any sense
attractive, but her powers of mind were considerable, and since
these were all directed towards making herself agreeable to
people more fortunately placed than herself it was not surprising that she was successful. She soon made herself pleasant to
the rich, voluptuous young widow, then useful and at last
indispensible. Dr Gulley meanwhile, in 1872, sold his practice and retired from Malvern. His retirement was a civic
event; demonstrations of respect and gratitude were made by
every clas of society and the town acknowledged that it was
his working there for thirty years which had brought pros-
perity to it. He did not immediately settle upon a house. He
took lodgings opposite to Mr Brooks's house on Tooting
Common.

That Florence had no friends of her own did not mean that she
felt able to do without them. Her infatuation for Dr Gully was
the most important thing in her life, but their liaison could not

supply the want of a social circle. The usage of the time obliged the lovers to behave with the utmost secrecy and discretion. They could enjoy very little of each other's society in an open manner. Florence still needed a friend for daily wear, and as a rich and somewhat self-indulgent young woman she also wanted somebody to take the troubles of her establishment off her hands. It was not long before the idea of Mrs Cox presented itself to her, irresistibly. Mrs Cox seemed to have every qualification that Florence could imagine as desirable. She was excellent in household management, and she knew how to order an establishment for rich people, how to control a large staff of servants and to see that a high standard of comfort and elegance was maintained. Nothing was irksome to her, no trouble was too great; in a quiet and unobstrusive way she whole-heartedly identified herself with the owner of the establishment. Then, too, she was a gentlewoman; and though personally unattractive and in narrow circumstances, she was presentable as a companion, and in her tact, sympathy, affection and common sense she was quite invaluable. Mrs Cox, on her part, was exceedingly happy to exchange the drudgery and poor pay of a governess for the luxury and freedom, the authority, of friend and companion to such an employer as Florence Ricardo. The opportunity was indeed exceptionally fortunate. The generosity of Florence's nature had had few outlets, and she thoroughly enjoyed being good to Mrs Cox. Their footing was one of complete social equality; they called each other Florence and Janie. And Florence not only did everything possible to make her companion happy under her roof—Mrs Cox received a salary of one hundred pounds a year, but her incidental expenses, which were all paid for her, including many items of her dress, came to three times this amount—but her employer took a warm interest in Mrs Cox's three boys. Their school holidays were spent with their mother in Mrs Ricardo's house.

When Florence left Mr Brooks's house, taking Mrs Cox with her, she settled herself for the time being in a house in Leigham Court Road, Streatham Hill. The house she had occupied in Malvern, where the great bliss of her life had come to her, had been called Stokefield, and she named this house Stokefield

also. At her suggestion Dr Gully bought a house which was
available on the opposite side of the road. That a woman so
astute as Mrs Cox should not have realized on what terms her
employer and Dr Gully were anyone may believe who likes; but
at least the polite fiction was kept up that the relationship was
merely one of devoted friendship. Dr Gully often came to meals.
He called his hostess by her Christian name, and they kissed
each other. In Mrs Cox's opinion, he was 'a very fascinating
man, likely to be of great interest to women'. She went so far as
to say that, though she believed the friendship to be quite
innocent, had Dr Gully been unmarried it would no doubt
'have been a match.'

In this year, 1872, Dr Gully and Mrs Ricardo went for a
holiday to the baths at Kissingen. They attempted no deceit;
they travelled under their own names and occupied separate
rooms in their hotels, but as a result of their time abroad
Florence had a miscarriage when she came home. Dr Gully
attended her, but she was nursed by Mrs Cox. She said that she
had at the time entirely concealed from Mrs Cox the cause of
the illness, and made out, what she had in fact at first thought to
be the case, that it was the result of a severe internal derange-
ment brought on by the baths at Kissingen. Mrs Cox's untiring
devotion to her during weeks of illness and prostration established the companion's claim on her more firmly than ever.

In 1874 Florence decided upon a permanent house. This was
an estate of ten acres known as the Priory at Balham. The house
had been built in the early 1800s and was a charming example
of the Walpole Gothic, simple, airy, graceful, that was later to
be submerged in the hideous Municipal Gothic of the Victorian
age. The Priory, with its pale tint, its crenellated roof, its arched
doorway, and windows with pointed upper panes, belonged to
the last era in English social life that produced charming
architecture. On the front lawn stood a giant oak tree, said to be
a hundred and fifty years old. Behind was the sunny 'garden
front', laid out in turf, gravelled paths and numerous flower-
beds. There were a greenhouse, a grapehouse, a melon pit,
large strawberry beds and a vegetable garden. Florence filled
the house with luxury, gaiety and comfort. Her morning-room
housed a sparkling collection of Venetian glass and opened into

The Priory, Balham.

a small conservatory. She liked this effect so much that she repeated it in the drawing-room, where she threw out one of the windows to make a fernery. Here she assembled a grove of exquisite ferns, for some of which she had paid twenty guineas each. Horticulture was one of her keenest enjoyments and she kept the garden in a high state of perfection, filling the beds with flowers and planting standard rose trees everywhere. The Victorian age was one of hot summers, and the windows of the Priory were shaded with striped awnings, which added their inimitable touch of festivity to the scene of a well-kept English garden on a hot summer day. Another of Florence's pleasures was driving. She kept one carriage horse for her landau—this was driven by her coachman; but she drove herself in a phaeton with two 'handsome actioned' cobs, called Victor and Cremorne. The pamphlet, *The Balham Mystery*, issued in seven numbers in 1876, contains instead of press photographs a series of pen-and-ink drawings of remarkable vividness. The press photographer has superseded the press artist, and it comes as a surprise to our generation to see how excellent the latter was. One of the illustrations shows Florence driving her cobs. The tiger sits behind with folded arms while she bowls along at a smart pace. The drawing shows a woman who drove very well. She wears a close-fitting jacket with a bow under her chin, and a wide-brimmed hat shaded by a feather, under which her hair streams away behind her ears. By her side, upright, collected and demure, sits Mrs Cox.

Within a few months of Florence's having bought the Priory Dr Gully bought a house in Bedford Hill Road, a few minutes away from the Priory lodge. The long slope of grass and trees terminating in the level ground of the Priory was unbuilt on, except for six houses, all of the same design, halfway up on the left-hand side. Dr Gully took the first, which was called Orwell Lodge. He, like Florence, seemed to regard his new establishments as a permanent one. He furnished it from top to bottom and installed his own servants, of whom the chief was his butler Pritchard, who was devoted to him and had been with him for twenty years. The neighbourhood in 1875 was still extremely retired. Bedford Hill Road was so quiet that when Florence built a second lodge to open the estate on that side, though the new lodge stood directly upon the road without the protection even of a paling, the climbing roses she trained all over its front hung undisturbed. There were no censorious neighbours to overlook their private lives. Dr Gully had a key to one of the doors of the Priory. The parlour-maid said: 'I never opened the door to him, but I have found him in the house.' He came frequently to lunch and stayed to dine. Once or twice when Mrs Cox was away he stayed the night. The Priory coachman, Griffiths, had previously been in Dr Gully's service. Now that Dr Gully had left off practice, he did not keep a carriage and Florence had taken Griffiths on. He and his wife lived in the new lodge. Three or four times a week Griffiths drove the doctor and Mrs Ricardo out in the landau. He would take up Dr Gully in one of the quiet roads near his house, and set him down again before he reached the gate of Orwell Lodge. Sometimes they drove in to London, but more often their drives were through the undisturbed country about Tooting Common. On frequent occasions Florence, accompanied by her chaperone, would come to meals at the doctor's house. When this happened, the butler Pritchard could see that, though his master and Mrs Ricardo were still very much attached to each other, the affair had become worn down to the level of ordinary existence. 'They often quarrelled,' he said.

The Bravos who had befriended Mrs Cox lived in a large house on Palace Green, Kensington. The family of three were Mr and Mrs Bravo and the latter's son by a previous marriage. Charles Bravo, who had taken his stepfather's name, was the idol, not only of his mother, but of his stepfather also. He was a good-looking young man, with dark hair, rounded features and an expression at once pugnacious and egotistical. Mr Joseph Bravo had brought him up from a child, educated him and seen him established at the bar. He doted on what he took to be the young man's great cleverness, and he loved him as fondly as if Charles had been in fact his son. Charles Bravo would not appear to have been strikingly gifted in the profession had had chosen. He was nearly thirty and his gains as a barrister were still almost nominal; but despite the fact that his stepfather gave him as much money as he could want, and that he had therefore no financial incentive to work very hard at an unrewarding

profession, he did not the less devote himself to it. He went
to his chambers every day and followed his profession as if
his bread had depended on it. He had kept a mistress for the
past four years, but the intense possessiveness of his mother and
the indulgent kindness of his stepfather had so far prevented
him from any inclination to be married.

One day Florence Ricardo went in the carriage to London to
do a day's shopping and arranged to drop Mrs Cox at Palace
Green to call upon her friends, and to pick her up again on the
way home. When, later in the day, Mrs Ricardo's carriage was
announced at the Bravos' door, Mrs Bravo courteously sent out
a request that Mrs Ricardo would come in for a few minutes. It
so happened that Charles Bravo was in his mother's drawing-
room when the lady with bright auburn hair was shown in, but
neither he nor she seemed at that time to take much notice of
each other. The visit was short and, though extremely civil, was
purely formal one.

In 1875 Dr Gully went abroad with some of his own relations. Though she might quarrel with him, Florence found her
house dull and wearisome when he was not at hand, and to
relieve the tedium of her lover's absence she took Mrs Cox on a
visit to Brighton. It was autumn, and Brighton was not gay.
The beauty of the Regency squares and terraces was not
appreciated by the taste of the 1870s, and the half-empty streets
and the sea under autumnal mists and gales did not restore
Florence's spirits. They had themselves photographed, but
there was really very little to do.

Brighton, however, is within very easy distance of London
and its advantage as a resort is that so many people run down
from London for the day. By a really remarkable coincidence,
in one of their walks they met Charles Bravo. The first meeting
between him and Florence had passed off apparently in complete indifference on both sides, but on the second one it seemed
as if a seed, long germinating, had suddenly burst into flower.
Mrs Cox was of course polite and cordial. It was not open to her
to be anything else. Her paramount duty to herself and her
children was to be pleasant to her employer, and whatever her
opinion of the rapidly-forming intimacy might have been it
would have had no weight with Florence. The latter might be

dependent on her friend up to a certain point, but in anything which concerned her pleasures she was entirely her own mistress and intended to remain so.

Florence had not an admirable character, but one of her strongest charms was naturalness, and though her actions might be unwise or even discreditable they were always understandable and such as would arouse sympathy. Her passion for Dr Gully was almost inevitable and the same might be said of its termination. She needed the love and protection of an elderly man to restore her after the shattering experiences of her first marriage, but when this influence had done its work and her being had recovered its normal balance she was ready to fall in love again with a man of her own age. Charles Bravo and she were both nearly thirty. She was independent by legal settlements and he was virtually so through the affection of his stepfather. If they chose to marry there would be no need of a long engagement. Charles Bravo was undoubtedly much attracted by Florence, but it is equally certain that what induced him to think of marrying her was her income. They were, however, well suited personally: young, vigorous, pleasure-loving, a virile man and an extremely feminine woman. The growth of mutual attraction went on fast and it was obvious that Charles Bravo's proposal would soon be made.

In October Dr Gully returned to England and he came down to see Florence at Brighton. She now acted with great duplicity. She told Dr Gully that the estrangement from her family, which could never be ended as long as her liaison with him lasted, had made her very unhappy for some time, and as her mother was now ill she wished earnestly to be reunited to her parents. She had decided therefore that the time had come for them to part. Dr Gully behaved with the unselfish kindness of real affection, in spite of having received a very disagreeable shock. He had had no preparation for this event. He said afterwards: 'I was very much attached to her at the time, and I had thought that she was fondly attached to me.' But he said that she must do whatever she felt was necessary to her own happiness and well-being. In November Charles Bravo proposed to her and she accepted him. When Dr Gully heard of this, he was at first thoroughly angry. After giving up his practice and his public position as one of the most eminent doctors of the day, and being at her beck and call for five years, he now found himself cavalierly thrown over for another man and shamelessly deceived as well. He wrote her one angry letter, but after that his anger subsided. He was sixty-six; and though the love affair had been an enchanting embellishment to his existence, what he really wanted now was peace and quiet, and a connection with a spoilt and exacting young woman, particularly one who was inclined to drink too much, was probably, as Sir John Hall suggests, something that on calmer reflection he was quite prepared to give up.

In the rest of Florence's small circle feeling was much mixed. Her own parents were delighted, first that she should have put an end to the liaison for which they had felt obliged to disown her, and secondly that she was going to marry a man of suitable age, steady character and the prospect of great wealth. Their reconciliation with their daughter was complete. On the other side, however, the idea was received with open animosity Mr Bravo's feelings were not disclosed, but Mrs Bravo, who would have been unwilling to see her son marry anybody, was horrified that he should marry Florence, whose independence, worldliness and sensual attractions filled her with hostile dismay. She would have stopped the marriage if she could, and once it was an accomplished fact she did the little that was in her power to upset its smoothness.

Mrs Bravo's enmity to the match was open enough, but there was some elsewhere that expressed itself in a more subtle and tortuous manner. Florence had not been candid with Dr Gully, but it was to the credit of her good feeling and also her common sense that she was perfectly open with Charles Bravo about her past. She told him the whole story of her affair with Dr Gully and he in return told her of his having had a mistress for the past four years, and each agreed that now all had been admitted they would never speak of the past again. Charles Bravo even discussed the matter with his future wife's companion. He said he should imagine that a woman who had once gone wrong would be even more likely to go straight in the future than one who had never strayed. What, he asked, was Mrs Cox's opinion? Mrs Cox had no doubt that he was quite right; but she did not stop there. She so much approved of the frankness the parties had shown to each other, that she wanted to see it carried even further. She suggested that the whole story of Dr Gully's relation with her future daughter-in-law should be explained to Mrs Bravo. Charles flatly refused to consider any such idea. His mother was so much against the marriage already that to tell her such a thing as that was absolutely out of the question. It was, in any case, a private matter between his wife and himself and no concern of anybody else, even of his mother's. Still Mrs Cox was urging her opinion to the contrary. It would be so much better, she thought, to have everything open and above-board. She was obliged, however, to give up the point. Charles Bravo, brusque, determined and short-tempered, was not amenable to unwelcome suggestions, especially from a paid companion.

The wedding was fixed for December 7, and meantime the settlements were being prepared. The Married Woman's Property Acts were not yet in operation and therefore everything in Florence's possession would become her husband's unless it were previously secured to her by settlement. Charles Bravo made a disagreeable impression on her solicitors because when he came to discuss the settlements and one of the firm offered him congratulations on the approaching marriage, he exclaimed: 'Damn your congratulations! I have come about the money.' His overbearing nature showed itself again on the question of the settlement itself. Florence's solicitor had wanted to secure to her, besides the income from her first husband's fortune, the Priory and all its furniture and movables. Charles Bravo acquiesced in her keeping the four thousand pounds a year in her own hands, but he demanded that the house and furniture should be taken out of the settlement and therefore become his. Florence took a keen delight in her charming estate and all her pretty furniture, her horses and carriage, and her jewellery, and in love though she was, a streak of her wilfulness showed itself. She refused to have these things removed from the settlement. The violence of Charles Bravo's temper now showed itself. He swore that rather than submit to sitting on a dining-room chair that was not 'his own' he would break off the marriage, and she might take it or leave it.

Florence was in a quandary, and she did what she had done for the last five years, what was now second nature to her. She consulted Dr Gully. They met in the Griffiths' lodge, and she told him her perplexity and asked his advice. She had already written to say that they must never see each other's face again, and Dr Gully had accepted this decision as perfectly proper in the circumstances; but now that he had been sent for, he did not refuse to come. He behaved with the utmost kindness and sense. He said it was natural that Bravo should feel as he did, and the matter was not worth upsetting the marriage over. He advised her to give way. Then he wished her every happiness, kissed her hand and said good-bye.

Though it was Florence herself who had stated dramatically that they must never meet again, she did not seem entirely prepared to carry out her own edict. Dr Gully, however, was prepared to do it for her. He saw that no other course was possible to a gentleman and a man of sense. He sent back the key he had made use of by Griffiths to Mrs Cox, and he told Pritchard that in no circumstances were Mrs Bravo or Mrs Cox ever to be admitted to Orwell Lodge. Pritchard was pleased enough to receive such orders; he said, 'I had had quite enough trouble before when we had to do with them. I did not want my master bothered any more with them.'

Florence was married on December 7, 1875, from her parents' house in Lowndes Square. It was a pleasant occasion, a marriage of affection between a good-looking young pair, with family approval and excellent prospects. The bridegroom's mother, however, had not brought herself to be present at the ceremony. She would only say that she hoped she might, in time, be able to feel more charitably towards her daughter-in-law.

Notwithstanding this piece of bad behaviour from old Mrs Bravo, life at the Priory appeared to begin very happily; but there were indications, even in a month's time, that causes of disquiet existed, and that they showed themselves unusually soon. There was no doubt that husband and wife were strongly attracted to each other, but their happiness was made by their mutual passion, and it was sometimes threatened by the conditions of their daily existence. Charles Bravo had the power of arousing strong affection, but he was violent, and egotistical to the point of arrogance. On his marriage, twenty thousand pounds had been settled on him by his stepfather, and Mr Bravo had afterwards given him another present of one thousand two hundred pounds; but apart from the stable expenses of the Priory, which he paid himself, all the expenses of the establishment, of any kind whatever, were paid out of his wife's income, while he had seen to it that all the property of the house was his. Florence spent freely, but she had always lived within her means; now, however, her husband began to domineer over her expenditure. Charles Bravo had certainly not been demoralized by the prospect of inherited wealth; not only did he work hard, but he was what his friends called careful, and those who disliked him mean. To a man of this temper a wife who would spend twenty guineas on a fern was a subject of considerable disquiet. Using his legal powers as a husband and his influence as a newly married bridegroom, he began to consider where retrenchments might be made. As he visited his mother in Palace Green almost daily, he had plenty of opportunity to discuss his ménage with her, and old Mrs Bravo was at no loss to suggest ways in which her daughter-in-law's pleasures might be curtailed. Florence had always kept a personal maid, but Charles, primed by his mother, persuaded her that she could do without one and manage with the help of the head housemaid. The fact that this housemaid, Mary Ann Keeber, was an exceptionally nice and sensible girl, perhaps made Florence acquiesce in the arrangement more easily than she might otherwise have done. The Priory gardens required the services of three gardeners; this, old Mrs Bravo thought, and Charles agreed, was excessive, and he discussed with Florence a scheme for letting some of the beds go under grass. She was reluctant to give up one of her favourite pastimes, but to please her husband she was willing to entertain the idea. On her marriage the landau had been replaced by a carriage, for which two horses were jobbed. With Victor and Cremorne, this meant a stable of four. 'What does one couple want with four horses?' exclaimed Charles. His mother agreed with him; Florence's cobs, she thought, were a quite unwarrantable expense. Florence was much annoyed at this final piece of interference, the more so because she knew who was behind it. She would not agree to parting with the cobs, and Charles Bravo relinquished the idea for the time being. His mind, however, was still earnestly bent upon saving his wife's money, and it occurred to him that with a husband, a butler, a footman, six women servants, three gardeners, a coachman and a groom, she really did not need the services of a companion. He began to look into the financial aspect of Mrs Cox's employment. One day at his chambers, as he sat with his pen in his hand, calculating, he said to the barrister beside him that with salary, board and incidental expenses Mrs Cox was costing them four hundred pounds a year. 'Why,' exclaimed his friend, 'you could keep another pair of horses for that!'

Charles Bravo had no personal objection to Mrs Cox. She lived as a member of his family and called him by his Christian name, and he spoke highly to his stepfather of her usefulness and her devotion to Florence; but the matter of four hundred pounds a year weighed on his mind considerably. Old Mr Bravo knew that Mrs Cox had an aunt in Jamaica from whom she had some modest expectations, and he advised her to go back to Jamaica with her boys. Mrs Cox did not enlarge upon the topic; she merely said that she was not going.

She could of course decide whether or not she would go to Jamaica, but it would not be open to her to remain at the Priory once Charles Bravo had made up his mind to get rid of her. Florence was wilful and self-centred, but beneath her bright, petulant manner there was a pronounced weakness and dependence; she could be overpersuaded by affection and though emotional she had very little stamina. It would be only a matter of time before the cobs were laid down, and any other retrenchment Charles had in view would inevitably come about sooner or later. He had a passion for his wife and considerable affection for her when everything was going as he liked, but his method of achieving domestic tranquillity was by crushing all opposition.

Yet the recipe for a happy marriage cannot be defined like the recipe for a good pudding. Though Charles Bravo sounds as if he were in some ways almost as odious as Captain Ricardo, he and Florence were happy. Their domestic servants who saw them at all hours, and especially Mary Ann Keeber, who was often in their bedroom, all said that the pair were on the most affectionate and happy terms. His wife was not even disturbed by his occasional violence. Once he struck her, but the next moment his passion had subsided. 'It was like a child's anger,' she said.

Unknown to the servants, however, unknown to anybody except themselves and Mrs Cox, there was, it is believed, one cause of very serious discord between husband and wife. That it existed is almost certain, but how acute it had become or what degree of importance was attached to it was never found out, and for more than seventy years the matter has aroused speculation and bewilderment. Florence Bravo asserted, and her statement was supported and amplified by Mrs Cox, that after the marriage Charles Bravo developed a violent, re-trospective jealousy of Dr Gully. Though Mrs Cox's statements are highly suspect, the wife's story, even though supported by no more trustworthy witness than Mrs Cox, deserves at least a hearing. In their mutual confessions before the marriage she and Charles Bravo had agreed to overlook the other's past. It was common enough for a man to have had pre-marital entanglements, but in overlooking one on the part of his future wife Charles Bravo did what few men of the time would have been prepared to do. But just as he was not a sensitive man, so, too, he was not imaginative, and it was not until he himself was in possession of the woman he loved that the full realization of her having been Dr Gully's mistress was brought home to him. The torment of sexual jealousy grew side by side with the delight of sexual love. Florence said that in spite of his promise he frequently upbraided her with her past love, that he cursed Dr Gully as 'a wretch' and said he would like to annihilate him. Meantime, so strictly did Dr Gully keep to his seclusion that Charles Bravo had never once set eyes on him.

In spite of her brilliant colouring. Florence was not robust. In January, the month after the wedding, she had a miscar-riage, and in February 1876 she went to Brighton to recover. While she was there her husband wrote to her every day; the letters were afterwards read at a legal inquiry, and they were put in as showing nothing but the feeling of an anxious, devoted young husband who missed his wife. But one of them, Florence maintained, referred to their cause of distress. It was dated February 15 and written from Palace Green. It said: 'I hold you to be the best of wives. We have had bitter troubles, but I trust every day to come the sweet peace of our lives will not so much as be disturbed by memories like those. . . . I wish I could sleep away my life till you return.' It was suggested that the bitter troubles and the memories of them were those of the miscarriage. Florence declared that they were the raking up of burning grievance over Dr Gully.

Neither Charles nor Florence Bravo had seen a sign of Dr Gully since November of the previous year, but Mrs Cox had seen him more than once. She fairly frequently made the short journey to town, on business about her house in Lancaster Road or to see her boys at St Ann's School. On one occasion she met Dr Gully in Victoria Street outside the Army and Navy Stores and he spoke civilly, and asked her to send him a book of press cuttings which he had once lent Florence and which had never been returned. Another time she met him on Balham Station. Dr Gully had a cure for what was known as Jamaica fever, and Mrs Cox asked him to let her have the prescription. He promised to do so, and a few days later it came to her by post addressed to the Priory. It was Charles Bravo's habit to meet the postman, take his wife's letters and open them before he gave them to her. On this occasion, Mrs Cox declared, he met her with the letter in his hand and asked her if he might open it as it was addressed in Dr Gully's hand. Mrs Cox providently added that she had no idea how he had been able to recognize Dr Gully's writing. She resented the request, she said, but she opened the envelope before his eyes and showed him that it contained nothing but the prescription. In the extraordinary maze to which the clue has never been found, incidents like this, with their double-edged aspect, add to the confusion like mirrors which are placed so to reflect turnings that the eye is lost between the reflection and the reality. Was this statement true? Grave doubts are cast upon it by the fact (of which Mrs Cox's parenthesis looks like a clumsy attempt at covering-up) that it was scarcely possible that Charles Bravo should have been able to recognize Dr Gully's handwriting. If it were not true, then it was obviously designed as an alibi for another incident, and if the second incident were not accounted for by the first's being true, then a new vista of murky possibilities is opened.

Florence returned from Brighton in recovered health, but shortly afterwards, on April 6, she miscarried again. The second miscarriage was more serious. She suffered much pain, weakness and sleeplessness. She stayed in bed for ten days, and her husband moved out of their bedroom and went to a spare room on the same landing, on the other side of an adjoining dressing-room. Mrs Cox, whose own bedroom was on the floor above, came down and shared Florence's bed. During these ten days she met Dr Gully again, on his way to Bayswater to stay with his son and daughter-in-law. Mrs Cox told him how ill Florence was, of her pain, her backache and her sleeplessness and asked him what he would advise. The discreet reply on Dr Gully's part would no doubt have been that Mrs Cox should consult another doctor, but it was scarcely to be expected that Dr Gully would make it. He recommended spinal washings and cold sitz baths, and knowing from his experience of her that Florence was 'driven frantic by ordinary opiates' he said he would try to think of some sedative that might suit her and would sent it to the Priory. Mrs Cox hurriedly interposed, and giving as her reason the vigilance which Charles Bravo exercised over the post, asked Dr Gully to send his prescription instead to her own house in Lancaster Road, where she would call for it. Dr Gully did so. He left a half ounce green bottle, with a stopper covered in white kid, to be called for by Mrs Cox. It contained laurel water. He had chosen it as something mild and incapable of producing disagreeable results.

Good Friday that year came on April 14. The weather was lovely, and Florence was getting up in the middle of the day. Over the holiday, Charles Bravo did not go up to his chambers; he stayed in the Priory, and Florence wrote a letter to his mother — so binding was the family etiquette of the time — in pleasant, domestic vein, saying, 'Charlie is walking about the garden with a book under his arm, as happy as a king.' He was in good spirits at the holiday, the fine weather and at his wife's recovering. Yet there was a slight upset after lunch. Florence

had gone to her room to lie down, and her husband followed
her, wanting to talk and be amused. She was weak and irritable
and wanted him to go away and leave her to her rest. At last she
absolutely ordered him out of the room. He was angry, and Mrs
Cox followed, attempting to soothe him. It was her own version
of the affair that he shouted: 'She's a selfish pig,' and then said:
'Let her go back to Gully.' According to her, he was still angry
that evening, and threatened to leave the house. By her own
account, she went to his bedroom door and spoke to him in a
placating manner. He replied, she said, by saying that he had
no quarrel with *her*. 'You are a good little woman,' he said, and
kissed her cheek.

As the weather was very fine, the Easter moon at its full must
have filled the sky with light. In the tranquillity and silence of
that quiet scene no sound from the outside world disturbed the
sleeping Priory. On the garden side gravel paths glistened and
conservatory panes glittered. In front, against the pale stuc-
coed façade, the giant oak tree stretched its arms, its black
shadow thrown across the grass. The servants were all sleep in
their quarters, the master was shut away in his single room. In
the large bedroom at the head of the stairs Florence was in her
bed, and beside her was Mrs Cox. In the moonlight and the
silence, what was said? It is as if the box containing the secret
were in full view but the key is irretrievable.

On Easter Saturday the weather continued brilliantly fine
and Florence and Mrs Cox drove in the carriage to Streatham,
meaning to bring the three boys to the Priory for the weekend,
but the headmaster would only allow them out for Easter
Monday. Florence arranged to send for them early on Monday
morning and they drove back to Balham. Charles Bravo had
had a tennis court laid out and was superintending the putting
up of the net. He had a vigorous game with the butler, and
when the boys arrived on Monday morning he at once started
to play with them. He wrote a letter to his father (those daily
letters which telephone conversations now replace) saying that
he had 'loafed vigorously' and thoroughly enjoyed the
weekend.

To help Florence's recovery, they had decided to go to
Worthing, and to take a house there as more comfortable than

lodgings. On Tuesday, April 18, Mrs Cox set off to Worthing to find a suitable house. Good living was the rule of the Priory and Mrs Cox took a flask of sherry with her to recruit her in her exertions. Meanwhile Florence ordered the carriage to drive in to town and her husband was to accompany her. The carriage turned out of the gates into Bedford Hill Road and when a few minutes later it passed Orwell Lodge Florence turned her head away in the gesture that had become instinctive. Charles Bravo noticed it and said savagely: 'Do you see anybody?' 'No,' she said. He then muttered some abuse of Dr Gully, and she exclaimed that he was very unkind to be always bringing up that name after the solemn promise he had made never to refer to the past. He would not like it, she said, if she were to be always taunting him about that woman! Her husband was touched by this, and asked her to forgive him. Then he said pleadingly: 'Kiss me!' She was too much ruffled, and refused; whereupon, she afterwards declared, he exclaimed: 'Then you shall see what I will do when we get home!' This frightened her, she said, and she did kiss him.

The carriage put him down at the Turkish Baths in Jermyn Street, and then took her to the Haymarket Stores, where she did some shopping. She drove back to the Priory for lunch. Charles Bravo lunched with a friend at St James's Hall, and came back to Balham in the afternoon. Florence gave him some tobacco she had bought him at the Stores, and he was very much pleased by the little gift, which was indeed a gesture of reconciliation, since in the 'seventies the mistress of the house, so far from encouraging smoking, was understood barely to tolerate it. Charles Bravo said he would now go and smoke in his room, for it was out of the question that he should do it in his wife's drawing-room or morning-room. Florence thought that he would spend the time up there till dinner, but, to her surprise, in the late afternoon he came down dressed for riding and said he was going out on Cremorne. His horsemanship was characteristic of him; he rode badly but with pertinacity and courage. This was the first evening that Florence had stayed up to dinner since her illness, but the meal, which should have been a little domestic celebration, did not go off well. First, Charles Bravo arrived home much shaken, saying the cob had

run away with him. The groom told him it was his own fault for
riding it on a snaffle instead of a curb. Charles admitted this
and said he would not do so next time. When he came in he
looked pale and complained of stiffness. Florence said he must
have a mustard bath and sent the butler upstairs to get it ready.
She then went upstairs herself to dress. Meanwhile the butler,
having prepared his master's bath, came down to the dining-
room to finish laying the table. A bottle of burgundy was
decanted and placed in the middle of the table. Dinner had to
be kept back because Mrs Cox had not returned, but she
arrived a little after half-past seven. She went upstairs, but did
not stay to dress as it was too late. When she came down a few
minutes afterwards they all went into the dining-room.

The meal was a simple one: whiting, roast lamb and a dish of
eggs and anchovies. Charles Bravo seemed unwell and was
certainly ill-humoured. Mrs Cox produced a photograph of the
house she had chosen, but he brushed it aside, and said the
whole project of going there was an unnecessary expense. Then
he was annoyed because a letter from a stockbroker addressed
to himself had been sent by mistake to his stepfather. The letter
gave an account of some very mild flutters in which Charles had
engaged and showed that he had lost twenty pounds. The elder
Mr Bravo disapproved of gambling on the Stock Exchange
even to such a trivial extent as this, and he forwarded the letter
with a few grave observations of his own. Charles Bravo was the
more irritated because his stepfather had had no business to see
the letter, anyway. He said he should 'write the governor a
shirty letter about it.' The butler noticed that his master was
pale and quite unlike himself, and put it down to the shock of
being bolted with; but though he did not complain of it that
evening, Charles had been suffering a good deal from toothache
and this trouble may have accounted for some of his pallor and
moroseness. He drank three glasses of burgundy, about his
usual measure. The ladies, it is somewhat startling to learn,
drank nearly two bottles of sherry between them.

At a little after half-past eight Charles told his wife she had
sat up long enough for a first evening. She agreed and went
upstairs, followed by Mrs Cox, but half-way up the staircase
she asked Mrs Cox to bring her up another glass of sherry. Mrs

Cox at once returned for it to the dining-room and carried it upstairs. She helped Florence to undress, because Mary Ann Keeber, who would ordinarily have done so, was now at her supper. It therefore happened that the two women were quite alone on the first floor, from just after half-past eight until Charles Bravo came upstairs at about half-past nine.

Mary Ann was going upstairs to Mrs Bravo's bedroom at the same time, and she stood back to let her master go up first. She particularly noted his distraught appearance. He was extremely pleasant and friendly with servants, and it was unlike him to walk upstairs with one of them without speaking. As it was, he looked round at her twice, and she thought he seemed angry. It must be admitted, however, that this would describe the appearance of a man gnawed by toothache. He went to his bedroom and she went to Mrs Bravo's. Florence asked the girl to bring her a glass of Marsala from the dining-room. Mary Ann went downstairs and returned with half a tumbler full. The master followed her into the bedroom and began to reproach his wife with taking too much wine. As she always took a glass of sherry while she was dressing, she had now swallowed more than a bottleful and half a tumbler of Marsala in the course of the evening. Mary Ann had discreetly gone away into the dressing-room, where she was busy in tidying away Florence's clothes. When she had finished, she went back to Florence's bedroom. Florence was lying in bed, and Mrs Cox was sitting at the bedside. Mary Ann was accustomed to seeing her sitting there. The maid asked if anything more were wanted and Mrs Cox said softly, 'No,' and asked her to take the dogs downstairs. Mary Ann collected the two small dogs who were in the bedroom and was half-way down the stairs with them when Charles Bravo appeared at the door of his room in desperate plight, calling loudly: 'Florence! Florence! Hot water!'

The startled maid turned back and ran to the big bedroom. Strange as it might appear, Mrs Cox had not heard these frantic cries which were uttered a few feet away from her. She still sat dreamily in her post by the bed. In the bed, Florence, overcome by the fumes of alcohol, was already fast asleep.

Roused by Mary Ann, Mrs Cox bustled off to Charles

The victim and suspects in the Bravo case.

Bravo's room, and as she and the maid came in they saw him standing at the window, vomiting. Mrs Cox at once sent Mary Ann down to the kitchen for a can of hot water. When the girl came back with it Bravo was lying on the floor and Mrs Cox was rubbing his chest. She now told Mary Ann to go for mustard, for an emetic, and in the course of her errand Mary Ann, thinking it strange the wife should not have been called to a husband in such an alarming crisis, went into Mrs Bravo's bedroom and succeeded in rousing her from her stupor. As soon as Florence could be made to understand what had happened, she hurried on her dressing-gown and rushed to the spare room. From that moment everyone who saw her agreed that her behaviour was that of a completely innocent woman, distracted with anxiety at her husband's state. Mrs Cox had sent one of the servants for Dr Harrison of Streatham, but Mrs Bravo now insisted on Dr Moore's being sent for, since he was much the nearer, as he lived in Balham itself.

When Dr Harrison arrived, Mrs Cox met him in the hall and told him she was sure Charlie had taken chloroform. She said afterwards that she had not mentioned this to Dr Moore because the latter was a local man and Charlie would not wish anyone in the neighbourhood to know what he had done. Harrison at once went up to join his colleague and they both tried to detect any odour of chloroform on the patient's breath, but there was none.

In her recent illness Florence had been attended by Mr Royes Bell of Harley Street, who was a connection of her husband's and an intimate friend of the Bravo family. She now suggested that he should be sent for. Dr Harrison wrote a note asking Mr Royes Bell to come at once and to bring someone with him. This note was given to the coachman, who drove with it to Harley Street, and at the end of the two hours necessary to go and come, returned bringing Mr Royes Bell and Dr Johnson.

Meantime Florence, with every sign of passionate distress, threw himself on the bed beside her husband; but, weak from illness, overpowered by grief and having had far too much to drink, she soon fell asleep. Dr Harrison roused her and got her off the bed; he was afraid she would interfere with the sick man's breathing. Presently Charles Bravo came to again; he

began to vomit, and the doctors could now be sure that he had
taken a strong dose of irritant poison. When Mr Royes Bell and
Dr Johnson were brought up to the bedroom and had made
their examinations, Mr Royes Bell took advantage of the
patient's returning consciousness to ask him what he had
taken. 'I took some laudanum for toothache,' he said. 'Laudanum will not account for your symptoms,' said Dr Johnson.

Mrs Cox now glided up to Mr Royes Bell and, drawing him
aside, she made the extraordinary statement that when she had
answered Charles Bravo's cries for help he had said: 'I have
taken poison. Don't tell Florence.' Royes Bell was astonished
that she had not said so at once. 'It's no good sending for a
doctor if you don't tell him what's the matter,' he said, and
hurriedly returned to his colleagues with the news. Dr Harrison
was extremely annoyed that Mrs Cox had not made the
disclosure to him. Mrs Cox, blandly obstinate, replied that she
had done so. 'I told you when you arrived,' she said. 'You did
nothing of the sort,' replied Dr Harrison heatedly; 'you said he
had taken chloroform.' The night passed with no improvement
and at five o'clock in the morning Dr Harrison, Dr Moore and
Dr Johnson went home, the latter taking with him a specimen
of the vomit for analysis. Mr Royes Bell, who was now in charge
of the case, remained at the Priory.

The day was Wednesday, April 19. It wore on slowly, the
patient suffering agonies of pain succeeded by periods of profound exhaustion. During one of his calmer moments he saw his
wife bending over him. A memory seemed to cross him of their
miserable altercation in the carriage. 'Kiss me!' he pleaded.
She did so. Many times during the day he asked her to kiss him.
At noon he had a short will made in which he left her everything, and he told Royes Bell that if his mother arrived too late
to see him alive she must be given a message from him. It was:
'Be kind to Florence.'

At three o'clock that afternoon the three doctors, once more
gathered at his bed, tried again to make him say whether he had
taken anything. The butler heard his master exclaim in weak
but irritable accents: 'Why the devil should I have sent for you
if I knew what was the matter with me?'

That same afternoon old Mr and Mrs Bravo, who had been

telegraphed for, arrived from St Leonards. They brought with them Mr Bravo's brother-in-law, Dr Henry Smith, Miss Bell, the surgeon's sister, and their maid Amelia Bushell, who had known Charles from a small child. Mrs Cox met them at the station with the appalling news that Charles had poisoned himself. The whole party disbelieved it, and Mr Bravo stoutly denied that such a thing was possible.

When they arrived at the Priory, Mrs Bravo told Florence that she had always nursed Charles in all his ailments and begged that she might take charge of the sickroom now. Florence, distracted and incapable, agreed willingly. She gave up the double bedroom to the Bravos and went upstairs to share Mrs Cox's.

Next morning, Thursday, the twentieth, there was no alteration and very little hope, and Florence, acting on a natural impulse, sent Mrs Cox round to Orwell Lodge. She afterwards said pathetically that she had always thought Dr Gully 'the cleverest doctor in the world'. When everyone else had failed, she instinctively turned for help to him. There was no room for embarrassment. Mrs Cox presented herself boldly, and Pritchard, putting her in the drawing-room, went to announce her to his master. 'You shouldn't have let her in, Pritchard,' said Dr Gully, but he went to see what was the matter. When he heard the trouble, he suggested mustard plaster, and small doses of arsenicum. Within five minutes of her arrival Mrs Cox was walking down the drive again.

Meanwhile Florence, in her desperate search for succour, had bethought her of a friend of her father's, the famous Sir William Gull. This doctor, who was short-tempered and domineering, and bore a curious resemblance to Napoleon, was the most eminent physician of the day and was considered to be unrivalled in diagnosis. Though, as Mr Royes Bell was in charge of the case, she ought not to have summoned another doctor without consulting him, the distraught wife sent Sir William Gull a note saying her husband was desperately ill and could he come at once? This note made no mention of poison.

Sir William Gull and Mr Royes Bell agreed to ignore this breach of etiquette and they drove out to Balham together, arriving at the Priory at six o'clock that evening. When Sir

William Gull entered the bedroom he told everybody to leave it except the five other doctors there already. Then he made his examination. Bending over Charles Bravo, he said: 'This is not disease. You have been poisoned. Pray tell us how you came by it.' In weak but unfaltering tones the dying man swore solemnly that he had taken nothing except laudanum for his toothache. 'You have taken a great deal more than that,' said Sir William Gull. Dr Johnson from his post at the foot of the bed said that if the patient could tell them no more, someone might be accused of poisoning him. 'I cannot help that,' said Charles Bravo; 'I have taken nothing else.'

Mrs Cox had already made two statements, to Dr Harrison and Mr Royes Bell, each one more important than the last. She now capped them with a third to Sir William Gull. She explained that what Charles Bravo had really said to her was: 'I have taken poison for Gully. Don't tell Florence.' How Sir William Gull received this is not known, but he, alone of the seven doctors, inclined to the theory of suicide. Dr Johnson's analysis of the vomit proved useless, for it had been tested for arsenic only, of which it contained no trace. It appeared at first as if no other specimen were obtainable, for when Mary Ann had attended Charles Bravo in his first seizure Mrs Cox had ordered her to wash the basin and throw away the contents. However, Sir William Gull stood at the window from which he had been told that Charles Bravo had vomited, and he saw traces of the rejected matter on the leads beneath. He ordered some to be collected and took it back with him to London. He had left the sickroom for a few moments only when he was hastily called back; but the patient only wanted to repeat his solemn assurance that he had not poisoned himself and to ask if there were any hope? Sir William Gull would not deceive him. He told him that he was half dead already. To the parents he said he doubted if their son would last the night. He then left the Priory and his prognostication was soon fulfilled.

At four o'clock on the morning of April 21 Charles Bravo died, within five months of his wedding day.

In the shock of grief, terror and dismay that swept the household, the only person to remain calm, useful, practical and thoughtful for others was Mrs Cox. There could be no question of granting a death certificate, and it was realized that a coroner's inquest must be prepared for. The coroner for East Surrey was Mr Carter, and Mrs Cox at once got into touch with him. She gave him to understand that this was a case of suicide and that it was an object to spare the family's feelings as far as possible. She suggested that the inquest should be held in the Priory itself, to avoid distressing publicity, and added, with her usual attention to detail, that refreshments would be provided for the jurors. Mr Carter fell in with these arrangements in the most obliging way. No notice of the inquest was sent to any of the papers, and no reporters were present. The ceremony, conducted in the pleasant seclusion of the Priory dining-room, was almost a family affair, except that a few of the late Charles Bravo's barrister friends had wormed themselves in. However, no one paid them any attention.

The proceedings opened on April 28, and the coroner had clearly taken it for granted that the case was one of suicide about which it would be well to say as little as might be. Meanwhile, however, the pathologist to whom Sir William Gull had submitted the specimen for analysis had revealed the fact that Charles Bravo had died from a large dose of antimony, taken in the form of tartar emetic. On the advice of Dr Smith, Mr Bravo took this report to Scotland Yard, who sent down Inspector Clarke to see if he could trace tartar emetic in the possession of anyone in the Priory. This he entirely failed to do. The rooms both of Mrs Bravo and Mrs Cox were full of patent medicines, but all of a quite harmless character. Meanwhile, evidence was given at the inquest that was difficult to reconcile with the idea of suicide, for Mary Ann Keeber showed that the couple were on terms of devoted affection, and Mr Royes Bell repeated the impressive denials of the victim that he had taken anything to poison himself. Nevertheless, Mr Carter appeared anxious to hurry through a verdict in accordance with his own view. He refused to hear the testimony of Dr Moore and Dr Johnson, both of whom wanted to speak, and he refused to allow Florence to be called, as he understood that she was prostrated by shock. The jury, however, were far from satisfied. They returned a verdict to the effect that Charles Bravo had died from a dose of tartar emetic but that there was no proof as to how he had come by it.

The next day, April 29, the funeral took place at Norwood

cemetery, and on the thirtieth, Florence retired with Mrs Cox
to Brighton, where Mrs Cox had found them apartments at 38
Brunswick Terrace. Mr Joseph Bravo remained at the Priory,
and he had all his son's drawers sealed up. Florence heard of
this in her retreat, and she at once wrote to her father-in-law
about it. She said that all her husband's possessions belonged
now to her, and no one else had the right to touch 'one single
thing'. At the same time she took the opportunity of suggesting
to Mr Bravo that any money he had been in the habit of giving
his son should now be considered as due to her. 'What he died
possessed of I must leave to you; he told me that he had two
hundred pounds a year from investments, and of course his
books and pictures and private papers at Palace Green are now
mine. . . . P.S. Poor Charlie told me that you promised to allow
him eight hundred pounds a year.'

Such a letter, at such a time, does not put her in an amiable
light; but a childish greed and selfishness was the reverse side of
her emotional nature. Charles Bravo had insisted, with brutal
and insulting harshness, that all her possessions should be his;
he had said if he were not to have everything for his own then he
would not marry her at all. She had acquiesced at the time, but
now she was particularly alive to the idea that she ought to reap
her side of the bargain. She wrote a little later apologizing to Mr
Bravo for the disagreeable tone of her last letter; she had quite
misunderstood his intentions, she said; she added that a letter
from Mr Royes Bell had convinced her that poor Charlie had
committed suicide, and she believed it had been because 'that
dreadful woman' had been pressing him for money; this, too,
was why he had been so anxious to cut down their expenses.
This was the letter of a woman who was either genuinely stupid
or a very incompetent deceiver. There had been no trouble
from Charles Bravo's mistress, who had made no claim on him
at all; she would not have got very far with such a man if she
had; whereas the cutting down of expenses required no explanation beyond the fact that Charles Bravo was exceedingly
careful about money and was supported by a woman who
disliked and disapproved of her daughter-in-law.

Dissatisfaction with the conduct of the inquest was growing.
It showed itself in a flood of anonymous letters which reached

Florence in her rooms at Brunswick Terrace, but it was also making its way among the reputable part of society. One of Charles Bravo's friends who had been present at the inquest, a Mr Willoughby, went and explained his uneasiness at Scotland Yard; while several newspapers, notably the *Telegraph*, began an agitation to have the proceedings reopened. Florence felt herself to be in a position of odious notoriety, which threatened to become something worse. On her father's advice she published the offer of a reward of five hundred pounds to anyone who could prove the sale of tartar emetic in the neighbourhood of the Priory.

The result of the pressure that was brought to bear was that an enquiry was held at the Treasury, at which Mrs Bravo and Mrs Cox each made a voluntary statement. The latter's was so startling that a second inquest was ordered to take place on July 11.

This time it was entirely out of private hands. Far from the pleasant seclusion of the Priory dining-room, the jurors met in the billiard-room of the Bedford Hotel, outside Balham Station. It was very hot, and the billiard-room windows were open, with the Venetian blinds half down. Public interest was enormous. Every available inch of space not occupied by the performers of the inquest was filled with a mob of intensely curious spectators. The possible issues were of the utmost seriousness, and the persons chiefly concerned were all able to pay for the best legal assistance, and consequently a most impressive collection of counsel was assembled in these incongruous surroundings. The Crown counsel were Sir John Holker, Mr Gorst, Q.C., and Mr, afterwards Sir, Harry Poland. For Mrs Charles Bravo there appeared Sir Henry James, Q.C., and Mr Biron; and Florence had also retained Mr Murphy, Q.C., to act for Mrs Cox. Mr Joseph Bravo was represented by Mr Lewis, a partner of Messrs Lewis & Lewis, the famous firm of solicitors. Half-way through, the proceedings took such an ominous turn that Mr Sergeant Parry and Mr Archibald Smith presented themselves, saying they had been instructed to watch the case for Dr Gully.

The legal gentlemen were indeed eminent, so eminent that they defied all control. In a court of law a judge would have managed them, but in the billiard-room of the Bedford Hotel there was nobody but Mr Carter. His unhappy position was rather that of Phaeton, who attempted to drive the coursers of the sun and was tumbled ignominiously into the ocean.

Before the inquest opened a macabre ceremony was performed. It was necessary for the jurors to view the body, and the coffin was therefore taken up out of its brick vault in Norwood cemetery and placed on wooden blocks under a canvas shelter. That the formality of viewing might be accomplished, the undertakers had cut away a square of the lead casing and left the dead man's face in sight under a pane of glass. The face was as dark as a mummy's, the teeth, exposed by rigor, were entirely black. The jurors filed past the coffin, raising their tall hats as they did so. A heavy, overpowering smell of disinfectants added to the oppressiveness of the sultry day.

The inquest was considered afterwards to have been conducted in a most undisciplined manner. Not only was Mr Carter unable to control the loud-voiced comments of the crowd or to prevent the jury from making unsuitable demonstrations; he could not prevent the lawyers from extorting by relentless cross-examination, much material that would probably have been ruled as inadmissible in a proper court. A domestic picture of the most graphic detail was built up by the statements of a wide variety of witnesses, but the three most important were Mrs Bravo, Dr Gully and Mrs Cox.

In Mrs Cox's examination, which was the longest, she quietly and persistently maintained that Charles Bravo had committed suicide and that he had done so out of retrospective jealousy of Dr Gully. Her story which had grown in circumstantial detail from the time she made her first communication to Dr Harrison now received its crowning touch. She said that at one of the moments when she was alone with Charles he had said: 'Why did you tell them?' and she had answered: 'I had to tell them. I could not let you die.' The only creature who could have contradicted her was now a blackened corpse. When she was asked why she had not at once reported that Charles Bravo had said he had taken poison 'for Dr Gully', she replied that it had been with a view of shielding Mrs Bravo's character.

As she and Florence both adhered to this story of the death, the story of the liaison with Dr Gully was pushed forward into a position of the utmost importance. It acquired in fact an importance in the minds of the lawyers which Mrs Cox had perhaps not foreseen, for if the liaison could account for the suicide, if still existing, it might equally be held to account for a murder. This perhaps accounts for the remarkable lengths to which the Crown counsel and Mr Lewis went in attempting to find out when the relationship had begun — a matter, after all, of some four years before Charles Bravo and Florence had ever set eyes on each other. When Mrs Cox was asked twice over whether she was not aware of the fact that her employer and Dr Gully were lovers, she looked down and gently brushed the tablecloth with her gloved hand. She admitted at last that she had suspected it. She was now called upon sharply to speak up, and this request was received with clamorous delight by the onlookers. Mr Sergeant Parry was appalled by these proceedings. 'Applause in a court of justice!' he exclaimed. 'It is terrible! It is fearful!' But Mr Carter was helpless.

When Florence Bravo was called her appearance created a sensation. In her widow's dress of black crêpe, her bright hair strained back under a bonnet with a crêpe veil, her large blue eyes sunken in her pale face, she appeared on the verge of breaking down, but she spoke with unexpected firmness, until Mr Lewis, after a long cross-examination on her relations with Dr Gully, began with savage persistence to demand at what point they had begun. She denied that this had been while she was at Malvern, but Mr Lewis produced a letter she had written six years ago to a maid called Laundon, in which she promised to recommend her to another place and said, 'I hope you will never mention what passed at Malvern.' 'What did that mean, Mrs Bravo?' asked Mr Lewis and he repeated the question until her merciless reiteration broke her self-control. Sobbing wildly, she implored the coroner for protection, which he was powerless to extend. He could not control the counsel any more than she could.

Dr Gully's examination aroused a great deal of unfavourable comment, both in the press and at the actual scene of the inquest, where several jurors showed disapproval because the coroner allowed him to sit down during his lengthy ordeal.

There was by the end of the proceedings no shred of evidence, no shade of implication, to connect him with the crime, but public opinion was weighted against him almost as if he had been proved a murderer. It was of course right that so serious a breach of professional etiquette, particularly on the part of such an eminent man, should be strongly condemned, but the tragedy of Dr Gully's fall after a long and distinguished career seems to have passed unregarded. This was no doubt partly or even largely due to the fact that a fellow human being always arouses hostility and resentment if he or she is felt to have enjoyed a sexual success out of proportion to any physical or social advantages. That Dr Gully, a man well over sixty, should have had a pretty young woman as his adoring mistress, unloosed a flood of vindictive taunts and scathing vituperation.

Once the discreditable fact had been admitted in its full culpability the rest of Dr Gully's evidence was that of an upright, distinguished man with every instinct of a gentleman. He spoke honestly, simply, and with a keen sense of regret for his backsliding. 'Too true, sir, too true,' he said, when the Crown counsel flung his past indiscretion in his face. At one point of the proceedings the horrible implication was made that he had prescribed medicines for Mrs Ricardo to bring on a miscarriage. His prescriptions had been traced to the chemists who dispensed them. Dr Gully replied with effective simplicity that to any medical man the prescriptions would speak for themselves; they were not such as would be used to procure abortion. All his evidence went to show, just as Florence Bravo's had shown, that after she had dismissed him in October of 1875 he had never attempted to have any further communication with her. He had seen her once at her own request, when he advised her to give way about the marriage settlement. After that, he had never even laid eyes on her. Nor, apart from the one interview in the coachman's lodge, had she ever attempted to get into touch with him till she sent Mrs Cox to ask his advice for her dying husband. He had prescribed for her pains, and he had sent her a bottle of laurel water: both these acts had been brought about by the agency of Mrs Cox.

The dead man, according to the pathologist, had taken the enormous quantity of some forty grains of antimony, and a thorough search of the Priory, including the medicine chests of Mrs Bravo and Mrs Cox and the numerous bottles that were littered about in both ladies' rooms, had revealed no trace of anything likely to contain antimony in any form. The reward of five hundred pounds offered by Florence to anyone who could prove a sale of tartar emetic in the neighbourhood had produced no response. But now it came to light that a large amount of tartar emetic had been on the premises no later than the preceding January, three months before Charles Bravo's death. The then coachman at the Priory, Griffiths, had bought tartar emetic to doctor Florence's horses, and he had also used it in Dr Gully's stables at Malvern. Dr Gully had not known of this; he had forbidden Griffiths to physic the horses, as he himself treated them by hydropathy, 'with marvellous results'. In the Priory stables, however, Griffiths had it all his own way, and he made a profuse purchase of tartar emetic, regardless of the fact that he had only four horses under his charge. He was asked why he had bought physic enough for at least a hundred, and he explained that he liked to have things by him. On the day of the Lord Mayor's Show, 1875, he was driving his mistress, accompanied of course by Mrs Cox, in the London streets, and the carriage was involved in a serious collision. Griffiths denied that he was to blame, but Charles Bravo, harsh, impetuous and alarmed for Florence's safety, insisted on his being dismissed. He left the Priory in January. Griffiths bore Charles Bravo a bitter grudge in consequence, though he went at once into the service of Lady Prescott. He said that while the tartar emetic was in his possession he had kept it locked in a cupboard in the harness room, and that before he left he had poured it down a drain in the stable yard. Unfortunately, though there was no reason to suppose Griffiths a deliberate liar, he was excitable and loquacious and his evidence was full of contradictions and inconsistencies. That he said he had kept the poison locked up and thrown away the remainder before he left was nothing like so significant as the fact that a large quantity of tartar emetic had actually been on the premises.

It was an accepted fact that Charles Bravo must have taken the poison in some form of drink after the dinner hour of seven-thirty. As Florence had gone upstairs immediately after

dinner, no coffee had been served that evening. Therefore the
two mediums in which he could have taken the poison were the
Burgundy he drank at dinner or the water in the bottle on his
bedroom washstand from which he always drank a glassful
before going to bed. The medical evidence inclined to its having
been taken in the water, and this view was supported by the fact
that the butler had been near at hand, in dining-room or hall,
ever since the wine was decanted some half an hour before
dinner. Though it would not have been impossible, it would
have been exceedingly difficult for anyone to enter the dining-
room and doctor the Burgundy unobserved. But with regard to
the water in the bedroom: Florence and Mrs Cox had the first
floor entirely to themselves between the time of their going
upstairs at eight-thirty and Charles Bravo and Mary Ann's
appearance at about half-past nine. The matter could have
been decided by the examination of what remained of wine and
water; but by the same perverse good fortune which had
supported the criminal in every aspect of the crime the remains
of wine and water could, neither of them, be accounted for. The
butler had opened a fresh bottle of Burgundy for Dr Harrison
and Dr Moore; he could not say what had happened to the
remains of the other; the house had been in confusion and he
could not remember if anyone had drunk it or not. (Similarly he
would not, of course, have known if anyone had poured it
away.) The remains of the water bottle had not been noticed
either. The doctors had noticed the bottle in the room, but at
that time they had naturally attached no importance to it. They
were not continuously present with the patient, and any careful, attentive soul refilling the bottle with fresh water would
scarcely attract attention.

The verdict which was finally pronounced after the sittings
had lasted three weeks was that Charles Bravo had not died by
misadventure and not committed suicide, but that he had been
poisoned, though there was not sufficient evidence to say by
whom. This statement came as a stunning blow, because it at
once branded Mrs Cox as a liar, and therefore it was next door
to an indictment of murder of either herself or Florence or both,
with the possibility of suspicion resting upon Dr Gully. The
pamphlet, *The Balham Mystery*, is exceptionally interesting, as it

not only supplies an exhaustive account of the proceedings at the inquest and drawings of the scenes and people involved, but it conveys the public feeling of the time in three fanciful drawings, crude and morbid and of astonishing effectiveness. One is of the devil dressed as a showman at a fair, with three thimbles standing on a board. The drawing is headed: 'Rather a Poser. Under which thimble is the P——?' Does P stand for prisoner? At all events there is no doubt as to whom the three thimbles represent. The second of these full-page drawings is in vivid chiaroscuro. It shows the setting sun from which a stony road leads up to the foreground. Here in deep shadow a gallows stands, and beneath it, sitting at the edge of an open pit strewed with bones, is a figure of such terror as is seldom seen outside nightmare. The hooded cloak reveals one hoof, and a head that would be a skull except that the features are still there. The expression of intense personal misery such as the devil might be supposed to bear is combined with an indrawn, waiting look and a hideous smile. On the lap a skeleton hand holds a whip. The picture is called: 'Waiting for the culprit.' But even more interesting is a small illustration at the end. This is a murky-looking corner where several phials and a glass jar containing what looks like an anatomical specimen are standing on a shelf. A single beam of light illuminates a woman's hand which stretches out towards one of the small bottles. A careful examination of the drawings of Mrs Bravo and Mrs Cox shows that the sleeve, banded with dark ribbon and finished with a deep fall of lace, is not identifiable with any dress which either of them is shown as wearing; but it is an elegant hand, with a massive bracelet on the wrist; this, and the richness of the sleeve, suggests inescapably that it is meant for Florence Bravo, while the anatomical specimen carries an equally inescapable suggestion of Dr Gully.

There are two authoritative pronouncements on this crime which after seventy years still holds its secret. In his memoir of Sir Harry Poland, *Seventy-two Years at the Bar*, Mr Ernest Rowlands says that Sir Harry Poland told him that he had his theory, though it was not for publication, and there was not enough evidence for a prosecution. It is tantalizing to read such words, because this theory, formed by a man who was one of the

counsel, would be as near to the actual truth as the rest of us
could hope ever to come. But Sir Harry Poland's other observations are extremely interesting. He entirely exonerates Dr
Gully, and he mentions a possible motive for each of the
women: that Mrs Cox was threatened by Charles Bravo with
the loss of her pleasant life at the Priory to which the alternative
was drudgery and insecurity and the anxiety for her sons'
future, and that Mrs Bravo murdered her husband to avoid
losing her companion, but he says that the first motive was
scarcely sufficient and the second was not credible. Nevertheless
the effect of that paragraph is that he thought it was the
motive rather than the identity of the culprit which remained
obscure.

Sir John Hall in *The Bravo Mystery and other Cases* also clears Dr
Gully from all suspicion of complicity in the murder and says
that there is no evidence of Florence Bravo's having wanted to
renew her liaison, of her having procured poison, or behaved in
any way but one natural to an affectionate and single-hearted
wife; but he also says that what lays her open to grave suspicion
is the way in which she supported every statement of Mrs Cox,
and the extraordinary intimacy in which she lived with her; not
only were they the closest friends, but for the last fortnight they
had been sleeping in the same bed. Sir John Hall says: 'If one be
guilty the other cannot be innocent.'

It would be presumptuous to hazard any theory which was
not closely conformable with what has been said by these two
writers, but it is, one hopes, not going beyond the lines thus laid
down to say that the murder was certainly done and almost
certainly planned by Mrs Cox, and that all that is doubtful is
her motive for it. The Marxist trend of present-day thought
perhaps inclines our generation to attach more importance to
economic motive than the men of Sir Harry Poland's day were
prepared to allow. To us it does not seem incredible that a
woman of such calibre as Mrs Cox should be prepared to
commit murder in order to maintain her own security and that
of her children. On the other hand, it seems likely that though
Florence Bravo did not know that the crime was to be committed at that time, or, perhaps, that it was ever actually to be
committed at all she knew afterwards how and by whom it had
been done. Though very little is known of her subsequent story,

that little is of extreme significance: it is simply that she died within fourteen months of the second inquest. It is not generally known whether her support of Mrs Cox continued during the short remainder of her own life. A theory (in default of any evidence) is sometimes suggested, more or less facetiously, that her death may have been a second murder, but by far the most probable explanation is that after the second inquest the truth about her husband's death became known to her, and that the strain of enduring this knowledge was more than she could bear. What is dreadfully clear is the influence of the controlled, secretive, ruthless character over the sensuous, impulsive, helpless one. Had Florence Bravo been another sort of woman she might be thought the victim of some morbid attachment to Mrs Cox, but the history of her love affair and her marriage puts this out of court. Mrs Cox dominated her because she ran her house, attended to her wants, promoted her comforts and pleasures and enabled her to lead her life as she wanted to lead it. Mrs Cox was the evil spirit whose power over us is the power we ourselves have given it. Florence's character, self-indulgent, greedy, impetuous, pleasure-loving, had its exact complement in the character that was vigilant, cautious, hard-working, self-reliant, capable of any self-denial to achieve a particular end, just as her appearance with its Rubens-like colouring, its feminine softness and grace, was the opposite of the plain, dark, unobtrusive figure, which had developed a self-protective obscurity.

In the infinite complexities of the mind it is possible to know without realizing the knowledge, until circumstances force the mind to admit it. In their extreme intimacy before the death of Charles Bravo, when Mrs Cox nursed her, waited on her and slept in her bed, Florence must have confided to her friend whatever causes of resentment and dislike she may have had against her husband, and she must have felt assured that her own feelings were met by a profound agreement. Yet nothing would be more natural than that she should accept, at first, Mrs Cox's version of the tragedy which had overtaken the household when she herself was weak from illness and bemused by a drunken sleep, and that at the actual moment of calamity all her other feelings should be submerged in dismay and terror at the sight of her husband's agonies.

It is of course impossible to say what may have been the extent of her complicity, whether she were an accessory before or after the event, whether her silence were willing or unwilling, but her early death seems to speak volumes on her sufferings. Hers was an organism that collapses in physical ill health whenever it is placed under a nervous strain, and if she ceased to want to live there would be no recovery. The force that killed her husband killed her also.

Mrs Cox was heard of many years after, visiting an elderly invalid with fruit and flowers. 'She was quiet and so *very* kind,' said those who remembered her visits.

Dr Gully died seven years later, and for those remaining years his penance was heavy. During a long life he had built up for himself a position of public respect and admiration such as very few men enjoy. As a result of the disclosures at the Balham inquest this was blasted overnight. Not only was his name trampled on by the public, but he had to bear the ruin of his professional reputation. His name was removed from all the societies to which he belonged and from all the journals and papers to which he had been one of the most distinguished contributors. That he bitterly regretted the love affair that had proved fatal to him, he had said himself; but however much his feelings might have altered towards her, the anguish and death of the woman he had loved must have caused him deep grief. He was a man of unusual gifts of personality and intellect, but, with all his good qualities, he had neglected the Wisdom of Solomon:

'Discretion shall preserve thee, understanding shall keep thee.
'To deliver thee from the strange woman, even from the stranger which flattereth with her tongue.
'Which forsaketh the guide of her youth and forgetteth the convenant of her God.
'For her house inclineth unto death, and her paths unto the dead.'

AFTERWORD by Elizabeth Jenkins

Since I wrote this account of the Balham Mystery in 1949, I have read a great deal more about the matter and I do not now altogether hold the view of it I presented then. I assumed that the murder had been committed by Mrs Cox, as this was the opinion of the distinguished authority Sir John Hall (The Bravo

Mystery and other cases); also, it would appear, of Sir Harry Poland, one of the Crown counsel at the second inquest, and of Sir George Lewis, the solicitor who represented the Bravo family. This is a formidable body of opinion, but in this century a more modern alternative suggests itself. Florence Bravo had had a miscarriage on December 7, 1875, seven weeks after her marriage; she suffered another one on April 7, 1876. (Had she been brought to trial this would, today, almost certainly have entitled her to plead diminished responsibility.) In the 19th century, contraception, though known, was not widely practised, and a device sometimes resorted to by women anxious to postpone another pregnancy was to administer an emetic to make the husband sick. Charles Bravo had shown signs of wanting to return to his wife's bed, and I, for one, subscribe to the theory that with Mrs Cox's connivance, she doctored the water-bottle on his wash-stand with a dose that she meant to incapacitate him for the time being; as she was half-tipsy, she put into the water a quantity of tartar emetic that was lethal. It was only when Mrs Cox, summoned to his bedroom, found him passing out on the floor, that the dreadful consequences were brought home to them. Florence, who, innocent of attempted murder, had none the less brought about her husband's death, was too much frightened to admit what she had done; this theory would account for Mrs Cox's self-contradictions in her first statements made to the doctors impromptu, and for Florence's desperate anxiety to save her husband, by calling in six doctors one after another. In their frantic attempts to protect themselves from a capital charge, she and Mrs Cox claimed that Charles Bravo had committed suicide out of retrospective jealousy of Dr Gully, and to build up this statement, Mrs Cox, in her cross-examination at the inquest, remorselessly exposed the love affair between himself and Florence which had existed before her marriage to Charles Bravo.

I was wrong in accepting, on the authority of the article on Dr Gully in the Dictionary of National Biography, the statement that after the inquest his name was removed from the medical societies to which he belonged. I have learned from the Library of the Wellcome Institute of the History of Medicine that this was not so; it should be added that the Garrick Club, of which he was a member, did not ask for his resignation. The attendance at his funeral and his obituary notices proved that though his reputation had ben injured much of it was left to him.

SYDNEY HORLER

Starr Faithfull, Beautiful Wanton

SYDNEY HORLER

Starr Faithfull, Beautiful Wanton

Perhaps the most famous of all unsolved crimes is that of the murder of a beautiful American girl named Starr Faithfull, whose body, clothed only in a dress—the shoes, stockings and underclothing were all absent—was found floating very near the edge of the waves at Long Beach, Long Island, at nine o'clock on Monday morning, June 8th, 1931.

The discovery was made by a man named Daniel Moriarity, who was strolling idly along the shore near the water's edge.

After taking one horrified glance at the corpse, he ran to find the nearest policeman, and in a few minutes Officer Patrick O'Connor arrived and superintended the carrying of the body up on the beach.

Long Beach, Long Island, is a fashionable summer resort, and soon many residents from the neighbouring cottages flocked to see what had happened.

Even in death the features of the unfortunate girl showed refinement and outstanding beauty; everyone who was present remarked on this fact. Naturally enough, the newspaper reports made the most of these attributes, and before many hours had passed, the affair had become an outstanding newspaper sensation.

The Police early came to the conclusion that the girl had been murdered, but there was no jewellery on the body and very few characteristics from which any attempt at identification could be made. The corpse was taken to the nearest Morgue, where Dr Otto Schultz made a post mortem. He declared that death had been caused by drowning, and that before her end the girl had been the victim of a criminal attack. As evidence of this, he pointed out that both arms and eyes were

Starr Faithfull.

covered with many marks and bruises which must have been made before death, and which from their positions on the body bore out the other indications that the girl had been violated.

It was not long, in spite of the lack of clues, before the Police were able to identify the body. The Long Beach authorities had only to glance through their file of persons reported missing to find that they had the exact description of a girl calling herself Starr Faithfull—here was a melodramatic nomenclature, if you like!—which tallied exactly with that of the corpse found on the beach.

The bereaved parents were quickly found, and Mr Faithfull, upon being notified, identified the corpse in the Nassau County Morgue as that of his daughter, Starr.

It was a shocking revelation to this man, a retired chemical manufacturer, who was not only wealthy but well respected.

Mr Faithfull informed the Police that his daughter had been missing since the previous Friday—that was since June 5th. On the next day, he had made a confidential report to the Charles Street Police Station saying that his daughter was missing. He described her as being twenty-five years of age, five feet three inches in height, and weighing 110 lbs. He added that his daughter was a graduate of two New England finishing schools, and had travelled extensively, having only returned recently from Europe.

Soon everyone in America was asking this question: *How did Starr Faithfull meet her end?* Not only was the mystery discussed in the newspapers, but it became a subject of universal conversation.

The situation was complicated by the fact that Dr Schultz, as a result of his autopsy, had announced that sand had been found in the dead girl's lungs. This indicated, of course, that she had been drowned in shallow water. But Starr Faithfull was known by all her intimates to be not only a strong but an expert swimmer. How was it possible then that such a girl could be drowned under those conditions? Could the explanation be found in the fact that someone had forcibly held her down under water until she died?

Such a case was naturally enough the cause of heated

controversy: experts were equally divided: some said that it was an open and shut murder case; others declared that Starr Faithfull had committed suicide.

The adherents to this latter theory pointed out that the bruises on the body could have been caused after death through contact with heavy objects—rocks, piers, etc.,—as the corpse floated in the water. Dr Schultz, when pressed on the point, admitted that such a possibility certainly existed, but that, in his opinion, it was a remote one. He still clung to the theory that the girl had been murdered.

It was whilst the controversy was raging at its height that another medical man, a Dr Alexander G. Goettler, and an eminent toxicologist, caused a fresh sensation by stating that death was undoubtedly due to submersion, as he had found traces of salt water in the left ventricle of the heart.

Dr Goettler went further; he was able to provide sensation in a large way. After making this first announcement, he stated that he had also found a large quantity of veronal in the girl's kidneys. Veronal is an opiate which may be bought in any chemist's shop and is taken by many people to induce sleep. It has its dangers, however, for it is habit-forming, and there have been many cases on record in which an overdose taken to induce sleep has ended in death.

But in this case the quantity of veronal found in the girl's system was proved not to be sufficient to have made her even unconscious; nevertheless, Dr Goettler persisted that Starr Faithfull must have been a veronal-addict. He said further that he had definitely come to the opinion that the girl had not been drinking at the time she died, and that in all probability she had been in full possession of her faculties.

Well, here was mystery indeed! Whilst the adherents of the suicide theory maintained that they alone were right, the opposite camp were more than ever convinced that this lovely girl of twenty-five had been done to death by a criminal lunatic.

A fresh development was soon forthcoming; as a result of an immediate investigation into Starr Faithfull's movements on the day she disappeared, it was discovered that the dead girl had been in love with a Dr James Carr, who acted as ship's surgeon on the *Franconia*. It was also disclosed that on May 29th she had gone down to the 14th Street Dock, New York, to see the ship off. There had been a cocktail party on board, and Starr had over-indulged with the result that when the gangway was taken off, the girl was still on the ship and had to be taken ashore in a tender. The famous *Mauretania* had sailed for a southern trip on the Friday on which the girl had disappeared, and as Starr Faithfull had a large acquaintance among the officers on board, it was presumed that she might have gone to say farewell to some of these friends and had remained on board in similar circumstances to what had happened to her in the case of the *Franconia*.

Spurred on by the previous melodramatic features of the case, several amateur investigators thought it was quite likely that once on board the *Mauretania*, the girl had been attacked and thrown overboard. Completely exhausted after her long swim, she might have been drowned in shallow water. There was certainly some point to this, considering that the course of the *Mauretania* had lain close to Long Beach.

One disclosure led to another. The investigators soon learned that Stanley Faithfull was not Starr Faithfull's father! The girl's real father was declared to be a Stanley Wyman. The latter had secured a divorce from Starr's mother in 1924, and in 1925 Faithfull had married the divorcée and Starr had taken his name.

Arrangements were quickly made for the body of the unfortunate girl to be cremated in the Fresh Pond Crematorium, but when the private cremation ceremonies were about to begin, the Police entered and stopped the proceedings. They explained that they wanted several taxi-drivers, steamship company agents and other people to view the body.

One cab-driver testified that the remains were undoubtedly those of a girl whom he had driven to the Cunard Line dock on the very day that Starr Faithfull was reported to have disappeared. The Faithfull family had all along been of the opinion that Starr had been murdered, and on hearing this evidence, they declared themselves willing to postpone cremation, so that more witnesses, if the latter could be found, might also give evidence.

Ever since the finding of the body, the New York Police had

been delving industriously into the past of the dead girl. It was not long before they were able to learn that in the previous March the girl had been brutally beaten by a man in an hotel room. Both Starr and this man had been taken to the psychopathic ward of the famous Bellevue Hospital. They were both stated to be suffering from acute alcoholism.

A page boy, in telling the Police of this occurrence, said that other guests in the hotel had reported a 'row' in a room occupied by a 'Mr and Mrs Collins.' The witness had entered the room with a pass key and had found there a young woman—later identified by him as Starr Faithfull—lying completely nude on the bed, while the man in his underwear was sitting on the edge of the bed. The girl showed signs of having just received a terrific beating. A policeman was called, and the pair, who were both still very drunk, were removed to hospital.

The detectives employed on the case also discovered that Starr Faithfull had been under observation at the Channing Sanatorium for a short period during 1925—that was six years before. She had been discharged nine days after entering the institution, and her card marked 'improved'.

It was also discovered by the detectives that in the previous autumn, Starr Faithfull had visited Europe with her mother and sister, and that whilst there she had spent a good deal of time buying clothes and frequenting nightclubs. A reluctant witness, who had known Starr in London, told the detectives that one night the girl had danced in the nude in a certain night-club upon being challenged to do so. One of the group of people who had accompanied her to the club tried to hide her nakedness with his overcoat, whereupon Starr's escort had taken a revolver from his overcoat pocket and fired at the Puritanic interrupter. The incident, it was stated, had caused a 'good deal of comment in the English Press'. And small wonder!

A scenic artist by the name of Rudolph Haybrook, now came on the scene. He told the Police that he was absolutely certain that Starr had been murdered, the reason being the result of a 25,000 dollar settlement case in which she was the principal witness. It was in order to stop these fresh sensational rumours, that Stanley Faithfull issued a statement to the Press declaring that his adopted daughter had never been involved in any such type of litigation.

Meanwhile, fresh inquiries were being prosecuted in England, and these disclosed the fact that Starr Faithfull had attempted suicide whilst a guest in a certain London hotel; she had only been thwarted by a chambermaid coming in at a critical moment.

It can easily be imagined that all this sensational rumour and counter-rumour was greedily printed by the New York Press—indeed, by a Press of the whole world. The Faithfull case was a 'natural' as a news story. But the vital questions, (1) How Starr Faithfull had died? and (2) Who was her murderer? still remained unsolved.

It was while the investigations were in this unsatisfactory state that District Attorney Edwards came into prominence. Placed in charge of the case, he declared that he was convinced that the dead girl's family was not telling the whole truth about her, but was trying to hide many vital facts. He went to the Faithfull home and asked to examine the dead girl's room. Here, behind a volume of Tennyson's poems in the bookcase, he found a small book marked 'My Diary'.

It did not take Edwards long to be convinced that the contents of this small volume was bound to add more sensation to the case, and increase the fury of the 'murder v. suicide' controversy.

For the diary made frequent references to a man whose initials were 'A.J.P.' Excitement followed upon excitement, for these initials were those of a former mayor of Boston, by the name of Andrew J. Peters! It was not determined, however, whether or not the notations in the diary referred to Mr Peters; the former Mayor, when questioned, admitted readily that he had known Starr but that he could give no information which was not already in possession of the Police.

But the diary certainly revealed that the dead girl had had a peculiarly warped and morbid mind. For instance, there were several references to suicide and the general futility of modern existence; and—an even more sensational feature—there were frank confessions of sexual perversion and promiscuity.

Faced by these disclosures, the Faithfull family were forced

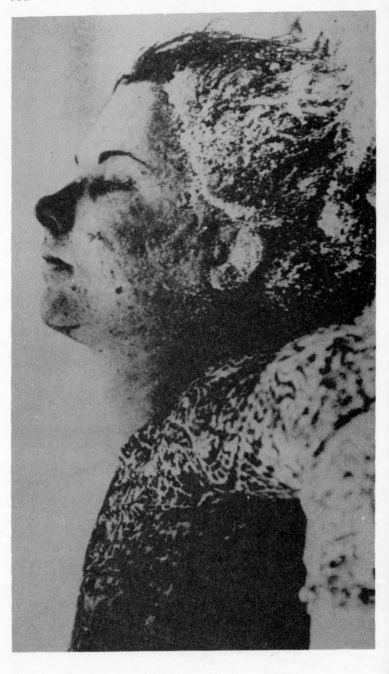

to admit that the girl's conduct had been a constant worry and problem to them. Mr Faithfull even went to the extent of revealing that when Starr was only eleven years old, she had allowed herself to be seduced by a man four times her age. It was this man who had taken her on various trips to Europe and had entirely warped her personality as well as her outlook on life. In her diary, Starr had told with the utmost frankness of her relations with this man—and even the Press of America could not print the full details, because of their revolting nature.

It was as a result of these sexual relations that the girl had had to be confined in a sanatorium, where she remained under the care of doctors for some time. A relative of the family, a lawyer by profession, had advised Mr Faithfull to sue Starr's 'lover' for the medical expenses. The result of the suit was that the man had settled out of Court, giving Starr 22,000 dollars in cash.

Ten days after the discovery of the body, Dr Carr of the *Franconia*, with whom it had been stated the girl had been in love, returned to New York and submitted to questioning by detectives. He showed the police officials a letter which Starr had written to him a few days before her disappearance. In this letter, the girl had said that she intended, at some time in the future, to take her own life, as she was 'fed up'.

Naturally enough, this statement was seized upon by the adherents of the suicide theory who claimed that the letter clinched their case, and that there could no longer be any possible doubt that Starr killed herself in a fit of morbid despondency.

But those on the other side were still not satisfied. They pointed out that there were yet many questions about the case that remained mysterious. Why, they put forward, had the girl been criminally violated before she committed her last dread act? Undoubtedly, they went on, she had been murdered. The assault would be ample motive for the killer.

Then again, if Starr had committed suicide (by jumping off a pier), why were her undergarments, coat, hat, shoes and stockings not found at the spot where she had entered the water?

These burning questions have been unanswered to this day.
The Starr Faithfull case is still unsolved. But one point of
interest in the affair has developed quite recently: a taxi-driver
has come forward to state that on the afternoon of Starr
Faithfull's disappearance, he carried a man and woman in his
cab away from the Manhattan dock. They were both quite
drunk. After riding for a few blocks, the man got out of the cab
and the girl returned to the docks from whence she had come.

When asked why he had kept this story for so long, the
taxi-driver explained that he was forced to keep silent for
'personal reasons'.

Will the truth ever be known? After this long period it seems
doubtful, but even to this day the Starr Faithfull case is
numbered amongst the most notorious murder-mysteries of
modern America.

AFTERWORD

*The passage of time has, alas, added absolutely nothing to our knowledge of how
Starr Faithfull met her end. The case continues to fascinate, however, and
regularly pops up in newspapers, magazines and books. For anyone wanting
to pursue the problem, an entertaining solution is to be found in Sandra
Scoppettone's 1977 novel,* Some Unknown Person.

WILLIAM LE QUEUX

Bela Kiss, the Mystery Man of Europe

WILLIAM LE QUEUX

Bela Kiss, the Mystery Man of Europe

In the early spring of 1912 a tall, rather elegant man of exquisite manner, thin-faced, black-haired, with high cheek-bones and a countenance of almost Tartar type, arrived with his young and pretty wife from Budapest at the charming little summer resort of Czinkota, a few miles from the Hungarian capital. The place is much frequented by holiday folk on Sundays, it being a centre for excursions to Visegrad, Nagy-Moros and Budafok. The stranger, who was about forty years of age, was named Bela Kiss, his wife being about fifteen years younger. After searching the district for a house he eventually took a rather spacious one standing back in a large garden on the Matyasfold road, in a somewhat isolated position, and for a few months lived happily there, going into Budapest alone about once or twice a week. It afterwards transpired that he had been a tinsmith in a large way of business, but had retired.

The pair formed few friendships, for Kiss seemed a some-what mystical person, and had often been heard to discuss psychic subjects with his wife. He was also something of an amateur astrologer and possessed many books upon the subject, while his wife had a small crystal globe into which she was fond of gazing. The pair seemed a most devoted couple, and went about together in the small and rather dilapidated car which the husband possessed, and in which he often went into Budapest.

The wife was extremely good-looking, and Kiss was apparently extremely jealous of her. Indeed, he forbade her to make any male acquaintances. She was a native of Zimony, on the Danube, in the extreme south of Hungary, a place long noted for its handsome female inhabitants. According to village

173

gossip, however, little Madame Kiss had a friend in a certain Paul Bihari, an artist of Budapest, who sometimes spent the day with her wandering in the acacia woods and picnicking together during her husband's absence. The handsome young fellow was well known in the capital and especially at the Otthon Club, where Hungarian authors, artists and journalists assemble nightly.

I

Matters proceeded in this manner for nearly six months, Paul being a frequent visitor to the house, and the pair making many excursions to the beauty spots in the vicinity. One evening, however, Bela Kiss on his return from Budapest found the house locked up. After waiting till near nightfall he broke open the door, and found, lying upon the dining-table, a note from his wife saying that she had fled with her lover, and asking forgiveness. In a frenzy of anger he burnt the note, and then rushing to a neighbour named Littman, who lived in the vicinity and who was one of the few persons with whom he had formed a friendship, told him of the staggering blow he had received.

Next day all Czinkota was agog, knowing what had occurred. But it was only what they had long expected.

Crushed by his disillusionment, the heart-broken husband shut himself up and became almost a recluse. He drove sometimes to Budapest, but he had no servant and did his own cooking and looked after his few daily wants himself. In fact, he became a woman-hater and devoted his time to the study of psychometry and mysticism. His eccentricity now became the more marked, but as months wore on his health appeared to be failing, until it was noticed that he had not been seen out for over a week, while the house appeared to be closed. Yet each night there appeared a light in his bedroom.

The neighbour in whom he had confided how his wife had deserted him began to wonder, so one day he called. The knock on the door's brought Bela, pale, half-clad and very feeble. He told his friend that he had been ill in bed for some days. The friend at once suggested that he should have somebody to nurse him, and that the village doctor should be called. At first Kiss demurred, saying: 'After all, if I die what matters? I have nothing to live for, now that my dear one has left me!'

The neighbour uttered comforting words, and eventually the doctor visited him—much against his will—and an old woman from the village, named Kalman, was left in charge.

His eccentricity had, it seems, increased to a marked degree. In one room there were laid out carefully upon the table the clothes and shoes that his wife had left behind, and into that room the invalid forbade the old woman to enter. For nearly three weeks the village woman was most assiduous, and carefully nursed him back to health, until at last he became quite well again. So he paid her and she left, leaving him to the dull, isolated life which he had lived ever since his young wife had gone.

II

Soon he resumed his business visits to Budapest, usually leaving the house in the afternoon and often not returning until midnight and after. Very naturally the woman Kalman was questioned by her friends as to the condition of the house of the poor grief-stricken man. It was also but natural that she should describe to her neighbours what she had seen—how, though forbidden to enter the room where the erring wife's clothes were displayed, she had entered it in secret while her patient was asleep, and passing through it had peered through the keyhole of the room beyond, where she saw five large tin drums ranged along by the wall.

The old woman's curiosity had been aroused by sight of these, and soon her friends, to whom she described what she had seen, suspected the eccentric, grief-stricken man to be in league with some illicit distillers who had their secret factory somewhere in the neighbourhood. The gossips were naturally sorely puzzled to account for those big receptacles for fluid. Some laughed and said that he had a big store of wine bought at the previous year's vintage. Littman, his neighbour and confidant, hearing about it, one day mentioned to him what the old woman Kalman had seen, whereupon Kiss laughed heartily and replied:

'Well, that is really amusing! They think I am one of those

who distil alcohol against the law and sell it in secret to the night cafés in Budapest—eh? Well, let them think so! I would be afraid to engage in such a dangerous trade, lucrative as it is. No. The fact is that I have my store of petrol there. I bought it cheaply from a man who was about to be made bankrupt.'

Quickly the truth went round the village, and suspicion was at once allayed. Indeed, a man of such exemplary conduct as Bela Kiss surely could never be engaged in any illicit transactions.

Once Littman expressed surprise that he had not followed the runaway pair and divorced his wife. To this, Kiss replied: 'If they are happy in Vienna, as I hear they are, why should I wreck her life? I loved her more than anything on earth. So that is enough. I was a fool! That's all!' And he refused to discuss the matter further.

From that moment, however, suspicions regarding Kiss became increased. His many journeys to Budapest were regarded as mysterious, and an evil-tongued woman who distrusted him declared that he practised black magic. He had drawn the horoscope of a woman of her acquaintance who believed in astrology, and thus a fresh theory was set up to account for his aloofness and eccentricity.

Whenever he motored to Budapest, as he did twice a week, it was noted that he never returned until the early hours of the morning, when the whole village was asleep. The villagers heard his noisy, ramshackle car speeding through the streets homeward bound. Of money this retired tinsmith had plenty. The village policeman, who, by the way, had also had his curiosity aroused by the malicious gossip, struck up an acquaintance with him, and soon discovered him to be a real good fellow, kind, generous and hospitable. They often spent evenings together, for the representative of the law was, in addition to Littman, the only person he ever invited to cross his threshold since his wife's flight. The constable naturally reported the result of his inquiries to his chief, and all suspicions were set at rest.

III

One wintry morning in January 1914, the exquisitely dressed Bela Kiss was seen walking with a pretty young woman, also handsomely attired in furs, about half a mile from the village, and this fact, which soon got about, gave rise to the theory that the disillusioned husband had fallen in love again. The gossips kept watch, but only on that one occasion was the lady seen. It, was, no doubt, an illicit meeting, for the well-dressed lady had, it was known, come from Budapest and had spent the day with her admirer.

About a month later a farmer driving from Czinkota to Rakosfalva noticed a man and a woman walking in the afternoon along a secluded footpath on the edge of a wood, and on approaching recognised Kiss arm in arm with a well-dressed young girl, to whom he was earnestly talking. The spot was nearly four miles from the village, and near by stood Kiss's old motor-car, muddy and unwashed.

Just about that time a strange story was told to the police of the Josefvaros quarter in Budapest by a young girl named Luisa Ruszt, daughter of a well-known draper in the Karoly Korut, one of the principal shopping thoroughfares.

She said that one evening she had met a man in the Somossy variety theatre, and he had taken her next day for a long motor drive. On their way back to Budapest, they had stopped at his country house and there had some refreshment. Afterwards they returned to the city, when he invited her to his flat somewhere near the Margaret Bridge. They had had dinner at a restaurant, when he told her that if she cared to go back to his flat he would tell her fortune. Like most girls she was eager to know her future, therefore she consented and went.

On arrival he offered her some pale yellow liqueur which seemed very strong, and then setting her at a table he told her to gaze intently into a small crystal globe. In fun he promised that she would see her future husband.

She did as he instructed, and had been gazing intently for some time when she began to experience a strange dizziness, probably due to the liqueur. Suddenly, on looking up from the crystal she saw in a mirror at her side the man standing behind her with a piece of green silk cord in his hand. It had a noose and a slip-knot, and he was about to place it over her head!

Sight of the changed face of her friend—a pale, evil countenance, with glaring dark eyes which had in them the spirit of murder—held her breathless. She fainted, and knew no more until she found herself lying beneath the trees in the Erszebet Park at dawn with all her jewellery and money gone.

She described to the police, as well as she could, the man with his house in the country and his flat in the town, but, though some inquiries were made, neither flat nor house could be identified, and they apparently dismissed the story as the imaginings of a romantic girl.

Curiously enough, however, about three weeks later a very similar story was told by a young married woman of good family, and whose husband was a wealthy merchant, to the police of the Belvaros quarter of Budapest. The lady, who lived on the handsome Franz Josef's Quai, facing the Danube, had met a smartly dressed man one Sunday morning as she came out alone after service in the Terezvaros Church, which is highly fashionable during the Budapest season. She was nearly run down by a passing taxi when he had grabbed her arm and pulled her back. Thus they became acquainted. They walked together for some distance, when he told her that his name was Franz Hofmann, a jeweller's traveller, and that he was greatly interested in spiritualism. She happened to be also interested in spiritualism, hence a friendship was formed. Her husband was away in Paris, therefore she invited him to dine at her house a few days later, and at the dinner she appeared wearing some valuable jewellery, while he, as a jeweller, admired it greatly.

Later that evening Hofmann invited her to go to one of the most select night cafés for which Budapest is famous, and she accepted. Afterwards, at two o'clock in the morning, he persuaded her to accompany him to his flat, where he would tell her fortune by the crystal. She went, and almost the same thing happened. She drank the liqueur, and he tried to strangle her. She fought with him, was overpowered, and when she came to her senses found herself in the hands of the police devoid of her jewellery. She had been found lying in a doorway unconscious.

This second story aroused the interest of the Budapest police, and inquiries were made, but neither woman could say where the flat in question was situated. They had been taken there, they said, by a roundabout route. The taxi had been dismissed in what seemed to be a cul-de-sac, and they had walked the remainder of the distance. They both described the interior in identical terms, and their description of the man left no doubt that it was the same individual in each case.

Then, when a third girl told a similar story a fortnight later, and when a dealer in second-hand jewellery had shown the police a ring the description of which had been circulated, a real hue and cry was raised. But just at that moment war broke out, and the country was thrown into disorder. The police system quickly broke down, and every available man was called up to fight against the Allies on the side of the Germans.

Bela Kiss was among those called up. He had been living a quiet, lonely, uneventful life, and as soon as the call to arms came he ordered from a blacksmith a number of iron bars, which he fixed inside the windows of his house to keep out thieves during his absence. Then, a week later, he left Czinkota and joined the colours.

IV

Eighteen months passed. He fought in Serbia, and once wrote to his friend Littman from Semendria, on the Serbian shore of the Danube, after a great battle had been fought. Littman, who was over military age, replied, but the letter was returned some four months later with an official intimation that Kiss had died of wounds in a military hospital near Belgrade. Then the village gossips of Czinkota knew that the poor deserted husband, who had led such a lonely life, had given his life for his country, and his name was later on engraved upon the local war memorial.

In the meantime, however, a sensational discovery had been made, quite by accident, of the body of a young woman in an advanced state of decomposition buried under about six inches of earth in the same wood of acacias wherein the farmer had seen Bela Kiss walking with a young woman. Upon the finger of the corpse was a wedding-ring engraved on the inside by which she was identified with the young wife of a furrier in a large way of business in Vienna, who had before the war run away with a middle-aged man, taking with her a quantity of jewellery and the equivalent of two thousand pounds in money. She had left her husband and entirely disappeared, after sending a letter to a friend from Budapest.

Inquiries were at once instituted, of course, and it was found that her husband had been killed within the first week of the war. Therefore, as far as the police—unfortunately a very inefficient service in those days—were concerned, they could do no more. But within three months yet another body was turned up by the plough in the vicinity. The records of missing persons were inspected, and they found that the unfortunate woman was named Isabelle Koblitz, a niece of the Minister of Commerce, who was known to have studied spiritualism, and who had disappeared from Vienna in July 1913.

The chief of the detective police of Budapest then began further inquiries. From Berne a report came that a wealthy Swiss lady named Riniker, living at Lausanne, had been staying at a well-known hotel in Budapest, from which she had written to her sister in Geneva, but had, in October 1913, mysteriously disappeared. A description was given of her, together with the fact that she had a red scar upon her cheek and that she had a slight deformation of the left leg. Within three days the Hungarian police established the fact that the body of the lady was that which had, six months before, been found in a disused well at Solymar, a little place about twenty miles away, at which the festival of the Queen of the Roses is celebrated each year.

The police now became much puzzled. Yet they did not connect the stories of the women who had gazed into the crystal with the discovery of the bodies of others.

Suddenly an order to commandeer all petrol went forth, and all garages and private persons were compelled to deliver it over for military purposes and receive receipts for it, which the Government eventually paid. At first the commandeering took place only in the big towns, but after three months a further thorough 'comb-out' of petrol was ordered, and commissioners visited every village, including Czinkota. There they searched for petrol, whereupon the old woman Kalman recalled the fact that poor Kiss who had died possessed quite a stock of petrol.

This quickly reached the ears of the commissioner, who went at once to the dead man's house, broke down the iron bars, and found the big drums of spirit. From their appearance both the commissioner and a constable suspected them to be full of smuggled brandy. Indeed, the constable obtained a tin mug from the kitchen in order to sample the spirit when they bored a hole. They did so—and found it to be crude alcohol.

Further investigation, however, led to a most ghastly discovery. On cutting open the top of the big drum a quantity of female clothing was seen. This was removed, and beneath was the nude body of a woman bound with cord and so well preserved in the spirit that her features were easily recognisable. Indeed, around her neck was a thin red line, showing plainly the manner in which she had been murdered—namely, by strangulation with a cord and slip-knot!

And each of the other drums contained the body of a woman, each showing traces of strangulation. Upon these gruesome facts—perhaps the most horrible discovery ever made in the annals of the police of Europe—we need not dwell.

Search of Bela Kiss's belongings brought to light a number of receipts for advertisements inserted in several of the most important newspapers in Vienna and Budapest, and upon examination of the files of those papers the advertisements in question were easily identified.

One, which was repeated in ten different issues of the paper, read:

> Bachelor: aged 40: lonely; good income from commercial enterprises averaging £3000 per annum, is desirous of corresponding with educated lady with a view to matrimony. Address: De Koller, Poste Restante, Granatos, Budapest.

A number of other similar advertisements were traced by the receipts, all of which were either alluding to matrimony or trying to induce girls to learn their futue. Indeed, when the police came to inquire at the Post Office in Budapest they found no fewer than fifty-three letters awaiting the mysterious De Koller undelivered!

In a Vienna daily newspaper the following advertisement was found: 'Know Yourself!—Those who wish to know their future and thus frame their lives should consult Professor

Hofmann of Budapest. Write: Poste Restante, Vienna.' To this one advertisement there were twenty-three replies awaiting him, all from women eager to have their fortunes told. It then became plain that the fellow's habit was to lure women possessing even paltry sums of money or modest jewellery, either to his flat in Budapest, or to take them out by night to his house at Czinkota, and there strangle them. The tin drums of spirit he evidently used in order to preserve the bodies of his victims until he could bury them in secret or otherwise dispose of them.

A number of prisoners of war were at once set to work digging in Kiss's garden and in the acacia woods, the result being that no fewer than twenty-six other bodies of women and girls were found at various spots. Over one hundred and sixty pawn-tickets relating to women's clothing were found concealed under the carpet of the dining-room, and by the recovery of the clothing and some jewellery, fourteen of his victims were eventually identified. They were mostly of women of the better class, and in every case had worn jewellery and had money in their possession when they had gone to consult him.

The method he adopted never varied. His first crime was committed by means of a cord slipped over the head and drawn tight ere his victims could utter a cry—thus adopting the method of the notorious Frenchwoman Gabrielle Bompard—and so successful was he that he always pursued the same course. Among the bodies recovered in the garden was one which was identified as the young wife who was supposed to have fled with the artist, Paul Bihari. The latter was found in Agram, and when questioned by the police stated that one day, while at the house in Czinkota, Kiss came home unexpectedly, and after a fracas he left and had not seen the lady or heard of her since.

The monster Bela Kiss had, however, died of wounds received while fighting in Serbia, therefore the police hushed up the terrible affair, and soon the gruesome discovery was forgotten by all except the villagers of Czinkota.

About a year later, however, Inspector Resch, of the detective force of Budapest, learned that a man closely resembling Franz Hofmann had been seen a week before by the girl Luisa Ruszt—who had had such a narrow escape while gazing into the crystal globe. At first he was not inclined to believe her, but so positive was she that she had actually seen him in the flesh, that the police officer decided to go to the hospital at Belgrade and learn details at first hand of the assassin's death.

On arrival he found that Bela Kiss had died from wounds, and he was given the dead man's papers, which proved his identity beyond question. By mere chance the nurse who had tended him in his dying moments was still there, and naturally the inspector questioned her as to the end of such a callous and elusive criminal.

'But surely,' she remarked, 'such a very frank and pious-minded boy could not have committed such awful crimes!'

'Boy!' echoed the inspector. 'What do you mean? Bela Kiss was over forty years old.'

'Well, the Bela Kiss who died here was about twenty!' was her reply.

Again the surprised detective examined the identification papers, and saw that without doubt they were the genuine ones belonging to Bela Kiss of Czinkota. Hence the assassin had, no doubt, exchanged papers with the poor young fellow who had died and been buried under his name.

With this astounding knowledge Inspector Resch sped back to Budapest, and a thorough search was at once made for the assassin. The police of Europe were warned, and as it was believed that the assassin had fled to London, Scotland Yard became active, as well as the Paris Sûreté. But the fellow managed to slip through their fingers, and today they are still searching for him all over Europe and America.

AFTERWORD

Five years later, a man who has just emerged from the French Foreign Legion informed the Sûreté that a fellow-soldier called Hofmann was in the habit of amusing his friends with lurid stories of garrottings; moreover, he answered the description of the wanted man. But by the time the authorities acted, Hofmann too had deserted.

There were rumours that he had fled to the United States, and in 1932 a detective in New York's Homicide Squad claimed to have spotted Kiss in Times Square, but again he proved too elusive to be apprehended.

He was never caught.

EDMUND PEARSON

The Borden Case

EDMUND PEARSON

The Borden Case

The Borden case is without parallel in the criminal history of America. It is the most interesting, and perhaps the most puzzling murder which has occurred in this country. There are in it all the elements which make such an event worth reading about, since, in the first place, it was a mysterious crime in a class of society where such deeds of violence are not only foreign, but usually wildly impossible. It was purely a problem in murder, not complicated by scandals of the kind which lead to the *crime passionel*, nor by any of the circumstances of the political assassination. The evidence was wholly circumstantial. The perpetrator of the double murder was protected by a series of chances which might not happen again in a thousand years. And, finally, the case attracted national attention, and divided public opinion, as no criminal prosecution has done since—nor, to the best of my belief, as any murder trial in the United States had ever done before. People have become disputatious, even quarrelsome, over the probability of a verdict, one way or the other, over the justice of a verdict rendered, or over the wisdom of a commutation of sentence, in cases in which there was no doubt at all as to the identity of the slayer. In many celebrated cases the actual murder has been done openly and in public.

But during the investigation of the Borden mystery, and during the thirteen days of the trial, families throughout the United States were divided upon the question, and argued its points with a vehement interest for which no comparison suggests itself to me except the excitement in France over the Dreyfus case. And since there were no political and no racial matters at issue, there becomes apparent the extraordinary

187

fascination of this case as a problem in human character and in human relations.

A murder may attract national attention for any one of a number of reasons. The actors may be persons of good position and respectability, as in the slaying of Dr Parkman by Professor Webster, which amazed everybody in the days of our grandparents, and is still discussed by many writers on criminology. In later days, those who follow the art of yellow journalism became agitated about that miserable affair in the Madison Square Garden in 1906. In this was no mystery whatever, and there would have been little interest except for the publicity of the crime, the scandals which attended it, and the fact that the victim was famous, and the other persons notorious. Otherwise, it was cheap and shabby; a carnival for the Sunday supplements. The warfare of gamblers, half a dozen years later, which came to a climax in front of the Hotel Metropole in New York, was really an incident in the history of municipal corruption; the killing of Rosenthal belongs in the class of crimes committed during feuds, rather than that of private murders. The lonely death of Mr Elwell in his own home, was the subject of great interest; the opening chapter from a novel by Anna Katharine Green had been translated into reality. But it happened upon a verge of a world where such events are neither rare nor astonishing. More unusual was that scene in De Russey's Lane, New Brunswick, upon whose horrors the discoverer casually wandered, as if stepping upon a stage laden with the dreadful quarry of an Elizabethan tragedy.

No one of these, I venture to assert, equals in peculiar interest the Borden murders in Fall River. Here were concerned neither gamblers, wasters, nor criminals, but quiet folk of a kind known to all of us. They were not members of a class among which killing is a matter of momentary impulse. They were so obscure that except for the event which put their names upon everybody's lips, we should never had heard of them. They became important in the light of what happened; the case was not like a play by a lazy dramatist who shirks his work of creation, and fills his scene with personages already famous. The crime itself—unexpected, hideous, unexplained—was the central point of interest. When the trial came to an end, ten months later, and the jury considered their verdict, there was before them, of course, only the task of answering, by yes or no, the question: was the accused person guilty? Apparently, they had little trouble in finding an answer to this, but the verdict did not clear up the astonishing puzzle. If, instead of a jury bound by our laws, they had been a committee of inquiry, charged with discovering an explanation of the crime, their task would have been as perplexing as anything which twelve men ever attempted. Each of the principal theories advanced at the time had its dark and doubtful points, and was moreover, as many reasonable men believed, in itself grossly improbable, and nearly contrary to human experience. Hardly ever was a murder committed where the limits of time and space so closed in upon the act, leaving such a narrow gap for the assassin to slip through to security.

The name Borden is found in all parts of the United States. It has been honorably associated with more than one important business, and in Canada two of the names have been eminent in politics. Many of the American Bordens are descendants of Richard and Joan Borden who came from England in 1638 to live in Rhode Island. In that State, and even more in the adjoining county of Bristol, Massachusetts (which includes the cities of Fall River, New Bedford, and Taunton), the Bordens have always been numerous. The name has often been associated with that of Durfee. In 1778, when Fall River was attacked by a detachment of British troops, a Major Durfee led the citizens in a successful defence. Two of the houses burned during the fight were owned by men named Borden; one of these men was captured. In 1844, a Borden and a Durfee represented the district in the Legislature; and, in 1892, the year of the tragedy, these family names were borne by one or the other of the victims. Orin Fowler's 'History of Fall River', in 1841, mentions the name Borden as second in frequency in the town. When the name came into painful notoriety in 1892, there were a hundred and twenty-five Bordens—representing, of course, many more than that—listed in the Fall River directory. It is illustrative of the frequency of the name that the indictment for murder, found in that year against a Borden, should have been attested by two others of the name, father and son, clerk and assistant clerk of the Superior Court, but not related to the accused person.

Fall River, like Dover or Calais, is one of those cities to which few go for its own sake, compared with the thousands who pass through on their way elsewhere. To the traveler into New England from New York or the South, it is associated with the name of a steamship line, and with an early morning change from boat to train. Reuben Paine, the hero of Mr Kipling's 'Rhyme of the Three Sealers', as he lay dying in the fogs of Bering Sea, let his mind travel far over the world to regret:

> No more I'll see the trawlers drift below the
> Bass Rock ground,
> Or watch the tall Fall steamer lights tear blazing
> up the Sound.

And if nobody except Reuben Paine, that I have heard of, ever referred to them as 'Fall steamers', it is best to remember not only the exigencies of verse, but that the sight of the Fall River boats, from either shore of Long Island Sound at night, or from the water, is one that might well return to a man after many years. Current and local speech has not always been so respectful toward this steamship line, but Mr Conrad Aiken has not hesitated to make one of the Sound steamers the scene of a poetical romance of much beauty.

The overwhelming importance of one industry, the manufacture of cotton goods, is perhaps what has prevented Fall River from becoming either interesting or attractive. It has its full complement of ugly streets, but of pleasant ones, fewer than such cities as Providence and Salem. Any American can see the town in his mind's eye, for there is a tedious similarity in places of this size; and the fact has been noted in the saying that West Newton, Massachusetts, extends all the way to the Pacific Coast. All have their Main Streets, under that name or another. Fall River has both the name and the thing itself. In 1892 there were a few more trees and a few less brick buildings upon it; the street-cars were not so noisy nor so many; the motion picture theatre, the motor-car and the traffic policeman were still to arrive. Otherwise it looked nearly as it does today. The city had not then grown to have a hundred and twenty thousand inhabitants, but there were about seventy-five thousand, already including many of foreign birth, who were helping the native-born in their work, and sometimes perplexing them, and rendering them doubtful of the blessing of their presence. Citizens whose families had long been established in this country were inclined, as always, to suspect that any unusual offence was necessarily the deed of 'some of those foreigners', forgetting the strange twists and distortions of which the oldest American stock has sometimes shown itself capable.

The newspapers of August, 1892, curiously prim and almost quaint to us today, contained small matter for excitement in that hot, dull season. There were speculations upon Mr Cleveland's popularity; he was about to turn the tables on President Harrison, and defeat him in the November election. Mr Gladstone's health was not too good. That aspiring sportsman, the Emperor Wilhelm, was racing his yacht at Cowes. John L. Sullivan was training for his last fight—with Corbett. From the port of Palos had set forth a replica of the caravel *Santa Maria*, to take part in the celebration of the 400th anniversary of Columbus's discovery. Chicago was raising money for its World's Fair, and hoping that the cholera, reported in distant parts of Europe, was not coming as a guest. There were echoes of the Homestead strike and riot; Mr Frick was recovering from the assault which had nearly ended his life. The *Teutonic* had broken the ocean record by crossing from Queenstown to New York in five days and eighteen hours. And the London police had caught a strange and terrible creature, named Neill Cream, and in great perplexity were uncovering a series of crimes, fiendish and inexplicable.

On the intensely hot morning of Thursday, August 4, 1892, something more than an hour before noon, an elderly gentleman named Andrew Jackson Borden was walking through South Main Street, Fall River. He was returning to his home which was only a few steps from the principal business street, and little more than around the corner from the City Hall, and the center of the town. It is probable that his mind was chiefly concerned with business, or with his family affairs, which were disconcerting. For the personages mentioned in the morning newspapers, and for the events described in them, it is fair to suppose he had no thought. So securely is the future hidden from us, that there is no way to imagine the astonishment which would have been his, could he have had any intimation not alone of the sufficiently startling fact that the remainder of his life time was then numbered by minutes, but that his name was to engage his countrymen's attention, for weeks and months to come, as if he were somebody of national importance.

However little he may have been known elsewhere, in his own town he was certainly not obscure. He was president of the Union Savings Bank, director in one or two other banks, and a director in various companies, including the Merchants Manufacturing Company, the Globe Yarn Mills, the B.M.C. Durfee Safe Deposit and Trust Company, and the Troy Cotton and Woolen Manufacturing Company. His business affairs had taken him on that morning to one or more of these banks. In his early life he had been an undertaker, and either that, or the gloomy custom of mankind, led him to dress in black, and in black clothes he trudged along on this tropically hot morning. His hair was white, for he was about seventy years of age, and he wore a fringe of white whiskers under his chin and along the angle of the jaw. His expression could be kindly, but it was stern; the thin lips—he wore no moustache—met in a way that denoted a stubborn character. The New England phrase is suggested: 'He was as set as the everlasting hills of Zion'. I have heard him described by one who remembers him coming from his farm—a tall and erect old man, in his black clothes, carrying a little basket of eggs. That last bit is significant; Mr Borden owned farms across the Taunton River, in addition to more than one house in the city. He had built one of the best office buildings in Fall River and the value of his estate was between $250,000 and $300,000. Yet he was not averse to bringing a few eggs to town, and selling them to some dealer. His manner of living had not changed as he rose from lesser things to greater, from one small business to financial power which, in that time and place, was not so different from that of a millionaire in a large city today. His was the melancholy lot of a man grown old in the treadmill of business, with no idea that life could be enjoyed, and no diversion except the further

The Borden house.

accumulation of money. Yet a just and honorable man, respected by everybody, and loved, perhaps, by one woman. He lived simply—many would say narrowly—in a small wooden house, Number 92 (now 230) Second Street.

Mr Borden had married twice. His first wife was a Miss Sarah A. Morse, by whom he had three children. After the death of the first Mrs Borden, he married in 1865, Miss Abby Durfee Gray, who was six years younger than himself, and therefore in 1892 about sixty-four years old. With Mr and Mrs Borden there lived the two surviving daughters by the first marriage, Miss Emma L. Borden, about forty-one years old, and Miss Lizzie Andrew Borden, about thirty-two. These four persons, with a servant named Bridget Sullivan, made up the family at the Borden home.

On August 4th, however, Miss Emma Borden was visiting some friends in Fairhaven, but the number of the house in Second Street remained the same, since John Vinnicum Morse, a brother of the first Mrs Borden, had arrived the day before for a short visit. This was a man of sixty years, who lived in Dartmouth, Massachusetts. Visits to Fall River and to the Borden house were frequent with him after his return to New England from twenty years spent as a farmer in Iowa. Serious and disturbing as the consequences of this visit were to Mr Morse, it is almost impossible to regard his casual appearance in the household, on this occasion, without amusement. Arriving, quite without baggage, on August 3rd, and solemnly pursuing for about twenty-four hours the objects of his visit—which seem to have been calls upon other relatives and the inspection of Mr Borden's farms—he found himself entangled in events of the most dreadful and sensational nature. The innocent bystander proverbially deserves our sympathy, but seldom gets it. Excepting young Mr Monks, embarking upon the *Herbert Fuller*, for health, rest, and recreation (as recorded elsewhere) it is hard to recall any figure similar to that of John Vinnicum Morse.

Mr Borden continued through South Main Street, up Borden Street, and thence—it could have been only a few minutes' walk, even for an elderly man—into Second Street. He arrived at his home at ten or fifteen minutes before eleven. He had some little difficulty getting admitted, going first to the side door and then to the front, (for it was a peculiar household as regards locks, bars, and bolts) but at last he entered. Within about thirty minutes a report came to the police that Mr Borden had died—by violence—and the investigation began.

Out of the mass of rumors and assertions, of charges and denials, it is necessary now to select certain facts which are generally admitted, and to trace the happenings of the week in Mr Borden's home. It is useless to pretend that the family was either happy or contented. The presence in one home, of a step-mother and two daughters of mature years may be a fortunate combination with people of especially sunny disposition, but the Bordens seem to have been rather dour folk, to say the least. There was an aggrieved feeling about money on the part of the daughters, and this was of long standing. There was a perfectly comprehensible dissatisfaction with the manner of living, with the lack of such modern arrangements as a bathroom—which some parents then considered new-fangled, expensive and unnecessary. When all these difficulties were discussed in court, the best that could be done was to admit some of them, but vigorously to deny that they had any bearing on the murder, or that anything of importance could be deduced from them. But we have it, on the statement of a witness who was undisputed, that there was in the mind of that member of the family most concerned not to exaggerate the lack of harmony, a sense of impending disaster, and this only the night before the murder.

It had been a disturbing week. On Tuesday, August 2nd, Mr and Mrs Borden had been violently ill during the night. They were seized with vomiting. Miss Lizzie Borden said that she herself was affected, but not so as to cause vomiting. She went, she said, to the bedroom door of the older people, and asked if she could be of any help to them, but the offer was declined. Mr Morse who came to the house after the family had eaten their dinner, at noon, on Wednesday, was served with that meal, which he ate alone. He ate again at breakfast on Thursday with Mr and Mrs Borden, but seems to have suffered no harm, nor was there any other return of this mysterious sickness, except that the servant Bridget Sullivan, was, alone of the household,

sick on Thursday morning, the day of the murder, when she
went into the backyard where she vomited her breakfast.

On Wednesday afternoon, after his dinner, Mr Morse went
to Swansea, to Mr Borden's farm. He returned to the house on
Second Street after eight o'clock, and sat talking with Mr and
Mrs Borden. Miss Lizzie Borden was paying a call in a
neighboring street, upon Miss Alice Russell, a friend of the
family. During this call there was a remarkable conversation.
Miss Borden said that she had decided to follow Miss Russell's
advice, and go to Marion for a vacation. But she was apprehen-
sive and depressed. She said:

'I feel as if somethig was hanging over me that I cannot throw
off.'

She described Mr and Mrs Borden's sickness, the night
before, and expressed a suspicion that the milk might have been
intentionally poisoned! Miss Russell was incredulous, and in
this there is little cause for wonder. The suggestion that some
person, with the tendencies of the Borgias, was, in the early
hours of the morning, slipping deadly drugs into the milk can of
a respectable family in a New England town is not one that
ordinarily commends itself to the usual lady of good sense. The
caller, however, went on to say that she feared her father had an
enemy. He had trouble with somebody who came to see him.
One man got into a quarrel with Mr Borden and was ordered
out of the house. Then there were robberies: the barn had been
broken into twice. Miss Russell, who had formerly lived in a
house next to the Bordens, and was still a not-distant neighbor,
offered a more prosaic explanation of the barn robberies; they
were merely boys coming after the pigeons. There had also
been a daylight burglary, in the house, said Miss Borden. At
one time or another in the conversation, this prophetess of
disaster said that she slept in 'fear that they will burn the house
down over us'. She was not precise as to who 'they' were, but as
everybody knows there are no more dangerous nor malicious
beings in the world than 'they'. After a little more lugubrious
chat of this kind, Miss Borden left her friend to her meditations.
Like Cassandra's, her foreboding fell upon doubting ears, but
like Cassandra's, her prophecies were by no means empty.

Miss Borden returned home, and although her uncle John

Vinnicum Morse was seated in the room below, talking with her father and step-mother, and although she had not yet seen him, she did not pause nor speak to him. She went upstairs to her own room. She was the last one to enter by the front door, which she locked. Bridget was the last to enter by the side door, which she in turn locked. Mr and Mrs Borden that night as usual occupied their room in the rear of the second floor of the house; Miss Borden's room was next theirs. Mr Morse slept in the guest-room at the front. Bridget's room was on the third floor. It is hard to conceive how any person other than these five could have been in the house, and I believe that no serious contention has ever been made that any stranger was concealed.

The next morning, Thursday, Bridget Sullivan came downstairs at a little after six o'clock, built a fire in the kitchen stove, and began to prepare breakfast. Mrs Borden appeared about seven, and her husband and Mr Morse soon following, the three breakfasted together. This breakfast was subsequently discussed at more than one legal investigation, so it may be said that according to Mr Morse it consisted of mutton, bread, coffee, 'sugar cakes' and bananas. The servant, who prepared the food, said that there was *mutton-broth*, as well as mutton itself, johnny cakes, coffee and cookies. Bridget insisted, in answer to the specific question, that to the best of her belief, they had no bananas that day. At all events, for a hot morning and mid-summer it was a breakfast well adapted to set the stage for a tragedy. One trembles at the thought of beginning a day in August with mutton-soup.

A lady said to me recently that, after more than thirty years, the details of the Borden case had vanished from her mind—all except this awful breakfast.

Mr Morse departed from the house at a quarter before eight. Mr Borden let him out at the side door, and locked the screen door after him. A little later, Miss Borden came downstairs, and at first said to Bridget that she doubted if she cared for any breakfast. Finally, however, she decided to have coffee and cookies. Mr and Mrs Borden moved about the house; emptying slops and attending to other work of the kind, for Bridget was not expected to do this, nor was she even allowed in the rooms

The bodies of Mr and Mrs Borden.

on the second floor. Soon afterwards, the servant was attacked by the sickness already referred to, and went into the yard, for perhaps ten or fifteen minutes, where she was relieved by vomiting. She described her illness as a 'sick headache'. When she returned to the house, Mr Borden had gone downtown. This was between nine and half after the hour, and the three women were now, so far as anybody knows, alone in the house. Miss Borden was in the kitchen, still engaged, perhaps with her cookies and coffee, while Mrs Borden was wielding a feather-duster in the dining-room. The latter gave Bridget some orders for the morning; the windows on the lower floor were to be washed inside and out. A few minutes later, at about half-past nine, it would appear that Mrs Borden, having made up the bed in the guest-room, came downstairs again, and remarked that she was going back to put pillow-cases upon the two pillows of the bed in that room. She disappeared upstairs and nobody has ever admitted to seeing her alive again.

Bridget Sullivan went to the barn and to the cellar for brushes, pails, and other things for the window-washing. She came into the kitchen, the dining-room and the sitting-room to close the windows before beginning her work, and found those rooms empty. Neither Mrs Borden nor Miss Borden was there. She began her duties outdoors and in, washing windows on both sides of the house. It occupied some time; she had a talk over the fence with 'Mrs Kelly's girl,' and she made a number of trips to the barn for fresh pails of water. The Kellys were the next-door neighbors to the south. Neighbors' houses were close to the Borden house on both sides, and in the rear. Finally Bridget finished outside, and was occupied indoors, when she heard Mr Borden fumbling at the front door. He had already been at the side of the house where he found the wooden door open, but the screen door locked. Now he was trying his key at the front.

Bridget came from the sitting-room to let him in, but found the door not only locked, but triple-locked, with bolt, key, and spring lock. This is said to have been contrary to custom, and the slight annoyance caused her to make some exclamation, to say 'Oh, pshaw!'

At that moment she heard Miss Lizzie Borden at the head of the front stairs. She heard her *laugh*.

This little hall opens into Miss Lizzie Borden's room, and into the guest-room. Mr Borden entered his house and went to the dining-room. His daughter came to him, asked about the mail, and said:

'Mrs Borden has gone out; she had a note from somebody who was sick.'

Mr Borden took the key of his bedroom — it was a curiously well-guarded house — from a shelf, and went up the backstairs, to his own chamber. He came down again very shortly, and sat by a window in the sitting-room. Bridget finished her window-cleaning, going from one room to another. Miss Borden now appeared in the kitchen, to get an ironing board; this she took to the dining-room, and placing it on the table there, began to iron some handkerchiefs. All of this, from the entrance of Mr Borden, occupied but a few moments.

Miss Borden then made an inquiry of Bridget, addressing her, according to her custom, as 'Maggie,'' a name which had been inherited from a former servant.

'Maggie, are you going out this afternoon?'

'I don't know,' replied Bridget, 'I might and I might not; I don't feel very well.'

Apparently nobody did feel very well in that house. Miss Borden had herself made a meagre breakfast, as we have seen. But the mutton-soup may account for that.

'If you go out,' pursued the lady, 'be sure and lock the door, for Mrs Borden has gone out on a sick call, and I might go out, too.'

'Miss Lizzie,' Bridget asked, 'who is sick?'

'I don't know,' was the reply, 'she had a note this morning; it must be in town.'

And she went on ironing. Bridget rinsed the cloths she had been using, and hung them behind the kitchen stove. Miss Borden came into the kitchen, with another friendly bit of information.

'There is a cheap sale of dress goods at Sargent's at eight cents a yard.'

Bridget replied:

'I am going to have one,' and went upstairs, up the back-stairs, of course, to her own room where she lay down on the bed for a rest.

Surprise has often been expressed at this action on the part of a servant, at eleven o'clock in the morning. But Bridget had been up since six, she had been working steadily and there was nothing more to be done until half-past eleven or twelve, when she was to get the midday dinner. It was her custom, if time allowed, to take such a rest; the Bordens were not unduly hard or exacting towards their servant. It has been seen that she had few of the duties of a housemaid, and none as chambermaid. No astonishment could have been felt by any member of the family when she went upstairs. The dinner, moreover, was to be merely a repetition of the gruesome breakfast: 'soup to warm over and cold mutton.'

Shortly after she reached her room she heard the City Hall clock strike eleven. The house was quite; she heard no doors opened nor shut, nor any other sound. She denied that she slept or even became drowsy; on second questioning she weakened the force of her denial a little — she did not *think* that she slept at all. One rarely does know about this, and with many persons it seems to be considered a confession of breach of trust ever to admit closing the eyes, days or night. Second Street is a narrow street; wagons and carts probably rattled and rumbled past from time to time, but Bridget may well have failed to hear or to notice them. Nothing unusual was abroad in the house; nothing, at least, that came to the servant's ears, until some ten or fifteen minutes had passed. Then she heard Miss Borden's voice, and the tone of alarm was apparent at the first words.

'Maggie, come down!'

'What is the matter?' asked Bridget.

'Come down quick; Father's dead; somebody came in and killed him!'

Bridget descended instantly, and found Miss Borden standing near the side door. The servant started to enter the sitting-room, but was checked.

'Oh, Maggie, don't go in. I have got to have a doctor quick. Go over. I have got to have the doctor.'

There was no doubt who was meant by this. Dr Bowen, the family's friend and physician, who had already been consulted that week in regard to the strange illness, lived diagonally across the street, within a stone's throw. Bridget hurried to his house and reported the death to Mrs Bowen, but learned that the doctor was, at the moment, not at home. She came back and told Miss Borden, and at the same time asked the question which was destined to be asked by everybody:

'Miss Lizzie, where were you when this thing happened?'

The reply was:

'I was out in the yard, and heard a groan, and came in and the screen door was wide open.'

Bridget was then ordered to go to Miss Russell's house and bring her. She departed again. In the meantime the going and coming of Bridget, pale and agitated, had attracted the attention of the nearest neighbor, Mrs Churchill, who lived in the house to the north, hardly more than thirty feet away. Mrs Churchill went to the window, looked across at her neighbor's house, and saw the younger daughter of the family standing inside the screen door, and apparently excited or agitated. The distance was so slight as to make it possible to note that. She called to Miss Borden and asked her if there was any trouble.

'Oh, Mrs Churchill,' was the reply, 'do come over. Someone has killed Father.

Mrs Churchill hastened to her neighbor's house, went up the side-steps, and put her hand upon Miss Borden's arm.

'Oh, Lizzie!   Where is your father?'

'In the sitting-room.'

'Where were you when it happened?'

'I went to the barn to get a piece of iron.'

'Where is your mother?'

'I don't know; she had a note to go see someone who is sick, but I don't know but that she is killed too, for I thought I heard her come in . . . Father must have an enemy, for we have all been sick, and we think the milk has been poisoned.'

Mrs Churchill then learned that Dr Bowen could not be found, and she volunteered to go out in search of another doctor. She crossed the street to a stable, and asked for help. Among the men who heard her was one named Cunningham, who telephoned to the police station. City Marshal Hilliard thus received the news at 11:15 and sent an officer to the house.

Mrs Churchill returned to the Borden home, where in a few moments and before the arrival of the policeman, Bridget rejoined them, followed by Dr Bowen. Then, for the first time since the alarm was given, somebody entered the sitting-room. This was a small room, nearly square, with but two windows, both on the south side. The floor was covered with the usual garish, flowered carpet, customary in such houses at that time, and the wall paper was of a similarly disturbing pattern. The furniture was mahogany or black walnut, upholstered with the invariable black horsehair. On the north side of the room, opposite the windows, was a large sofa, and on this lay the dead body of Mr Borden with his head and face so hacked as to be unrecognizable even to his friend and physician, Dr Bowen.

The doctor noticed that Mr Borden had removed his coat, which was folded on the arm of the sofa, above the pillow on which his head rested. He had put on a cardigan jacket, in place of the coat. The body was stretched on the couch, but the legs from the knees down sloped toward the floor, and the feet rested on the carpet. It was his custom to take a nap in that position. Apparently, he had not altered his position after the attack. He wore congress shoes. There was no sign of a struggle; the fists were not clenched, and no furniture in the room was over-turned. Dr Bowen believed that he had been killed by the first blow, while asleep, but as to the other wounds which had been inflicted, in order to make death certain, he added:

'Physician that I am, and accustomed to all kinds of horrible sights, it sickened me to look upon the dead man's face.'

Mr Borden had been dead, so he thought, not more than twenty minutes.

Dr Bowen asked for a sheet with which to cover the body, and then, at Miss Borden's request, went to send a telegram to her elder sister at Fairhaven. He was asked to break the sad news as gently as possible. Miss Russell had arrived by this time, and with Mrs Churchill was engaged in the humane task of comforting Mr Borden's afflicted daughter: fanning her, bathing her brow with cologne, and otherwise offering such help as would naturally be suggested. It was not observed that she asked for any of these feminine consolations, nor that she shed any tears, showed hysteria, nor betrayed great agitation. Indeed, it would not be too much to say that she was, on the whole, as calm in her demeanor, perhaps calmer, than any of

Lizzie Borden.

the women who fluttered about, and made unsuccessful attempts to 'loosen her dress' and apply other forms of first aid. Grief shows itself in different ways in different temperaments; and it has often been noticed, even after natural deaths which have not come suddenly, that the person most bereaved does not, at once, exhibit the most sorrow.

Finally, Miss Borden said that she wished that somebody would try to find Mrs Borden, as she thought she had heard her come in. Dr Bowen had been sent for, and Miss Russell, and it now seemed appropriate to notify the person most concerned: the wife of the dead man. Bridget declined to go upstairs alone, but went with Mrs Churchill from the kitchen to the front of the house, and up the frontstairs. The neighbor said:

'As I went upstairs I turned my head to the left, and as I got up so that my eyes were on the level with the front hall, I could see across the front hall and across the floor of the spare room. At the far side on the north side of the room I saw something that looked like the form of a person.'

Bridget went into the room for an instant; Mrs Churchill did not. They went downstairs again, hastily. When they had joined the others in the kitchen, Mrs Churchill sank into a chair, with an exclamation or a groan. Miss Russell asked:

'Is there another?'

And Mrs Churchill said: 'Yes; she is up there.'

The situation was quite beyond the experience of any woman; it is not surprising that Mrs Churchill had no exclamation or remark in her vocabulary. Others went upstairs within a few minutes; Dr Bowen was soon back at the house; and if the scene in the lower room was shocking, that in the upper was both ghastly and pitiful. The furnishing of the 'spare room' would be homely and familiar to most of us. It had all the heaviness of the Victorian style of decoration: the carpet with gigantic clusters of impossible roses; the ponderous bed with carved head and frontboards in some dark wood; and beyond, against the north wall, another ornate piece of furniture, a dressing table, or 'bureau', with brass knobs and handles on the drawers, slabs of white marble on the top, ornaments and framed photographs, a lace-covered pin-cushion, and two white bottles or cruets, theoretically for scent or toilet water, precisely placed but purely ornamental, since nobody ever knew such receptacles to contain anything at all. The fringed bedcover was smooth and clean, and the two pillows were covered by the white cases with ruffled borders which had been the last care of the poor woman who had gone to make up the bed which her guest had occupied.

On the floor between the dressing table and the bed, face-downward in a pool of blood, was the body of Mrs Borden. Her head had been ferociously hacked and battered, like her husband's. But her wounds, unlike his, were not so fresh nor recent; the blood had ceased to flow from them, and that on the floor had coagulated; the temperature of her body was sensibly lower; she had been dead much longer than he. She wore a light dress of some cotton cloth. She was a short, heavy woman, weighing nearly two hundred pounds; how had she fallen at full length from an upright position without shaking the house, and alarming the others who were in it? Had she been caught by the assailant kneeling at the side of the bed to tuck in the bed clothes, and had there been, in consequence, no heavy fall? The position of the body, stretched out fully, with the arms under her; did not indicate this. If it were true, what evil fate was it that caused the two victims, the old man and his wife, she kneeling and he lying down, and both helpless, to be delivered thus into such savage and merciless hands?

The first policeman to arrive at the house was one named Allen. He was the committing officer at the police station, and happened to be there and available when the City Marshal (or chief of police) received the warning by telephone. He was dispatched to look into some 'row' on Second Street, and may have thought that it was merely another 'cutting affray' between some of 'those foreigners.' Certainly he did not know that he was to make the first report upon one of the most notorious and perplexing crimes which have ever engaged American police officers. It is one of the ironical circumstances of this case that upon the day when the Fall River police were for the first and only time to be brought into national celebrity, and to start an investigation which was to call down upon themselves unlimited criticism and abuse—quite undeserved, as best I can judge—that upon this day of days in their history, more than half of them were away on their annual picnic at Rocky Point! Their chief was at his post, however, while a few members of the day force were on double duty.

Officer Allen stayed but a few moments at the Borden house. He looked upon the body of Mr Borden, but at that time no discovery had been made of the other death, and he did not search the house. Instead of finding some fruit-vender, or vagrant, bleeding from one or two unimportant wounds acquired in a casual fight with a friend, he gazed upon the horrifying spectacle of a venerable and respected citizen barbarously murdered in his own home. A friendly writer says of Allen that he was, 'to put it mildly, taken considerably aback by the sight in the house, and, to put it not too strongly, was frightened out of his wits. He left no guard upon the house when he ran back to the station' to inform the Marshal. It is, however, said that he stationed a private citizen at the side door, with orders to admit nobody except the police and physicians. There have always been many to assert that a prompt and intelligent search of the house, with all that this implies, would have solved the mystery at once. This assertion seems to be based upon the knowledge gained after the fact and upon suppositions which may or may not be sound. It is not at all impossible that the police did, within twenty-four hours, discover nearly all the evidence which it was humanly possible to find. I think it can be put even more strongly: it is probable that they did so. This statement holds true, it seems to me, whatever view one takes of the commission of the crime. If one follows the opinion of those who hold that the murders were the work of a stranger, an outsider, then this assassin certainly carried with him, when he fled from the house, all the most important evidence. And while it is not possible to discuss other theories, except as one may speculate upon a mystery, it is not unreasonable to believe that the most telling clews as to guilt were suppressed, destroyed or removed before the alarm was given. Officer Allen did not act with composure nor acumen — but it may be that his omissions were less damaging than they have been considered.

What the police did not comprehend was that they were working in the dark against a person of considerable cunning and extraordinary audacity, who was, moreover, protected by an incredible series of lucky chances.

Before a great number of people had arrived in or near the house, Mr John Vinnicum Morse strolled down Second Street. He had been calling, at some distance, upon a nephew and niece, and now, as the dinner hour approached, returned to the Borden home, part of the way by street-car, but the rest of the way on foot. Although inside the house lay the murdered forms of his host and hostess, and although a small group of agitated persons had gathered in the kitchen, Mr Morse was not aware of anything unusual. He went through the side yard, to the rear of the house, picked up two or three pears, and began to eat them. Pears enter this case more than once, and to all who are familiar with the region and the time of year, they suggest the atmosphere of an old New England garden in August. Perhaps Mr Morse, as he thought of dinner, foresaw a recurrence of the mutton-soup and was fortifying himself against the blow, but in any event we should not begrudge him his pears, nor the two or three peaceful minutes he spent with them, before he went into the house. It was to be a long time before he was to know peace again, or to go mooning about Fall River and its vicinity upon his innocent errands. From a small expedition which he attempted, a day or two later, merely as far as the post-office, he returned with an escort of about one thousand people, and under police protection. Most unjustifiable suspicions were entertained against him for a number of days, but the police discovered promptly that his alibi was perfect, and that his account of his doings that morning was truthful and fully corroborated.

From shortly after midday it is impossible to think of Second Street as quiet, or of Number 92 as a house in which silence dwelt, as it had when Bridget heard the town clock strike the hour before noon. Crowds gathered in such numbers as to drive the newspaper reporters, in describing them, to the use of the phrase, 'a surging mass of humanity.' Friends, policemen, clergymen and doctors gathered in the yard, or swarmed through the house. The utmost pity was expressed for Miss Borden, since she had suffered a double sorrow through events far more distressing than natural deaths.

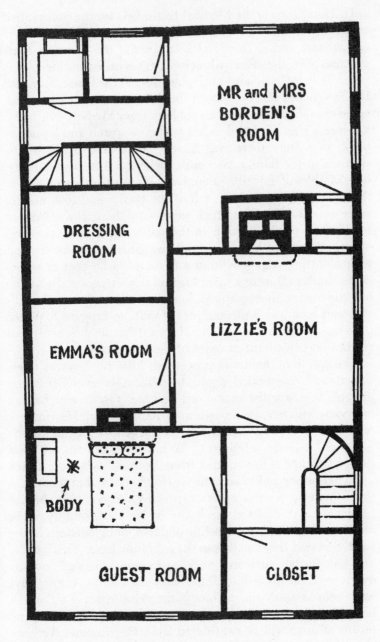

Upstairs at the Borden house.

Dr Dolan, one of the Medical Examiners for the county, had chanced to be passing the Borden house at 11:45, before the crowds had come. (Medical Examiner is the name in Massachusetts for the officer who elsewhere is called coroner. He is necessarily a physician.) Dr Dolan entered the house, and with Dr Bowen and others, viewed the dead persons. It was discovered that there had been no robbery from Mr Borden's body: he wore a ring, and had in his pockets a watch and a pocket-book; in money there was $81.65. Dr Dolan heard of the sickness in the family, two days earlier, and in consequence, took samples of the milk for analysis. He went with the police to the cellar, during their search of the house, and took note of some axes and hatchets which were found there. It was evident to all who saw the wounds in the skulls of the dead man and woman that these had been made by some heavy instrument, with a cutting edge—without any doubt, a hatchet or something similar. During a visit, later in the afternoon, Dr Dolan had the bodies photographed, and then removed the stomachs and sent them, with the samples of milk, to Edward S Wood, professor of chemistry in the Harvard Medical School, and celebrated consultant in cases of legal medicine.

The search of the house proceeded; Miss Borden was questioned and questioned again by almost every officer who arrived. It was a distressing ordeal. One of those who had an interview with her was a patrolman, named Philip Harrington, who was afterwards described by the Chief Justice of the Superior Court as 'intelligent.' To him Miss Borden said that during the time of her absence from the house, when the attack upon her father took place, she was in the barn, that she was in there for twenty minutes. He expressed surprise that she did not hear anything from the house or the yard, sounds of the attack, of the opening or closing of doors, or of footsteps in the yard. She said that she was in the *loft* of the barn. This caused him still further surprise, since, as he and others afterwards discovered, the dusty loft of that barn, on a sultry August day, was about as uninviting a place as the steam-room of a Turkish bath. He and others made investigations as to the barn and the results of them will be considered later. Harrington asked her about any men who might have borne malice against her father, and she narrated one or two semi-angry conversations between her father and some strange man, which she had overheard. The policeman warned her about talking to anybody else, and suggested that it would be well for her to make no further statements for that day. Owing to the atrocity of the crime, he suggested, she might well be confused. She answered, however, with what he called 'a stiff courtesy,' and said:

'No, I can tell you all I know now, just as well as at any other time.'

Mr Edwin H. Porter, historian of the Borden case, says that it was his conversation with Philip Harrington, as it was later reported to the City Marshal, which aroused suspicions 'in the minds of the police that the daughter knew more of the circumstances of the tragedy than she cared to tell.' The police were to pay dearly for such suspicions, but it seems hard to understand, in view of what has been related, to say nothing of what was yet to be discovered, how they could have avoided them. And yet it was a monstrous thing to suspect. As time went on, it took the form not of a mere accusation of complicity, or guilty knowledge of the crime, but of the part of principal and sole actor in it. And to suggest that a woman of good family, of blameless life and hitherto unimpeachable character, could possibly commit two such murders, is to suggest something so rare as to be almost unknown to criminology. It is beside the question to cite the many homicides of which women have been proven guilty. Nearly always, when the victim was an adult person, they have been murders by poison or by shooting. When, in modern times, the attack has taken a more brutal form, the murderess has usually been a woman of base antecedents, one from the criminal class, and acting in concert with a man. There is that about the act of battering in the skulls of an elderly man and woman which suggests the male butcher, not the more subtle though equally malicious methods of the murderess. The police of Fall River and the law officers of the county were not so inexperienced as to ignore this, and they could not have taken the step they did under the pressure of strong evidence. There was no lack of other and powerful influences working against it.

Mr Edwin Porter's book, 'The Fall River Tragedy' is a

comprehensive history of the case based upon intimate personal knowledge. It has the advantages and disadvantages of having been compiled, apparently, from current newspaper accounts, the result of the author's work as police reporter of the *Fall River Globe*. In the opening chapter, he sums up the perplexity which beset all early investigators. They were absolutely at a loss to explain how, in broad daylight, it had been possible for anybody to commit two murders and escape unseen, both by those in and outside the house. This difficulty was increased as the medical testimony made it apparent that from one to two hours had elapsed between the death of Mrs Borden and that of her husband. Mr Porter refers to the escape of the murderer in one apt sentence:

'The author of that hideous slaughter had come and gone as gently as the south wind, but had fulfilled his mission as terrifically as a cyclone.'

In the same chapter he describes the extraordinary series of chances that favored the murderer. I quote the passage:

'To those who stop to contemplate the circumstances surrounding the double murder, it was marvelous to reflect how fortune had favored the assassin. Not once in a million times would fate have paved such a way for him. He had to deal with a family of six persons in an unpretentious two-and-a-half story house, the rooms of which were all connected and in which it would have been a difficult matter to stifle sound. He must catch Mr Borden alone and either asleep, or off his guard, and kill him with one fell blow. The faintest outcry would have sounded an alarm. He must also encounter Mrs Borden alone and fell her, a heavy woman, noiselessly. To do this he must either make his way from the sitting room on the ground floor to the spare bed room above the parlor and avoid five persons in the passage, or he must conceal himself in one of the rooms upstairs and make the descent under the same conditions. The murdered woman must not lisp a syllable at the first attack, and her fall must not attract attention. He must then conceal the dripping implement of death and depart in broad daylight by a much frequented street. In order to accomplish this he must take a time, when Miss Emma L. Borden, the older daughter of the murdered man, was on a visit to relatives out of the city; Miss Lizzie A. Borden, the other daughter, must be in the barn and remain there twenty minutes. A less time than that would not suffice. Bridget Sullivan, the servant, must be in the attic asleep on her own bed. Her presence in the pantry or kitchen or any room on the first or second floors would have frustrated the fiend's designs, unless he also killed her so that she would die without a murmur. In making his escape there must be no blood stains upon his clothing; for such tell-tale marks might have betrayed him. And so, if the assailant of the aged couple was not familiar with the premises, his luck favored him exactly as described. He made no false move. He could not have proceeded more swiftly nor surely had he lived in the modest edifice for years. At the most he had just twenty minutes in which to complete his work. He must go into the house after Miss Lizzie entered the barn and he must disappear before she returned. More than that, the sixth member of the family, John V. Morse, must vanish from the house while the work was being done. He could not have been counted on by any criminal, however shrewd, who had planned the tragedy ahead. Mr Morse came and went at the Borden homestead. He was not engaged in business in Fall River and there were no stated times when the wretch who did the slaughtering could depend upon his absence. Mr Morse must not loiter about the house or yard after breakfast as was his custom; he must take a car to some other part of the city and he must not return until his host and hostess have been stretched lifeless. The slightest hitch in these conditions and the murderer would have been balked or detected red handed upon the spot. Had Miss Emma remained at home she would have been a stumbling block; had Miss Lizzie left the stable [barn] a few moments earlier she would have seen the murderer as he ran out the side door; had Bridget Sullivan shortened her nap and descended the stairs she would have heard her mistress drop, as the axe fell on her head; had Mr Morse cut short his visit to friends by as much as ten minutes the butcher would have dashed into his arms as he ran out at the front gate; had Mr Borden returned earlier from his morning visit to the post office he would have caught the assassin murdering his aged wife, or had he uttered a scream at the time he himself was cut down, at least two persons would have rushed to his assistance.

It was a wonderful chain of circumstances which conspired to clear the way for the murderer; so wonderful that its links baffled men's understanding.'

There was still another and greater difficulty for this singularly astute and favored murderer to overcome. It is not clearly mentioned by Mr Porter, for the reason, it may be, that his first chapter was written early in the history of the case and never revised in the light of subsequent knowledge. It was established that Mrs Borden had been killed not less than an hour and possibly two hours before her husband. The autopsies proved this. Therefore it was necessary, assuming the murderer to have come from outside the house, for him to have killed Mrs Borden at about half-past nine, without attracting the attention of Miss Lizzie Borden or of Bridget Sullivan; to have remained concealed in the house until eleven, still eluding them, and then to have accompliuhed his purpose with Mr Borden, and to have left the house unseen. Even for those who advanced a different theory as to the identity of the murderer, that is, for persons who agreed with the contention of the Commonwealth, there were still unexplained difficulties—especially as to the time of Mr Morse's return and of Bridget's retirement upstairs. Who could have predicted when these would take place?

For those who like to exhaust every possibility, there is, of course, the wild hypothesis of a first and second murderer: one who killed Mrs Borden and then fled, and one who tracked down and slew Mr Borden in the same fashion, and with the same or similar weapon. Difficult, even absurd, as this theory is, it is no more impossible of belief than some of the notions which were entertained. Folk were almost ready to suggest a visitation of Providence, or other supernatural act of vengeance, although why the Heavenly powers should set upon this harmless pair was unexplained. Nor was the method exactly celestial.

The investigation went on during that hot afternoon, and before midnight the police had some astounding information. Dr Bowen had related the story of the illness, and the suspected poisoning — as Miss Borden had also done to Miss Russell and to Mrs Churchill. Two officers went to various pharmacies to learn if anybody had been purchasing poison, and at D.R. Smith's on South Main Street, the clerk, Eli Bence, said that an attempt had been made to buy prussic acid. This had happened on Wednesday, the day before the murders. A lady had come in the morning and asked for this deadly drug for the purpose of killing moths in a seal-skin coat. Mr Bence had refused to sell it, except on a doctor's prescription, and she went away disappointed. He identified this lady as Miss Lizzie Borden, and, being taken to her house to see her (although it is said that he knew her perfectly well by sight), persisted in the identification. In this he was supported by another clerk in the pharmacy, Frederick E. Hart, and by a third man who was also present, one Frank H. Kilroy. On the next day, August 5, the *Fall River Globe* printed a full account of it, under the headings: 'What did Lizzie Want of Poison? She is Identified by a Drug Clerk as Having Visited his Store Recently.' Newspapers elsewhere failed to accept the information, or else gave it slight attention. I have been told by one who knew him that Bence was a careful man, who was quite aware of the serious import of his state-

ment. The final disposition of the matter, as legal evidence, will
appear in an account of the trial.

The note, which, according to Miss Borden, had been received by her stepmother, remained elusive. Who had sent it?
Who brought it? Under what circumstances was it received,
and what action was taken? Did she really go out? If she did go
out, it is inconceivable that she went in the cotton dress in
which was doing housework, and so it must have required
agility to get back into that dress, for she wore it when death
overtook her. A New York paper, *Once a Week*, offered $500 for
the discovery of the writer of the note, and the *Fall River News*
begged its readers in the name of justice, to find this writer. But
the reward was unclaimed, and the appeal unanswered. Finally, Miss Borden told Dr Dolan that she believed the note must
have been burned up in the kitchen stove. Nobody suggested
that the person who sent it and the messenger who brought it
had been carried away by giant eagles. But the land knew them
no more.

Within a single day the attention of the newspaper readers of
the country was directed toward the Misses Borden. Miss
Emma, the elder, had returned from Fairhaven in the evening
of the day of the murder. Information about her was of a rather
negative quality; she was reputed to be less active in church
work than her sister, and to have traveled less. As to the
younger, it never appeared that her parents had called her by
the glorious name of Elizabeth; her legal style was that less
pleasing diminutive, for which the best that can be said is that it
did not offend the delicate ear of Miss Jane Austen, since she
allowed the heroine of '*Pride and Prejudice*' so to be addressed by
her family. In our time, the Ford automobile has been called, in
derision, a Lizzie, and it is said that Miss Mary Pickford uses
this name as a sort of generic term to describe her spectators. It
can hardly be given in compliment. But in the years '92 and '93
there was only one 'Lizzie' for the people of the United States,
and it was that Fall River lady who was presently to be
confronted with the gravest of accusations. It is almost invariably noticed that a charge of murder, or of any serious crime,
acts automatically to rob a person of all right to polite address;
the public promptly makes free with the first name, especially if

it is a woman. There is some strange rule about this, exactly as with the custom by which a sedate middle-aged man, when he puts on military uniform, in time of war, instantly becomes a 'boy'.

Miss Lizzie Borden was a native of Fall River, and had been graduated from the high school. Some of her classmates described her as 'rather eccentric,' which, of itself, means exactly nothing. There is no human being who would not be described as 'eccentric,' by one or another of his or her acquaintances. She had traveled in Europe, with other ladies, in 1890. Perhaps the outstanding fact about her was her membership in the Central Congregational Church, in various charitable societies such as the Fruit and Flower Mission, and in the Woman's Christian Temperance Union. At her Church Mission she taught a class of young people. Her association with these religious bodies was no meaningless fact when clouds began to gather over her life, for her cause was warmly supported by them. The Rev. Mr Buck and the Rev. Mr Jubb, her pastors, became her pillars of support, and although after a time, through constant repetition of their names, some of the less devout were tempted to look upon them as the Box and Cox of the Borden cause, it could have been no small consolation and of no little value to her, when she appeared at public hearings, to enter the room on some occasions 'leaning on the arm' of the Rev. Mr Buck, and at other times escorted in similar fashion by the Rev. Mr Jubb.

The frank comments upon the case which appeared within the first few days may be typified by an interview given out on August 5th by Mr Hiram Harrington. He was the husband of Mr Borden's only sister, and is not to be confused with the officer, Philip Harrington. A few passages may be quoted:

> 'Mr Borden was an exceedingly hard man concerning money matters, determined and stubborn. . . . As the motive for the crime it was money, unquestionably money. If Mr Borden died he would have left something over $500,000, and in my opinion that estate furnishes the only motive, and a sufficient one for the double murder. Last evening I had a long interview with Miss Lizzie, who has refused to see anyone else. . . . She was very composed, showed no signs of any emotion, nor were there any traces of grief upon her countenance. That did not surprise me, as she is not naturally emotional.'

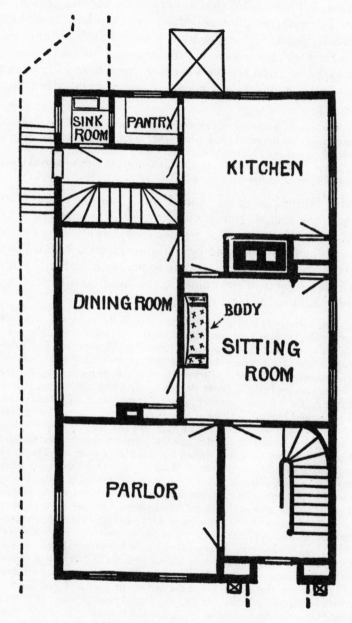

Downstairs at the Borden house.

Then followed a description, quoted by Mr Harrington, of Miss Borden's reception of her father when he returned on Thursday morning, her solicitous inquiries for his health, the assistance which she gave him in removing his coat, helping him to the sofa, and her offers to cover him with an afghan, and to lower the shades at the windows, so that he could have a 'nice nap.'

'On leaving the house, she says she went directly to the barn to obtain some lead. She informed me that it was her intention to go to Marion on a vacation, and she wanted the lead in the barn loft to make some sinkers. She was a very enthusiastic angler. I went over the ground several times and she repeated the same story.'

Miss Borden, when questioned as to a possible explanation of the crime, told Mr Harrington the story of the burglary in the house a year earlier, and of 'strange men' recently seen by her around the house. She had been frightened enough to tell her parents about them, and to write to her sister at Fairhaven.

On the subject of the domestic and business affairs of the Borden family, Mr Harrington said:

'Yes, there were family dissensions although it has been always kept very quiet. For nearly ten years there have been constant disputes between the daughters and their father and stepmother. It arose, of course, with regard to the stepmother. Mr Borden gave her some bank stock, and the girls thought they ought to be treated as evenly as the mother. I guess Mr Borden did try to do it, for he deeded to the daughters, Emma L. and Lizzie A., the homestead on Ferry Street, an estate of 120 rods of land, with a house and barn, all valued at $3,000. This was in 1887. The trouble about money matters did not diminish, nor the acerbity of the family ruptures lessen, and Mr Borden gave each girl ten shares in the Crystal Spring Bleachery Company, which he paid $100 a share for. They sold them soon after for less than $40 a share. He also gave them some bank stock at various times, allowing them of course, the entire income from them. In addition to this he gave them a weekly stipend, amounting to $200 a year. In spite of all this the dispute about their not being allowed enough went on with equal bitterness. Lizzie did most of the demonstrative contention, as Emma is very quiet and unassuming, and would feel deeply any disparaging or angry word from her father. Lizzie on the contrary, was haughty and domineering with the stubborn will of her father and bound to contest for her rights. There were many animated interviews between father and daughter on this point. Lizzie is of a repellent disposition, and after an unsuccessful passage with her father, would become sulky and refuse to speak to him for days at a time. . . . She thought she ought to entertain as others did, and felt that with her father's wealth she was expected to hold her end up with others of her set. Her father's constant refusal to allow her to entertain lavishly angered her. I have heard many bitter things she has said of her father, and know that she was deeply resentful of her father's maintained stand in this matter. This house on Ferry Street was an old one, and was in constant need of repairs. There were two tenants paying $16.50 and $14 a month, but with taxes and repairs there was very little income from the property. It was a great deal of trouble for the girls to keep the house in repair, and a month or two ago they got disgusted and deeded the house back to their father. I am positive that Emma knows nothing of the murder.'

The faction which held strong views about the stupidity of the Fall River police, and their brutal persecution of an innocent and bereaved woman, often said that the officers neglected all opportunities to catch the real murderer. The police formed a 'theory,' said their critics, and having done so, tried by all means—some of them unusually foul—to entangle their victim in it. In the opinion of the man in the street, who is supposed to be a devotee of 'good, plain common-sense,' it is, of course, a destructive thing to say of another man that he has a 'theory.' Nobody should ever have any theories at all: but just plunge ahead. As a matter of truth, the police of Fall River spent weary hours and days in running down every report, rumor, and suspicion.

The usual crop of 'strange,' 'wild' and 'crazy' men, of tramps and vagrants, of 'foreigners,' and other guilty-looking persons was more prolific than ever. There was a suspected Portuguese, who was called a Portuguese because he was a Swede; and there were miscreants who turned up in lonely places, days and weeks after the murders, still brandishing axes or hatchets dripping with gore,—just as the Russian soldiers in England in August, 1914, still had—on their boots—the snow of their native land. Pale young men had been seen on Second Street. There was a camp of wandering horse-traders in Westport, and with them, it was alleged, Mr John Vinnicum Morse had been darkly dealing. There was a disgruntled owner of property, across the river, whose business relations with Mr Borden might have roused him to dreadful vengeance against all who bore the hated name. One Dr Handy, who was on Second Street about an hour before the murders, had seen a very peculiar looking man, who attracted the doctor's most particular attention. This man was discussed, in column after column of newspaper space, as 'Dr Handy's Wild Eyed Man.' Some participants in the discussion held that the Wild Eyed Man was better, but still cryptically, known as 'Mike the Soldier.' Mike was run down and found free from all criminous taint, excepting that he was near Second Street ten o'clock that mcrning, that he was pale, as a result of a spree, and that he wore an odd and noticeable pair of trousers. It appeared that he followed the weaver's trade, when he was not going from one bar-room to the next, and by talking with his fellow-weavers, and various saloon-keepers, it was easy to learn all that he had been doing, and to find that it was unimportant. But the Wild Eyed Man lingered, off-stage.

A boy thought he had seen a man jump over the back fence of the Borden house. A Frenchman had helped the same man escape toward New Bedford, but how he knew it was the same man, in what way he helped him, and what he was escaping from, do not appear. Two officers found somebody like him in the person of the chief of the gypsy horse-dealers' camp. He had the satisfactory name of Bearsley S. Cooper, but he also had an alibi, which prevented anybody from visiting upon him the punishment which mankind always longs to inflict upon a horsedealer. The terror of the murders had spread throughout New England, and men seen getting on railroad trains, or getting off them, with dust on their shoes, or spots on their clothes, were asked who they were, and what they had been doing. A Bostonian was frightened half to death by detention and questioning. On Monday another bloody hatchet was discovered on a farm in South Somerset; it was the property of somebody called Sylvia, and the police rushed out there, with the first words of the famous song trembling upon their lips. But the blood was the blood of a chicken, and old Mr Sylvia was left undisturbed.

Petty offences hover close to great crimes, as the sucker follows the shark. When at some fête, during the French Revolution, two men were discovered lurking under a platform built for the spectators, they were charged with designs against the Republic, and promptly lynched by the mob. They went to their deaths, however, with the somewhat humiliating but probably truthful confession that gunpowder plots were far from their minds; they had gone there merely to gaze upwards at the sturdy legs of citizennesses. One man seen by a neighbor on the back fence of the Borden yard, was caught, and forced blushingly to admit that he had been attracted, as Mr Morse had been, by the pears. But his interest was, of course, illicit, and hence his confusion. The police investigated every plausible rumor, and in order to deal according to precept with unturned stones, spent much good effort in many searches which were hopeless from the start. Their work at first was undoubtedly open to criticism, although metropolitan police often do no better with perplexing crimes. They finally arrived at a conclusion, and its results will appear in the account of the four legal investigations which followed.

Something should be said now about Bridget Sullivan, since she was in the house, or within a few feet of it, when each murder was committed. It has often been asked why she was not suspected. The answer is simple: she bore a good character, she had no motive to such crimes, and she was exonerated by the person who was still nearer to the scenes of the murders, Miss Lizzie Borden herself. Vague suggestions of complicity, or guilty knowledge, arose against her, but evidently were not shared by the officers of the law. Bridget was an agitated and badly scared woman for a few days, and at last had to undergo a long cross-examination by one of the most skilful advocates in the State. It is said that she returned to her native land some years—not very long—after the trial, and there, an elderly woman, she may still abide, in the intermittent calm of the Irish Free State.

Of all the rumors as to murderers from the outside, only one had the charm of romance. Somebody attempted to inject a maritime flavor into the mystery, by recalling the trial, in 1876, of the mutineers of the schooner *Jefferson Borden*. This was not Mr Borden's name, but it was suggested that he had an interest in this vessel, and that the guilty mutineers, imbued with the combined spirits of Clark Russell and Conan Doyle, had nursed their vengeful feelings for sixteen years, only to strike at last in this telling fashion. Unluckily for the story, it was discovered that two of the accused had been acquitted on their trial, one had served his term and now lived, crippled, in St

Paul; while the two ring-leaders were safe in the State Prison at Thomaston, Maine. Mr Borden, moreover, had no connection with the schooner.

On the day after the murders, this notice was sent to and duly appeared in the newspapers:

'Five thousand dollars reward. The above reward will be paid to anyone who may secure the arrest and conviction of the person or persons, who occasioned the death of Andrew J. Borden and his wife. Signed,

Emma L. Borden and Lizzie A. Borden.'

The funeral services were held on Saturday, August 6. From three to four thousand people surrounded the house, and a passage was kept clear by twenty police officers. Other crowds of people lined the street as the hearses and the carriages with mourners proceeded to the cemetery. The coffins were not buried, but placed in a receiving tomb.

In the evening of that day, the Mayor of Fall River, Dr John W. Coughlin, with City Marshal Hilliard, went to the Borden house. The number of people standing on the sidewalks or in the street itself was still so great that the Mayor's carriage was driven with difficulty. Policemen were called and ordered to send the people away. The Mayor and the Marshal then went into the house to confer with the Misses Borden and Mr Morse. Dr Coughlin said:

'I have a request to make of the family, and that is that you remain in the house for a few days. I believe it would be better if you do so.'

Miss Lizzie raised the question:

'Why, is there anybody in this house suspected?'

The Mayor answered: 'Well, perhaps Mr Morse can answer that question better than I, as his experience last night, perhaps, would justify him in the inference that somebody in the house is suspected.'

Miss Lizzie persisted: 'I want to know the truth.'

And she repeated this remark. Then the Mayor said:

'Well, Miss Borden, I regret to answer, but I must answer yes; you are suspected.'

She replied: 'I am ready to go now.'

Her sister said: 'We have tried to keep it from her as long as we could.'

Dr Coughlin told the family that if they were disturbed in any way, or annoyed by the crowds in the street, they should either notify the officer in the yard, or sent word to him—the Mayor— who would see that the police department gave them protection. Miss Emma Borden then remarked: 'We want to do everything we can in this matter.' And the two officials departed.

On the following Tuesday an investigation began, when Bridget Sullivan was examined by the District Attorney, Mr Hosea M. Knowlton, assisted by the City Marshal, the Mayor, and the Medical Examiner. This investigation, on the same day, took the form of an inquest, before Judge Josiah C. Blaisdell of the Second District Court. A summons to attend was served upon Miss Lizzie Borden. Her family attorney, Mr Andrew J. Jennings, appeared and made an appeal to the Court for permission to be present, 'in the interest of the witnesses.' The Justice heard his argument, but denied admission. The inquest continued its sessions in secret, until Thursday, while Fall River waited in suppressed excitement and impatience, reading newspaper bulletins, and learning nothing. The case was of such importance as to attract to the city the Attorney General of Massachusetts, Mr Albert E. Pillsbury, who was in consultation with Mr Knowlton and other officers. In addition to Miss Lizzie Borden, Dr Bowen, Mrs Churchill, Mr Hiram Harrington, Mr John Vinnicum Morse, and Miss Emma Borden were examined. Another witness, who was followed about in Fall River, and unsuccessfully questioned by the newspaper reporters, was Professor Wood of the Harvard Medical School. On the third and last day of the inquest there appeared Eli Bence and the two other witnesses who were supposed to offer testimony as to the attempt to buy poison. On that same day autopsies were held, at the cemetery, upon the two bodies. Chiefly, they disclosed ten incised wounds on the head and face of Mr Borden; and on the body of his wife, one wound in the back, just below the neck, and no less than eighteen incised and crushing wounds on the head.

The inquest ended late Thursday afternoon, one week after

the murders. A short consultation was held and at the end of it, Mr Jennings was called, and Miss Lizzie Borden arrested for the murder of her father. No mention of Mrs Borden was made in the warrant. The prisoner was detained at the police station under charge of the matron, but she was not confined in the cell-room. Mr Porter writes:

'No other prisoner arrested in Bristol County had been accorded the delicate and patient consideration which Marshal Hilliard bestowed upon Miss Lizzie Borden.'

She was arraigned in the District Court, before Judge Blaisdell next morning. She entered the room 'on the arm of the Rev Mr Buck,' and is described as wearing a dark blue suit, and a black hat with red flowers. She was 'not crying, but her features were far from firm. She has a face and chin betokening strength of character, and on this occasion the sensitiveness of the lips especially betrayed itself. She was constantly moving her lips as she sat in the court-room in a way to show that she was not altogether unemotional.'

To the warrant, she pleaded not guilty. Mr Jennings protested against the proceedings as 'extraordinary,' in that the Judge had presided at the inquest and was now sitting to hear the case against her. This he called sitting in a double capacity and not ensuring his client an unprejudiced hearing. The District Attorney replied that the statutes required Judge Blaisdell to hold the inquest, which was in itself an action against no one, but an attempt to ascertain facts. The same procedure had been followed more than twenty times to his knowledge in cases which had not excited so much attention. The inquest was still proceeding, and the evidence before it had no bearing upon this hearing. The Judge was equally required by statute to hear this case. The Court overruled Mr Jennings's motion, and the point does not seem to have been raised again. The lawyers agreed upon August 22 for the preliminary hearing, and Miss Borden was taken by train to the jail at Taunton. At railway stations, and other places, crowds gathered to look at her.

On the date appointed Miss Borden was brought back to Fall River, but a postponement was made, until August 25. She remained in charge of the police matron, and was not taken back to Taunton. Finally, the hearings began. Crowds were present, inside and out of the court-room, and it is said that forty newspapers were represented by reporters. The prisoner entered the Court, leaning upon the practised arm of the Rev Mr Buck. There began a preliminary trial which lasted for six days. Few such extensive investigations, prior to the presentation of a criminal case to the Grand Jury, could ever have been held in the State. Mr Melvin O. Adams of Boston was now associated with Mr Jennings in the defence. The witnesses included the Medical Examiner, Dr Dolan; Thomas Kieran, an engineer, who gave technical details about measurements of the Borden house; officers of the banks which Mr Borden had visited the day he was killed; John Vinnicum Morse; Bridget Sullivan; Mrs Churchill; Miss Alice Russell, who testified only as to events on the day of the murder; Eli Bence and the other men from the pharmacy—whose appearance, says Mr Porter, 'in the judgment of many of the spectators . . . produced evidence of uneasiness on the part of Lizzie Borden,' and some officers of the police.

On the fifth day of the hearing, Professor Wood's evidence was given. It was to the effect that his tests and analyses of the two stomachs showed that digestion was much further advanced with Mr Borden than with his wife. No trace of prussic acid was found in either stomach; tests were not made for any other poison, but there was no evidence of irritation. He had made examinations for blood stains on a hatchet and two axes, found in the Borden house, and on a dress waist, two skirts, and shoes and stockings belonging to the prisoner. Except for a minute spot on one of the skirts, he found no blood upon any of these. This testimony was received with great relief and joy by the friends of Miss Borden; quite naturally and correctly they looked upon it as a strong point in her favor.

After some more police evidence, the District Attorney read the short-hand report of the testimony of Miss Lizzie Borden given at the inquest. This is an exceedingly interesting and important series of questions and answers. Miss Borden, as we have seen, talked to friends and neighbors and to the police, on the day of the murders. Afterwards, except for the inquest statement, she never opened her mouth. She acted upon what proved to be the best of legal advice, and at her final trial, availed herself of her right not to go upon the witness stand. Miss Borden's testimony at the inquest introduced at the preliminary trial, as part of the case of the Commonwealth, is significant not only for itself but for the point raised when it was offered as evidence at the trial before the Superior Court. It is to be found today in the press reports of that date, and in Mr Porter's book—to which I am so much indebted for information about this period in the history of the case. I quote his version of it.

My father and stepmother were married twenty-seven years ago. I have no idea how much my father was worth and have never heard him form an opinion. I know something about what real estate my father owned . . . 'two farms in Swansea, the homestead, some property on North Main street, Borden Block, some land further south and some he had recently purchased.' 'Did you ever deed him any property?' 'He gave us some land, but my father bought it back. Had no other transaction with him. He paid in five thousand dollars cash for this property. Never knew my father made a will, but heard so from Uncle Morse.' 'Did you know of anybody that your father had trouble with?' 'There was a man who came there some weeks before, but I do not know who he was. He came to the house one day, and I heard them talk about a store. My father told him he could not have a store. The man said: "I thought with your liking for money you would let anybody in." I heard my father order him out of the house. Think he lived out of town, because he said he could go back and talk with father.' 'Did you father and anybody else have bad feelings between them?' 'Yes, Hiram C. Harrington. He married my father's only sister.' 'Nobody else?' 'I have no reason to suppose that that man had seen my father before that day.' 'Did you ever have any trouble with your stepmother?' 'No.' 'Within a year?' 'No.' 'Within three years?' 'No. About five years ago.' 'What was it about?' 'About my stepmother's stepsister, Mrs George Whitehead.' 'Was it a violent expression of feeling?' 'It was simply a difference of opinion.' 'Were you always cordial with your stepmother?' 'That depends upon one's idea of cordiality. 'Was it cordial according to your ideas of cordiality?' 'Yes.' Continuing: 'I did not regard her as my mother, though she came there when I was young. I decline to say whether my relations between her and myself were those of mother and daughter or not. I called her Mrs Borden and sometimes mother. I stopped calling her mother after the affair regarding her sister-in-law.' 'Why did you leave off calling her mother?' 'Because I wanted to.' 'Have you any other answer to give me?' 'No, sir. I always went to my sister. She was older than I was. I don't know but that my father and stepmother were happily united. I never knew of any difficulty between them, and they seemed to be affectionate. The day they were killed I had on a blue dress. I changed it in the afternoon and put on a print dress. Mr Morse came into our house whenever he wanted to. He has been here once since the river was frozen over. I don't know how often he came to spend the nights, because I had been away so much. I have not been away much during the year. He has been there very little during the past year. I have been away a great deal in the daytime during the last year. I don't think I have been away much at night, except once when I was in New Bedford. I was abroad in 1890. I first saw Mr Morse Thursday noon. Wednesday evening I was with Miss Russell at 9 o'clock, and I don't know whether the family were in or not. I went direct to my room. I locked the front door when I came in. Was in my room Wednesday, not feeling well all day. Did not go down to supper. Went out that evening and came in and locked the front door. Came down about 9 next morning. Did not inquire about Mr Morse that morning. Did not go to Marion at that time, because they could go sooner than I. I had taken the Secretaryship of the Christian Endeavor Society and had to remain over till the 10th. There had been nobody else around there that week but the man I have spoken of. I did not say that he came a week before, but that week. Mr Morse slept in the spare room Wednesday night. It was my habit to close my room door when I was in it. That Wednesday afternoon they made such a noise that I closed the door. First saw my father Thursday morning down stairs reading the *Providence Journal*. Saw my mother with a dust cloth in her hand. Maggie was putting a cloth into a mop. Don't know whether I ate cookies and tea that morning. Know the coffee pot was on the stove. My father went down town after 9 o'clock. I did not finish the handkerchiefs because the irons were not right. I was in the kitchen reading when he returned. I am not sure that I was in the kitchen when my father returned. I stayed in my room long enough to sew a piece of lace on a garment. That was before he came back. I don't know where Maggie was. I think she let my father in, and that he rang the bell. I understood Maggie to say he said he had forgotten his key. I think I was up stairs when my father came in, and I think I was on the stairs when he entered. I don't know whether Maggie was washing windows or not when my father came in.' At this point the District Attorney had called Miss Borden's attention to her conflicting statements regarding her position when her father came in, and her answer was: 'You have asked me so many questions, I don't know what I have said.' Later, she said she was reading in the kitchen and had gone into the other room for a copy of the *Providence Journal*. 'I last saw my mother when I was downstairs. She was dusting the dining room. She said she had been upstairs and made the bed and was going up stairs to put on the pillow slips. She had some cotton cloth pillows up there, and she said she was going to work on them. If she had remained down stairs I should have seen her. She would have gone up the back way to go to her room. If she had gone to the kitchen I would have seen her. There is no reason to suppose I would not have seen her when she was down stairs or in her room, except when I went down stairs once for two or three minutes.' 'I ask you again what you suppose she was doing from the time you saw her till 11 o'clock?' 'I don't know, unless she she was making her bed.' 'She would have had to pass your room, and you would have seen her wouldn't you?' 'Yes, unless I was in my room or down cellar, I supposed she had gone away, because she told me she was going, and we talked about the dinner. Didn't hear her go out or come back. When I first came down stairs saw Maggie coming in, and my mother asked me how I was feeling. My father was still there, still reading. My mother used to go and do the marketing.' 'Now I call your attention to the fact you said twice yesterday that you first saw your father after he came in when you were standing on the stairs.' 'I did not. I was in the kitchen when he came in, or in one of the three rooms, the dining room, kitchen and sitting room. It would have been difficult for anybody to pass through these rooms unless they passed through while I was in the dining room.' 'A portion of the time the girl was out of doors, wasn't she?' 'Yes.' 'So far as I know, I was alone in the house the larger part of the time while my father was away. I was eating a pear when my father came in. I had put a stick of wood into the fire to see if I could start it. I did no more ironing after my father came in. I then went in to tell him. I did not put away the ironing board. I don't know what time my father came in. When I went out to the barn I left him on the sofa. The last thing I said was to ask him if he wanted the window left that way. Then I went to the barn to get some lead for a sinker. I went up stairs in the barn. There was a bench there which contained some lead. I unhooked the screen door when I went out. I don't know when Bridget got through washing the windows inside. I knew she washed the windows outside. I knew she didn't wash the kitchen windows, but I don't know whether she washed the sitting room windows or not. I thought the flats would be hot by the time I got back. I had not fishing apparatus, but there was some at the farm. It is five years since I used the fish line. I don't think there was any sinker on my line. I don't think there were any fish lines suitable for use at the farm.' 'What! did you think you would find sinkers in the barn?' 'My father once told me that there was some lead and nails in the barn.' 'How long do you think you occupied in looking for the sinkers?' 'About fifteen or twenty minutes.' 'Did you do nothing besides look for sinkers in the twenty minutes?' 'Yes, sir. I ate some pears.' 'Would it take you all that time to eat a few pears?' 'I do not do things in a hurry.' 'Was Bridget not washing the dining room windows and the sitting room windows?' 'I do not know. I did not see her.' 'Did you tell Bridget to wash the windows?' 'No, sir.' 'Who did?' 'My mother.' 'Did you see Bridget after your mother told her to wash the windows?' 'Yes, sir.' 'What was she doing?' 'She had got a long pole and was sticking it in a brush, and she had a pail of water.' 'About what time did you go out into the barn?' 'About as near as I can recollect, 10 o'clock.' 'What did you go into the barn for?' 'To find some sinkers.' 'How many pears did you eat in that twenty minutes?' 'Three.' 'Is that all you did?' 'No. I went over to the window and opened it.' 'Why did you do that?' 'Because it was too hot.' 'I suppose that it is the hottest place on the premises?' 'Yes, sir.' 'Could you, while standing looking out of that window, see anybody enter the kitchen?' 'No, sir.' 'I thought you said you could see people from the barn?' 'Not after you pass a jog in the barn. It obstructs the view of the back door.' 'What kind of lead were you looking for, for sinkers? Hard lead?' 'No, sir; soft lead.' 'Did you expect to find the sinkers already made?' 'Well, no. I thought I might find one with a hole through it.' 'Was the lead referred to tea lead or lead that comes in tea chests?' 'I don't know.' 'When were you going fishing?' 'Monday.' 'The next Monday after the fatal day?' 'Yes, sir.' 'Had you lines all ready?' 'No, sir.' 'Did you have a line?' 'Yes, sir.' 'Where was your line?' 'Down to the farm.' 'Do you know whether there were any sinkers on the line you left at the farm?' 'I think there was none on the line.' 'Did you have any hooks?' 'No, sir.' 'Then you were making all this preparation without either hook or line. Why did you go into the barn after sinkers?' 'Because I was going down town to buy some hooks and line, and thought it would save me from buying them.' 'Now, to the barn again. Do you not think I could go into the barn and do the same as you in a few minutes?' 'I do not do things in a hurry.' 'Did you then think there were no sinkers at the barn?' 'I thought there were no sinkers anywhere there. I had no idea of using my lines. I thought you understood that I wasn't going to use these lines at the farm, because they hadn't sinkers. I went up stairs to the kind of bench there. I had heard my father say there was lead there. Looked for lead in a box up there. There were nails and perhaps an old door knob. Did not find any lead as thin as tea lead in the box. Did not look anywhere except on the bench. I ate some pears up there. I have now told you everything that took place up in the barn. It was the hottest place in the premises. I suppose I ate my pears when I first went up there. I stood looking out of the window. I was feeling well enough to eat pears, but don't know how to answer the question if I was feeling better than I was in the morning, because I was feeling better that morning. I picked the pears up from the ground. I was not in the rear of the barn. I was in the front of it. Don't see how anybody could leave the house then without my seeing them. I pulled over boards to look for the lead. That took me some time. I returned from the barn and put my hat in the dining room. I found my father and called to Maggie. I found the fire gone out. I went to the barn because the irons were not hot enough and the fire had gone out. I made no efforts to find my mother at all. Sent Maggie for Dr Bowen. Didn't see or find anything after the murders to tell me my mother had been sewing in the spare room that morning.' 'What did your mother say when you saw her?' 'She told me she had had a note and was going out. She said she would get the dinner.' The District Attorney continued to read: 'My mother did not tell when she was coming back. I did not know Mr Morse was coming to dinner. I don't know whether I was at tea Wednesday night or not. I had no apron on Thursday; that is, I don't think I had. I don't remember surely. I had no occasion to use the axe or hatchet. I knew there was an old axe down stairs and last time I saw it it was on the old chopping block. I don't know whether my father owned a hatchet or not. Assuming a hatchet was found in the cellar I don't know how it got there, and if there was blood on it I have no idea as to how it got there. My father killed some pigeons last May. When I found my father I did not think of Mrs Borden, for I believed she was out. I remember asking Mrs Churchill to look for my mother. I left the screen door closed when I left, and it was open when I came from the barn. I can give no idea of the time my father came home. I went right to the barn. I don't know whether he came to the sitting room at once or not. I don't remember his being in the sitting room or sitting down. I think I was in there when I asked him if there was any mail. I do not think he went upstairs. He had a letter in his hand. I did not help him to lie down

and did not touch the sofa. He was taking medicine for some time. Mrs
Borden's father's house was for sale on Fourth street. My father bought
Mrs Borden's half sister's share and gave it to her. We thought what he did
for her people he ought to do for his own and he then gave us grandfather's
house. I always thought my stepmother induced him to purchase the
interest. I don't know when the windows were last washed before that day.
All day Tuesday I was at the table. I gave the officer the same skirt I wore
that day, and if there was any blood on it I can give an explanation as to
how it got there. If the blood came from the outside, I cannot say how it got
there, I wore tie shoes that day and black stockings. I was under the pear
trees four or five minutes. I came down the front stairs when I came down
in the morning. The dress I wore that forenoon was a white and blue stripe
of some sort. It is at home in the attic. I did not go to Smith's drug store to
buy prussic acid. Did not go to the rooms where mother or father lay after
the murder. Went through when I went up stairs that day.' . . . 'I now ask
if you can furnish any other suspicion concerning any person who might
have committed the crime?' 'Yes; one night as I was coming home not long
ago I saw the shadow of a man on the house at the east end. I thought it
was a man because I could not see any skirts. I hurried in the front door. It
was about 8.45 o'clock; not later than 9. I saw somebody run around the
house last winter. The last time I saw anybody lately was since my sister
went to Marion. I told Mr Jennings, may have told Mr Hanscom.' 'Who
suggested the reward offered, you or your sister?' 'I don't know. I may
have.'

Mr Knowlton stopped reading, and said: 'This is the case of
the Commonwealth.'

The defence called Dr Bowen and Marshal Hilliard. On the
sixth day of the trial, arguments of counsel were presented at a
length hardly less than at a trial before a jury. At the conclusion
of the speech of the prosecuting attorney, Judge Blaisdell said:

'The long examination is now concluded, and there remains
for the magistrate to perform what he believes to be his duty. It
would be a pleasure for him, and he would doubtless receive
much sympathy if he could say, "Lizzie, I judge you probably
not guilty. You may go home." But upon the character of the
evidence presented through the witnesses who have been so
closely and thoroughly examined, there is but one thing to be
done. Suppose for a single moment a *man* was standing there.
He was found close by that guest chamber, which, to Mrs
Borden, was a chamber of death. Suppose a *man* had been found
in the vicinity of Mr Borden; was the first to find the body, and
the only account he could give of himself was the unreasonable
one that he was out in the barn looking for sinkers; then he was

out in the yard; then he was out for something else; would there be any question in the minds of men what should be done with such a man?'

There was a pause, and the old Judge's eyes filled with tears.

'So there is only one thing to do, painful as it may be—the judgment of the Court is that you are probably guilty, and you are ordered committed to await the action of the Superior Court.'

If the tide seemed to set against Miss Borden, and if the preliminary skirmishes had given distress to those who had already acquitted her in their minds, it must not be supposed that her friends, including a number of highly respected and influential persons, were not gathering valiantly. The painful situation in which she found herself, her sex, and her religious associations, were summoning to her aid many people from all parts of the State—persons who had hitherto been strangers to her. The points which had told against her were the seemingly impossible nature of the story about the visit to the barn or yard; the alleged attempt to buy poison; the lapse of time between the two murders, which appeared to shake the theory of an outside murderer; the failure to find the sender of the note to Mrs Borden; and the fact that from the stairs which she descended when her father entered the house, the body of her stepmother could have been visible. But, on the other hand, the glaring improbability of such murders being committed by a woman; combined with the failure to find any definitely determined weapon; and above everything, the absence of blood from the clothing or person of the accused—all these not only strengthened the faith of those who were sure of her innocence, but convinced the authorities that they were far from having a strong case.

Her defence, so far as concerns those in whose hands it was officially placed, was conducted with wisdom and ability.

Elsewhere, however, there was more than the usual amount of irresponsible agitation, gushing sentimentality, and abuse of officers of the governments who were merely bent on the disagreeable task of carrying out their plain and imperative duties. The abuse was the more disgusting since much of it

originated with persons of education and self-professed moral
superiority. The lynching mob exists in America in two forms,
equally discouraging to those who cling to their faith in demo-
cracy: the mob which hunts down and kills some wretch of a
malefactor, or alleged malefactor; and the mob which rails
against legal officers who are engaged in protecting the community against crime Some newspaper writers and public
personages, men and women, took up Miss Borden's cause
with no other equipment than ignorance. Blatantly they
abused the Judge, the District Attorney and the police. One
editorial writer was outraged in his feelings because of the
'harshness' of the words used in the warrant for arrest, as if a
charge of murder should be conveyed in terms of delicate
insinuation. To tell him that the form of complaint was a
hundred and fifty years old would have availed nothing; so
excited was he in behalf of the 'unfortunate girl' that he would
have suggested an agreeable form for this case. The Rev Mr
Jubb said that the action of Judge Blaisdell in sitting on the
bench, after presiding at the inquest, was 'indecent, outrageous
and not to be tolerated in any civilized community.' To him it
was mildly remarked that the statute under which the Judge
acted had been in use in America nearly two hundred years,
and somewhat antedated his own personal knowledge of this
country, since he had come hither from England within about
one year.

Associations like the Woman's Auxiliary of the Y.M.C.A.
took up Miss Borden's cause, sometimes with enthusiasm and
knowledge; sometimes merely with enthusiasm. Prayers were
invited from religious societies all over the country, the verdict
was found in advance, and Heaven was to be implored or
advised to assist the 'unfortunate girl.' There was an un-
pleasant flavor of sectarianism about much of this agitation;
innocence must be assumed because of church membership. In
contradistinction to this, however, I have seen proof that some
of the more thoughtful of the lady's spiritual brethren, including clergymen in different parts of the State, had no sympathy
with the attempts to interfere with law by the methods of the
revival and the camp-meeting. As to the term which was
applied to her, it is, of course, conventional to refer to anybody

accused of a capital crime as 'this girl' or 'this boy' provided that she or he is still under sixty years of age. And for the other word, Mr Porter said that throughout the whole proceeding, Miss Borden was called 'unfortunate,' but that nobody, good, bad, or indifferent, was ever heard to say that the murdered man and woman were 'unfortunate.'

Ten thousand tears are shed in America for persons accused of murder, and even for persons convicted of murder, to every word of regret spoken for the victims of the murders. And that, according to thoughtful investigators, is one of the reasons why America leads the world in its shameful record for the unlawful taking of human life—although a few semi-civilized Oriental countries, and certain turbulent provinces of Italy, may be exceptions to this statement.

Advocates of suffrage for women came energetically to the defence of Miss Borden, almost as if her sex alone proved her innocence. One especially good result of the present status of women as voters, is a nearly complete abandonment on the part of their political leaders of the belief which was prevalent thirty of forty years ago: that all women accused of grave crimes should either be cleared in advance of trial, or if convicted, should not be liable for punishment. Their present attitude is a far more reasonable acceptance of women's duties and respon- sibilities to the State, as no more and no less than those of men. But in 1892, Mrs Mary A. Livermore, an estimable lady of very vigorous character, Mrs Susan Fessenden, president of the Woman's Christian Temperance Union, and Miss Lucy Stone, all distinguished in the struggle for what were then termed 'Woman's Rights,' came to the aid and comfort of Miss Borden. They did it so ecstatically as to leave doubt whether they were acting from logic or from emotion.

Miss Borden's name means little today to those who do not remember the year of her trial. Perhaps the younger folk in Scotland have never heard of Madeleine Smith, although their fathers and grandfathers followed her adventures with palpi- tating interest. Soon, perhaps, the name of Mrs Maybrick will have completely faded from memory in England and America. One may search old books on criminology and summon one's own recollections, in vain, to recall the name of any American

woman, resting under the capital charge, which was so widely
known as that of Miss Borden. Perhaps the equally unfortunate
Miss Nan Patterson is the only one for comparison, although
far in the past there was Mrs Cunningham, while more recently
arose the grim figure of Mrs Rogers of Vermont, and the
adventurous Clara Phillips of California. No *Ballade des Dames
du Temps Jadis* celebrates these names; they, too, are gone with
the snows of yester-year. But once, upon railroad trains, in
clubs, at tea-parties, and around every breakfast table could be
heard conversations about 'Lizzie.' A voice would arise from a
group of talkers, anywhere between the two oceans: 'I tell you,
she never did it in the world! It's impossible. I *know* she never
did it!' And nobody had to ask what was being discussed.

An account of the case would be incomplete if it did not
record the fact that, however unjustly, the event was celebrated
in rhyme, in one of those jingles which are never forgotten. Who
invented it, nobody knows, but everyone heard it:

> Lizzie Borden took an axe
> And gave her Mother forty whacks;
> When she saw what she had done,—
> She gave her Father forty-one!

This has been communicated to me, in one way or another, at
least half a dozen times, while I have been writing this article,
by persons to whom it was the most vivid recollection of the Fall
River murders—surpassing even the mutton-soup.

Similar folk-rhymes have been associated with two notorious crimes in Great Britain: one which delighted Sir Walter
Scott:

> They cut his throat from ear to ear
>   His brains they battered in;
> His name was Mr William Weare,
>   He dwelt in Lyon's Inn,

and that even grimmer quatrain which sums up the popular
notion—as these things do—of the West Port murders in
Edinburgh:

Up the close and doun the stair,
But and ben wi' Burke and Hare,
Burke's the butcher, Hare's the thief,
Knox the boy that buys the beef.

In America there is hardly a notorious murder which does not evoke one or two jokes or epigrams, sometimes witty, sometimes ribald, but only one other beside the Fall River murder, has, to my knowledge, brought forth any rhyme. In the early '90's, one Isaac Sawtell, living in New Hampshire, planned to do away with his brother, Hiram. He noted with approval that the neighboring State of Maine, more considerate toward gentlemen of his disposition than his own New Hampshire, had abolished the death penalty. So he took his brother out for a drive one evening, crossed, as he thought, into Maine, and killed him. But his topographical sense was at fault; the deed had really been done in New Hampshire after all, and in that State he was tried. The incident was described in a couplet by some rhymster:

Two brothers in our town did dwell,
Hiram sought Heaven, but Isaac Sawtell.

Miss Borden went back to the jail in Taunton, to await the action of the Grand Jury. It was with her as with the Napoleonic prisoners in *Peter Ibbetson:* she could not have found her durance very vile. I have been credibly informed that she was seen on the streets of Taunton, from time to time, having been taken out for walks. Whether this privilege was accorded because of the advance decision of her innocence, or because she was joint-heiress to a considerable estate, there is no information.

In October occurred a thoroughly discredible incident. At first it seemed to be a heavy blow at Miss Borden's interests, but its effect was almost instantly reversed, and in the end probably worked in her favor. A newspaper reporter with the felicitious name of Henry G. Trickey, and a detective named Edwin D. McHenry were concerned in the production of a long newspaper article with which they hoodwinked the *Boston*

Globe. Trickey and his friends blamed McHenry for it, while
McHenry and his friends blamed Trickey. Definitely it can be
said that Trickey was indicted by the Grand Jury for an
attempt to tamper with a Government witness, that he left the
country and did not live to return, nor to meet the accusation.

A newspaper seldom publishes such an article. It began on
the front page of the *Globe*, on October 10, and filled nearly two
and a half of its pages. In all these columns, which purported to
set forth testimony in possession of the Government, truth rarely
entered. Had one-quarter of it been fact, it would have convicted the prisoner. The *prima facie* case for the prosecution
must have seemed, to outsiders, to be strong indeed, or this
could not have appeared. The names of the newly discovered
witnesses were plausible, although they were nearly all imagin-
ary. A man called John H. Murphy, while passing the house,
had seen Miss Borden in Mrs Borden's room. Another mythic-
al person, 'Mrs Gustave F. Ronald,' had passed the house at
9:40, had heard a terrible cry, and had seen a woman whose
head was covered with a rubber cap, or hood. (It was a favorite
theory, at this time, that the mysterious assassin had worn some
outside covering for the hair to avoid being spattered with
blood. Some newspapers and their readers found a still greater
thrill in the notion that the assailant of the Bordens had dispensed with clothing altogether during the commission of the
deed.) A certain 'Peter Mahany' had witnessed all that 'Mrs
Ronald' had seen, and, in addition, had recognized the hooded
woman as the prisoner. The street opposite must have thronged
with witnesses! 'Mr and Mrs Frederick Chace,' calling at the
house on Wednesday evening, had overheard a quarrel between Mr Borden and his younger daughter—about a man, a
lover. This seemed at last to bring into the case the 'love
interest,' for which many newspaper reporters had almost
pined away and died. Bridget Sullivan (an actual person at last)
was to tell of a quarrel which happened the same evening. The
police matron was to amplify an adverse bit of testimony—
already in evidence—and to say that she had heard Miss
Borden tell John Vinnicum Morse to 'get those things out of the
way in my room, and then they can do their worst.'

On the following day the *Globe* made a partial retraction. 'It

[the story] has been proven wrong in some particulars.' Mr
McHenry, the *Globe* said, had furnished the story, and admits
that the names and addresses of witnesses were purposely false.
The other Boston papers were quoted as denying the truth of
the yarn. One part which was entirely withdrawn—to the sorrow of all good reporters—was the 'love interest.' Finally, on
October 12, the *Globe*, in a boxed article on the front page, made
a full retraction. It had been 'grievously misled,' suffered an
'imposition,' 'unparalleled. . . cunningly contrived' but 'based
on facts.' It expressed its 'heartfelt apology' for the 'inhuman
reflection' on Miss Borden's honor, and included in the
apology, Mr John Vinnicum Morse.

Mr Trickey soon left Boston, and in November he was killed
by a railroad train in Canada. It may be imagined that more
than one of Miss Borden's rural neighbors and sympathizers
solemnly remarked: 'It was a *jedgment* on him!' The final result
of this wretched affair may well have been to add to the number
of those who distrust the newspapers, and to persuade them
that if this damaging story were false, everything which seemed
to tell against the prisoner might equally be false.

The Grand Jury of Bristol met in November and listened to
the evidence for a week. An unusual course was followed in that
the District Attorney, Mr Knowlton, invited Miss Borden's
counsel, Mr Jennings, to be present and offer evidence for the
defence. It is not customary for the Grand Jury to hear others
beside the witnesses for the prosecution. The sitting was adjourned until December 1, when a curious thing happened.
Miss Alice Russell re-appeared and gave testimony which had
not been offered before. On December 2, the Grand Jury found
three indictments against Miss Borden: one for the murder of
her father, one for the murder of her step-mother, and one in
which she was charged with both murders. Mr Porter says that
there were twenty-one jurymen present when the vote was
taken; twenty voted 'guilty,' and one voted against that finding.

In the months which followed the preliminary trial, and
especially in the autumn of 1892, the District Attorney made a
careful study of the case, and pursued investigations in various
directions. The members of the Grand Jury, after they com-
pleted their work, had desired to draw up a paper certifying to

the impartial manner in which he had presented the case for the
Government, but he advised them not to do so. The question of
the prisoner's sanity had been raised, soon after the arrest, and
inquiries were made into the family history, but with negative
results. Miss Borden had more than once spoken of the burglary of the house, which had taken place a year before the
murders, and as the police had been consulted at the time, they
were asked for a report of the circumstances.

In the latter part of June, 1891, so it appeared, Mr Borden
had called upon City Marshal Hilliard, and asked that officer's
help. A police captain was detailed to go with Mr Borden to the
house on Second Street, where they found Mrs Borden, the
Misses Borden, and Bridget Sullivan. In a small room on the
second floor, Mr Borden's desk had been broken open. Eighty
dollars in bank-notes, twenty-five or thirty in gold, a large
number of street-car tickets, Mrs Borden's watch with a chain,
and some other small trinkets had been stolen. The family were
at a loss to see how any one could get in and out unseen. Miss
Lizzie Borden said:

'The cellar door was open, and someone might have come in
that way.'

The officer visited the houses in the neighborhood and
exhausted all the resources of the average detective who is not
the creation of a novelist: that is, he asked if anybody had seen a
mysterious stranger entering the Borden house. One 'clew' he
did get: Miss Lizzie Borden presented him with 'a 6 or 8 penny
nail' which she had found in the keyhole of a bedroom door.
Apparently nobody seemed to think that the robber, in leaving
this behind him, had made an adequate return for his thefts.
Three times within two weeks, said the officer, Mr Borden
remarked to him:

'I am afraid the police will not be able to find the real thief.'

He was right, and the robbery, like the greater crime in that
household, remains a mystery.

We usually read, during the investigation of a notorious
crime, that the police, or the prosecuting officers, or the attorneys for the defence, or the Governor, are receiving hundreds or
thousands of letters from cranks and others; suggestions, in-
sinuations, accusations, and threats. As few of us are police-

men, criminal lawyers, or Governors, we take this for granted and seldom expect to see such letters; perhaps we would rather not see them. It has been my privilege to read five or six large packets of communications received by the District Attorney during his investigation of these murders, and a more curious and varied collection could not be imagined. From all parts of the United States they came; written on all possible colors and shapes of paper, in every type of handwriting, and every degree of sanity. Excitable, calm, puerile, nonsensical, pompous, intelligent (a few), preposterous, or insulting, they poured in by the dozen. A railroad conductor in the West asked Mr Knowlton to lay aside his official duties, and embark upon genealogical research, which had no reference to the crime. An embattled Protestant from Vermont called upon him to clap Bridget Sullivan and her 'confessor' into prison, and extort admissions from them—apparently by torture. He ended: 'beware of jesuits.' A man in Albany gleefully admitted that he alone was guilty in this case (he had many a rival in his claim!), but that he was 'moving about so fast' that the police could not hope to catch him. Spiritualists, clairvoyants, crystal-gazers, and other seers had discovered strange things under the flooring of the Borden house, or concealed in the stuffing of the 'sopha.' The Ouija board had been invoked, and had answered a long series of questions in its maddening fashion—half devil and half child. Its control was much interested in 'Lizzie's cat,' that doubtful animal, which, according to a cruel and unfounded bit of gossip, had been carried down cellar, by Miss Borden, and beheaded, with an axe.

One bold blade, who signed 'Voter,' wrote an abusive post-card, to inform Mr Knowlton that he deserved to be 'kicked out' and that he would never again be District Attorney—a sound prophecy, since he was soon promoted by the voters of the State to the office of Attorney General.

Many of the letters began with apologies, and assurances that the writers were acting solely in the interests of justice, but a lady from Brooklyn with a romantic name, an adherent to the most popular theory of all, closed by saying: 'If the suggestions prove of any value, I shall expect to be suitably rewarded.' The attorney was advised to hunt for the missing weapon in the piano, in the back of the kitchen stove, in the barn, the outhouses, and the well. The thought that the police might have looked in some of these places did not occur to the letter-writers. One man, who sent in some curious and rather acute messages, wrote that if the search continued unsuccessful, the house should be burned down in order to find the weapon, as nobody, in his opinion, would ever wish to live in it again. He cited the Burdell and Nathan houses in New York, in support of this theory, but he was mistaken, since the house is cheerfully occupied at the present time.

A band of letter-writers were convinced that the weapon had been, not a hatchet, but a flat-iron, and upon this contention they wrote pages. (The nature of the wounds made this theory untenable.) A serious correspondent from Danvers, Massachusetts, proposed that both men and women should be set to work battering the skulls of subjects in the dissecting-room, in order to prove experimentally the difference between blows inflicted by persons of opposite sexes. Two or three correspondents suggested that the Fall River murderer was probably Such-a-One who murdered Somebody in 1884, or Another Man who killed Some-One-Else-Again in 1879—the fancy being that there only one or two murderers in the land, and that they go about from place to place, like traveling salesmen, or the public hangman in England. But by far the most popular theory was that held by the 'water-proof' or 'gossamer' school. The idea that the clothes of the assailant of the Bordens might have been protected from blood stains by a water-proof, to be washed or destroyed, was widely entertained and vigorously argued.

Perhaps the most intelligent letter of all came from a lady, who also wrote to the Attorney General. Her suggestion was that there was something curious in the action of the discoverer of the body of the dead man, in remaining in that fatal house, where for all anybody could know, the murderer was still lurking. Another suggestion was that the absence of blood stains from clothing, might well prove too much, when that clothing was worn by the child of a murdered man, who was the first to discover the death.

Six months elapsed between the indictment and the trial

before the Superior Court, one of the almost invariable delays of our law, but one which provoked no complaint from the defence. The situation was unusual, and it is best indicated by a letter from the District Attorney to the Attorney General, written in the spring. A capital case in Massachusetts is frequently prosecuted for the State by the Attorney General, but Mr Pillsbury was not in good health. Mr Knowlton, in this letter of April 24, 1893, said, among other things:

'Personally I would like very much to get rid of the trial of the case, and fear that my own feelings in that direction may have influenced my better judgment. I feel this all the more upon your not unexpected announcement that the burden of the trial will come upon me.

'I confess, however, I cannot see my way clear to any disposition of the case other than a trial. Should it result in disagreement of the jury there would be no difficulty then in disposing of the case by admitting the defendant to bail: but a verdict either way would render such a course unnecessary.

'The case has proceeded so far and an indictment has been found by the Grand Inquest of the county that it does not seem to me that we ought to take the responsibility of discharging her without trial, even though there is every reasonable expectation of a verdict of not guilty. I am unable to concur fully in your views as to the probable result. I think it may well be that the jury might disagree upon the case. But even in my most sanguine moments I have scarcely expected a verdict of guilty.

'The situation is this: nothing has developed which satisfies either of us that she is innocent, neither of us can escape the conclusion that she must have had some knowledge of the occurrence. She has been presented for trial by a jury which, to say the least, was not influenced by anything said by the Government in the favor of the indictment . . . I cannot see how any other course than setting the case down for trial, and trying it will satisfy that portion of the public sentiment, whether favorable to her or not, which is worthy of being respected.'

This remarkable letter, so accurate in its prediction, shows how clearly the man best informed understood both the strength and the weakness of the Government's case. The fact that every investigation, so far, had resulted in a decision adverse to the interests of the accused, makes many of the final comments in the newspapers seem absurd. Yet the facts that the evidence was still purely circumstantial; that the unquestioned weapon had not been found; that the absence of blood stains upon the prisoner's clothing was a telling point in her favor; as well as the difficulty in prevailing upon a jury to convict a woman except upon the most overwhelming proof,— all these points made the District Attorney understand the hopelessness of convicting a defendant whose guilt, he sincerely believed, was nevertheless certain.

Miss Borden was arraigned before Justice Hammond of the Superior Court, in New Bedford, on May 8, when she pleaded to the indictments. Early in the next month she was taken again to the Court House, in the same city, to be put upon her trial. Newspaper readers had almost forgotten her. In the first week in June they were amusing themselves with reports of one of the damage suits of Laidlaw against Russell Sage, for injuries received in the attempt to blow up Mr Sage. An archaic problem was under debate, whether the World's Fair in Chicago should be opened on Sundays. Lord Dunraven's *Valkyrie* was winning in English waters, and seemed the probable challenger for the *America's* cup. At the end of the week, Edwin Booth died at his home, *The Players*. These far off events were news, during the week that Miss Borden came, as the reporters said, 'to face her accusers.'

Three judges were on the bench on June 5, 1893, as the trial began. They were Chief Justice Albert Mason and Associate Justice Caleb Blodgett and Justin Dewey. Mr Knowlton was assisted in the prosecution by the District Attorney for the Eastern District, Mr William H. Moody. The defence was now entrusted to Mr George D. Robinson, together with Messrs Jennings and Adams. Mr Robinson had been Governor of Massachusetts thrice; he was held in peculiar and unusual esteem by the people of the State for the integrity of his character. The story, then current, that before accepting a retainer in this case he had spent two hours in consultation with Miss Borden in the jail, and that he had come forth declaring his firm belief in her innocence, had done much to hearten her friends and convince the doubtful.

On the first day one hundred and eight talesmen were examined before twelve were selected for the jury. Almost every town and city of the county was represented on this large panel, but not Fall River, and there were no Fall River men on the jury. The fine old question and reply, between the Clerk and the prisoner, have vanished from our courts: 'How will you be tried?' 'By God and my country.' 'God send you good deliverance!' But Massachusetts keeps some of the ancient phraseology, so after the reading of the indictment, the Clerk said to the jury:

'To each count of which indictment Lizzie Andrew Borden, the prisoner at the bar, has heretofore pleaded and said that thereof she is not guilty, and for trial puts herself upon her country, which country you are. You are now sworn to try the issue. If she is guilty on either or both of said counts, you are to say so, and if she is not guilty on either or both of said counts, you are to say so, and no more. Good men and true, stand fast together and hearken to your evidence.'

It is one of the great sensational moments in our civilization: the trial of a woman for her life. The newspapers, for the ultimate thrill, prefer to have a trial for the murder of a lover or a husband, but this was for a crime more rare and terrible—for parricide. If anybody in the crowded Court, on that warm June day, found the scene dramatic, it was merely because he comprehended its meaning. The proceedings were quiet and dignified, but without ceremony or circumstance; the surroundings were commonplace. There entered no judge in scarlet, acclaimed by trumpeters, as in the trial of Mrs Maybrick at Liverpool; these justices did not even wear the black silk gowns of our Supreme Court. The sitting was held in a bare, white-walled room, filled with desks, chairs and long settees. Three elderly and bearded gentlemen, with palm-leaf fans, sat a little above the rest, upon the bench. Another beard, a long one, on the chin of the Clerk. Beards, side-whiskers, or heavy moustaches in the jury-box; men still liked to surround their faces with hair. The prisoner came in 'walking steadily.' She wore a 'new dress of black mohair, cut in the latest style, with leg-of-mutton sleeves, which fitted her by no means inferior form to perfection. Upon her head was a jaunty black lace hat trimmed with rosettes of blue velvet and a blue feather. . . . She was altogether unembarrassed.'

Perhaps the most unusual figures in the New Bedford Court House were the thirty or forty newspaper men from Boston and New York, and from the press associations. They alternately amused and were amused by New Bedford. They sat upon uncomfortable stools and rested their papers upon narrow strips of board, called by courtesy, tables. Writers from the metropolitan journals gave their readers what they were supposed to desire, by describing almost every man in the trial as 'stern and Puritanical' and nearly every woman as 'an angular old maid.' The New Yorker visualizes the inhabitant of New England as looking more or less, in features and costume, like St Gaudens' statue of Deacon Chapin, 'The Puritan,' and if, in his expeditions to Newport, Boston or Bar Harbor, he has seen few of this appearance, he clings, nevertheless, to his secret belief.

There may have been women among the reporters; the sob-sister had made her appearance in journalism, and one who signed herself 'Amy Robsart' had already written sympathetic articles about Miss Borden languishing in the Taunton jail. Mr Algernon Blackwood, the novelist, was on the staff of the New York *Sun* at this time, and he refers in his autobiography, *Episodes before Thirty*, to the Borden case. None of the bizarre and terrible situations in Mr Blackwood's stories, with all their appropriate setting, is stranger than the contrast between the homely scene of the Borden house on that August morning and the Æschylean slaughter there enacted.

Probably the most distinguished correspondent present was Julian Ralph of the New York *Sun*, although nobody was so conspicuous as Joseph Howard, Jr., of *The New York Recorder* and *The Boston Globe*. At that time many citizens of New England considered it a solemn duty, between breakfast and church on Sunday mornings to read 'Howard's Letter' from New York in the *Globe*. Pontifical in style, and invariably ending with a description, in two words, of the weather in New York, these letters had become a sort of weekly necessity, for reasons difficult to explain today. Mr Howard had descended upon New Bedford with something of the grandeur of an

Oriental embassy, and with every provision for his comfort and convenience. Somehow he secured a chair next the Sheriff, and there, conspicuous in his summer clothes, among all the poor wretches in doleful black, he fairly dominated the scene. Mr Howard was said to have attended every notable trial in thirty years, including that of Mrs Surratt of the Lincoln conspiracy.

Before giving any narrative of the progress of the trial, it may be useful to show what the State tried to prove. I will condense into this paragraph and the next an analysis of the case made by Professor John H. Wigmore, author of *The Principles of Judicial Proof*. The State sought to establish that the prisoner had a motive for the crime, and the design to commit it; that she had the opportunity, and the means and the capacity; and finally, that she betrayed consciousness of guilt. The motive was supposed to arise in the family history; in the fact that she was not on good terms with her stepmother; that customarily she and her sister did not eat with the others in the house; and that she had made certain remarks about her stepmother which betrayed her animosity. There was no evidence of design to use an axe, but a general intention to kill was to be shown by the attempt to buy poison. The conversation with Miss Russell on Wednesday night, and the suggestion to Bridget that she go out to buy dress goods, were to support the theory of premeditation.

For opportunity, means and capacity, the State attempted to prove that she had exclusive opportunity; that physically she was not incapable of the deeds; and that one of the hatchets produced in Court—the 'handleless' hatchet—was not incapable of being the weapon. Consciousness of guilt, with exclusive opportunity, were the strong points of the prosecution. To establish the former the State relied, first, on the alleged falsehoods to prevent detection of the first death in the story about the note sent to Mrs Borden. Second, the falsehoods as to the visit to the barn, and the contradictory versions of this story. Third, her knowledge as to the first death. Fourth, her concealment of the knowledge. Fifth, that she concealed or destroyed evidence, as will appear in the testimony. So far, Professor Wigmore.

Mr Moody opened for the Commonwealth. He had begun a

career which was to reward him, before middle-age had passed, with two of the great prizes of his profession in America. Of medium-size and sturdy figure, he had a pleasant, youthful countenance, and a manner in public speech of sincere, often intense, conviction, not unlike that of President Theodore Roosevelt, whose Cabinet Minister he became. Mr Moody gave an outline of the history of the case which need not be repeated here, since I qave already drawn upon it, as well as other sources. He described the interior of the Borden house— fortunately this description was supplemented by an inspection, for which the jury were taken to Fall River. One or two points in the address may be mentioned. When he came to the remark which Miss Borden made to her father: 'Mrs Borden has gone out; she had a note from somebody who was sick,' he said:

'That, gentlemen, we put to you as a lie, intended for no purpose except to stifle inquiry as to the whereabouts of Mrs Borden.'

In regard to the stories about the visit to the yard or to the barn, he invited the jury's attention to certain minor differences and to one important discrepancy. To Bridget, to Mrs Churchill, and to Officer Mullaly, she said that she was in the barn, and came into the house because of a noise she heard. The noise was variously described, to the different persons, as 'a groan,' 'a distress noise' and a 'scraping sound.'

'All those, gentlemen, you see in substance are stories which include the fact that while she was outside she heard some alarming noise which caused her to rush in and discover the homicide. Well, gentlemen, as inquiry begins to multiply upon her as to her whereabouts, another story comes into view, and she repeats it again and again, and finally repeats it under oath, that at the time, after Bridget went upstairs she went out into the barn to get lead to make sinkers. Now, gentlemen, having in view the character of her statements, that she heard the noise, you will find that when she gave a later and detailed account, she said that she went into the loft of the barn, opened the window, ate some pears up there, and looked over some lead for sinkers, came down, looked into the stove to see if the fire was hot enough that she might go on with her ironing, found it was not, put her hat down, started to go upstairs to await the fire which Bridget was to build for the noonday, and discovered her father. It is not, gentlemen, and I pray your attention to it, a difference of words here. In the one case the statement is that she was alarmed by the noise of the homicide. In the other case, the statement is that she came coolly, deliberately, about her business, looking after her ironing, putting down her hat, and accidentally discovered the homicide as she went upstairs.'

Mr Moody also described other portions of the case for the prosecution, and these may be mentioned as they are reached in the testimony. At the close of his speech, the prisoner fainted. The witness first called included Mr Kieran, the engineer who measured the house; Mr John Vinnicum Morse; and a number of bank employees and shop-keepers who saw Mr Borden on the day of his death.

The first important witness was Bridget Sullivan, and her cross-examination by Mr Robinson seemed to elicit the first bits of information which had not been heard at the preliminary trial. Mr Robinson dwelt upon the matter of discord in the family. The witness testified that she had never observed any quarrels. Asked the direct question if the daughters came to the table for meals with the rest of the family, the answer was:

'No, sir, they did not.'

The lawyer persisted, and she replied:

'Most of the time they did not eat with their father and mother.'

He suggested that this was because they did not arise as early in the morning, and asked about the custom at dinner. She answered:

'Sometimes at dinner; a good many more times they were not.'

She testified that Miss Lizzie and Mrs Borden did speak to each other civilly. He asked about the stepdaughter's conduct toward Mrs Borden when the latter was ill, and brought out the disconcerting reply:

'I know that she was sick one time, and none of them went into the room while she was sick.'

He quoted her testimony at the inquest, which was in some degree opposed to this, but did not get her to alter the statement. He returned to the question of their eating together, until she finally said that

'They always ate at the same dining-room.'

He then asked:

'Always ate together in the dining-room?'

The answer was 'Yes.'

His treatment of the witness on this point seems somewhat disingenuous. Bridget testified that she had no duties in the bedrooms of the family. The most important facts which he brought out in favor of the prisoner were that while Bridget was on the other side of the house, talking with the Kellys' servant, she could not have seen anyone who might have entered the house by the sideyard; and that when she came downstairs, after the murders, she saw no blood on Miss Borden's face or hands. Mr Robinson touched upon the story of the note to Mrs Borden, learned that the witness heard the prisoner tell her father that such a note had been received, but then dropped the subject, and did not ask whether the witness had heard of the note from Mrs Borden, or from anybody except the prisoner. That omission was significant.

Dr Bowen and Mrs Churchill followed Bridget Sullivan. All of these witnesses were questioned about the dress which Miss Borden was wearing when they first saw her after the murders. Dr Bowen's testimony on this point was confused; Mrs Churchill described it as 'a light blue and white ground work . . . with a dark navy blue diamond on it.' Shown a dark blue *silk* dress, given to the police by the prisoner as the one worn by her that morning, and asked if this was the one she saw, Mrs Churchill replied:

'I did not see her with it on that morning.'

On cross-examination Mrs Churchill said that she could not tell much about Bridget's dress on that day; and that she saw no blood on Miss Borden, although she stood over her and had fanned her. Mrs Churchill also said that Bridget told her the story about the note. The defence promptly tried to clinch this apparently valuable testimony and made the witness repeat it again and again. But on the redirect examination, Mr Moody asked:

'Lest there be any mistake, Mrs Churchill, you don't speak of this talk with Bridget with reference to the note as in substitution, but in addition to what Miss Lizzie Borden told you?'

'It was after Lizzie had told me.'

'Then Bridget told you what you have told us?'

'Yes, after that.'

When Miss Alice Russell was called, 'Miss Borden straightened up in her chair and began to watch the door.' Miss Russell entered, and looked, says a reporter, in every direction but toward the prisoner. She related, at length, the conversation with Miss Borden on the night before the murders. When the witness came to relate experiences at the Borden house after the murders, she said that in answer to her question:

'What did you go to the barn for, Lizzie?' the answer was:

'I went to get a piece of tin or iron to fix my screen.'

A new and important part of Miss Russell's testimony was that on the Sunday morning after the murders (following Mayor Coughlin's call on Saturday evening) she—the witness—came into the kitchen of the Borden house and saw Miss Lizzie Borden at the stove, with a dress in her hand. Her sister, Miss Emma, asked what she was going to do, and the answer was:

'I am going to burn this old thing up; it is covered with paint.'

Miss Russell left the room without speaking, but on returning saw the prisoner ripping or tearing the garment. She said:

'I wouldn't let anybody see me do that, Lizzie.'

There was no reply. On the next day, Miss Russell said to the prisoner:

'I am afraid, Lizzie, the worst thing you could have done was to burn that dress. I have been asked about your dresses.'

The prisoner answered: 'Oh, what made you let me do it? Why didn't you tell me?'

This testimony about the dress, said Miss Russell, was not given at the inquest nor at the preliminary trial, nor at her first appearance before the Grand Jury. She further said that the burned dress was a 'cheap cotton Bedford cord' with 'light blue ground with a dark figure, small figure.'

Miss Russell, on cross-examination, said that in the diningroom, on the day of the murder, she found the handkerchiefs that the prisoner had been ironing. Some of them had been

ironed; two or three had not. She saw no blood anywhere upon
the prisoner. When the dress was burned, on Sunday morning,
there was a policeman in the yard at the time. She saw no blood
on the dress, and she did not actually see the prisoner put it into
the stove.

It was the Government's contention that the few handkerchiefs left unironed were significant: that there was no good
reason for leaving this work unfinished.

One of the first of the police witnesses was the assistant city
marshal, John Fleet. He had been early to arrive, and to talk
with the prisoner. In this conversation she made what was
considered a significant remark. In reply to Mr Fleet's question
if she had any idea who could have killed her father and mother,
she said:

'She is not my mother, sir; she is my stepmother; my mother
died when I was a child.'

One gathers from various sources the impression that there
was something in Miss Borden's manner, in all these early
interviews, which tended to arouse suspicion. This, of course,
did not reach the jury, but it is often alluded to in contemporary
accounts. The cross-examination of Mr Fleet was long and
severe; it was the policy of the defence to impeach all the police
testimony as incorrect, sometimes deliberately malicious. In
the opinion of some of the reporters, the police witnesses were
badly confused by Mr Robinson; this is not apparent in reading
the stenographic report. Officer Medley, who arrived at the
Borden house at twenty minutes before twelve and heard from
Miss Borden about her visit to the barn, promptly went to the
place himself. He testified that he especially examined the floor
of the loft for footprints, and found that he could see none. He
experimented to see if his own footsteps would be left in the
accumulation of dust on the floor, and found that they were.

On the seventh day of the trial, the prosecution offered Miss
Borden's own testimony at the inquest, and on Mr Robinson's
objection, argued for its admission, after the jury had withdrawn. Mr Moody said, without dispute, that the conduct of
the inquest had been in accordance with law; that her testimony was not a confession, but rather in the nature of denials,
which were evidences of guilt. He made the usual citations of

other cases in which similar evidence had been admitted.

In reply, Mr Robinson urged that an accusation had been made against his client, by the Mayor, on August 6, that the inquest was from August 9 to 11, and that from August 6 she was under observation of the police. The house was surrounded. A warrant had been issued—but not served—on August 8; she was arrested, later, under another warrant. She was surrounded by police, a defenceless woman, denied counsel, not told by the Court or the District Attorney that she ought not testify to anything which might incriminate herself.

'If that is freedom, God save the Commonwealth of Massachusetts!'

Mr Moody replied that all this was magnificent, but it was not law. He pointed out that it was agreed that Mr Jennings was told by the District Attorney that he might confer with his client on her rights as a witness, and that it was absurd to suppose that he had not warned her of her rights not to give evidence.

The Court withdrew for consultation, and on returning said that Miss Borden was practically under arrest at the time she gave this testimony, and it was therefore excluded.

Doctors Dolan, Wood, and Draper were among the medical witnesses for the State. They were examined and cross-examined at enormous length. They agreed that between one and two hours, probably about one hour and a half, had elapsed between the two deaths—a fact deduced from the progress of digestion, the warmth of the two bodies, and the condition of the blood from each. A valuable point for the accused woman was made when Professor Wood said that he believed the assailant of the Bordens could not have avoided at least a few spatters of blood. No doctor testified that many blood stains would necessarily be received.

During the medical testimony the skull of Mr Borden was produced in Court, for purposes of illustration of the nature of the wounds. The mawkish and sentimental newspapers—and this included three-quarters of them at this stage—made great play with this fact, and dwelt upon how it affected the poor prisoner. The newspapers were few which did not speak as if the deaths of Mr and Mrs Borden ought to have been forgotten long ago; that the officers of the law were little better than brutes to have prosecuted anybody; and that the sole concern of mankind was to rescue, from her grievous position, the 'unfortunate girl,' and send her home amid a shower of roses.

Mrs Hannah Gifford, a dressmaker, testified, under objection by the defence, as to a conversation which she had with the prisoner in the month of March, preceding the murders. Mrs Gifford, in referring to Mrs Borden had used the word 'mother,' whereupon Miss Lizzie had said:

'Don't say that to me, for she is a mean, good-for-nothing thing.'

To which the dressmaker replied: 'Oh, Lizzie, you don't mean that?'

'Yes, I don't have much to do with her; I stay in my room most of the time.'

'You come down to your meals, don't you?'

'Yes; but we don't eat with them if we can help it.'

Miss Anna H. Borden (not a relative) was produced to testify to a similar but milder remark on the ship during the voyage home from Europe, in 1890, but this was excluded as remote.

A mass of conflicting evidence surrounded the testimony of Mrs Hannah Reagan, matron of the Fall River Police Station. She said she overheard a quarrel between the Borden sisters, in which the prisoner said:

'Emma, you have given me away, haven't you?'

The reply of the elder sister was: 'No, Lizzie, I have not.'

The prisoner answered: 'You have; and I will let you see I won't give in one inch.'

A controversy had arisen over Mrs Reagan's testimony, and in it were included Mr Jennings, the police, the Rev Mr Buck, and others. At the time the conversation was first reported, in August, a determined attempt was made by Miss Borden's friends to induce Mrs Reagan to sign a retraction, and thenceforth the incident was like a football, kicked about by the Borden partisans and the reporters. The original conversation was evidently believed by the prosecution, and was repeated in detail by Mrs Reagan at the trial. But it was more flatly contradicted than almost any other point in the case for the Government.

The testimony of Eli Bence, as to the poison, was excluded on the ground that it was not shown that prussic acid might not have an innocent use! At this point the Government then rested its case.

The defence, to give Professor Wigmore's analysis in one paragraph, did not shake the evidence as to motive. It had excluded the prussic acid evidence. It did not destroy the proof of exclusive opportunity, but it did show that the screen door at the side was not locked at all times. It showed no traces of another person in the house, and only vague reports of others in the vicinity. It failed to prove that the handleless hatchet might not have been used, but tried to suggest that the evidence of the police was wilfully false. It could not shake the story of the note, but suggested that the note might have been part of the murderer's plot. The inconsistent stories about the trip to the barn were attributed to excitement, and the most damaging of them—the inquest testimony—was excluded. It was shown that lead was found in the barn loft, but no fish-line was produced, and no screen in need of repair was identified. 'The inconsistent stories as to her return and discovery of the murder were in part slid over, in part ignored, and in part discredited.' The stronghold of the defence was the utter absence of blood stains on the person of the accused. Five or six persons saw her within ten minutes, and saw no stains on her. 'It is safe to say that this was the decisive fact of the case.'

Mr Jennings opened for the defence. He dwelt upon the fact that not one particle of direct evidence had been produced against her. He quoted cases to show the unreliability of circumstantial evidence—often an effective argument, for although attorneys may argue and judges expound until the end of time, persons will still be found to say: 'I don't believe in circumstantial evidence.' He pointed out that the Government, for all the array of axes and hatchets they brought into Court, were not positive about any one of them. He denied the proof of exclusive opportunity. He asserted that others had been in the barn before Medley paid his visit.

The defence had little need of any witnesses. The previous good character of the prisoner had been conceded by the Government, so no testimony was offered on that point. A number of witnesses did appear; they were solemnly heard, and

duly cross-examined; but at this distance they appear in no
other light than as comic relief. Two ladies, neighbors of the
Bordens, named Chagnon, testified that they had heard a
thumping sound in the direction of the Borden barn, the night
before the murders. (It had been investigated, and shown to be
dogs upsetting barrels of waste to get at some bones. Even had
it been other than this, did the defence suggest that the
murderer, arriving twelve hours in advance of the crime, had
taken up quarters in the barn—perhaps to get an early chance
at the sinkers—and had announced his coming by thumping on
the floor?) One Mrs Durfee had heard a man, a year before,
make threats against Mr Borden; her testimony was excluded
as remote. One or two witnesses appeared to tell of a drunken
man seen sitting on the Borden steps, the night before. Dr
Handy described his Wild Eyed Man—not satisfied that he
was 'Mike the Soldier.' The appearance of Hyman Lubinsky,
an ice-cream peddler, gave an exotic flavor to the day's proceedings. He had driven through Second Street at some time
that morning, when he 'saw a lady come out the way from the
barn to the stairs from the back of the house.' This was offered
in corroboration of the story of the visit to the barn, but it was
discarded testimony, as he had already been carefully examined by the Government, and his idea of time shown to be
faulty. The Clan Lubinsky were more of a novelty in 1893 than
today, and Hyman's tart answers to the District Attorney
('What has a person got eyes for, but to look with?') must have
amused the auditors.

Better still were a pair of youthful witnesses, Everett Brown
and Thomas Barlow, a couple of boys who had apparently
determined to get into Court one way or another. The spirit of
romance burned in them, a far hotter flame than their passion
for fact. They had not had, like Huck Finn and Tom Sawyer,
the luck to witness a murder, and to be able to take a solemn
oath by midnight. But they did almost as well. They ate their
dinners at the surprising hour of 10:30 a.m., on August 4, and
arrived at the scene almost before the crime was committed.
    'We went in the side gate.'
    'You say "we." Who?'
    'Me and Brownie.'

They went up in the barn loft far ahead of anybody else, although they paused a while at the stairs, and dared each other to go first, each thinking that 'somebody might drop an axe on him.' They enjoyed the loft because it was 'cooler' up there than it was outdoors. The District Attorney was inhospitable toward these fairy-tales.

'The barn loft was a nice, comfortable, cool place?'

'Yes, sir.'

They had approached the Borden house 'fooling along,' and they were asked what that meant.

'He was pushing me off the sidewalk and I was pushing him off.'

Ah, 'me and Brownie,' the rest of the folk who were in the New Bedford Court House, that day, are either dead, or else they are old, old people. But you are not too old to recall with delight the day you had a trip over from Fall River, and a free ride on the train, chummed with the police, and for a while stood with the fierce light of fame beating upon you, the reporters taking down your words, to be printed that evening in all the papers. What mattered it to you if Truth blushed and turned aside while you spoke?

Joseph Lemay from Steep Brook, led forward the murderer of melodrama. On August 16 (twelve days after the crime), on a farm four miles from the city, he was in a deep wood, a savage place, holy and enchanted. Suddenly he heard a voice thrice repeating the words:

'Poor Mrs Borden!'

He looked over a wall and saw a man sitting on the ground. The man picked up a hatchet and shook it at him. Then he—the man with the hatchet—leaped over the wall and disappeared; he had spots of blood on his shirt. The Court, however, did not let Mr Lemay entertain the jury with this fable. It was unnecessary; the Court were to do far better for the prisoner than all these romancers combined.

Miss Emma Borden was one of the last witnesses for the defence, and she bore with some composure a long and skilful cross-examination. She was not allowed by the Court to tell about the custom in the family of burning old dresses. She admitted that there had been trouble between her father and

step-mother on one side, and her sister and herself on the other.
She said that it was Miss Lizzie, not herself, who had become
reconciled with the stepmother, and this statement was considered more gallant than veracious.

The prisoner did not testify in her own defence. The jury
were, of course, duly informed that she was within her rights in
refraining from the witness stand, and the justice who delivered
the charge gave a long explanation of why she might refrain.
They were warned not to consider it as telling against her. But
we, who are not jurymen, may wonder at it. She was not a
foreigner, unable to speak or understand the language, nor a
timid or feeble person, who could not make a calm appearance.
She had not an evil record in her past life, which might be
disclosed in cross-examination, unfairly to prejudice the jury.
The spotlessness of her life was acclaimed by her defenders. She
was known to have made the most unaccountable and contradictory statements about her actions at the time of her father's
murder. Here was her chance to explain them all away. She did
not accept it. Not any of the warm admirers who were soon to
throng around her, or to fill the mails and the wires with
enthusiastic messages of congratulation, ever seemed to notice
the fact. The law, in their opinion, owed her an abject apology
for having suspected her. At the close of the arguments, and
before the charge, the Chief Justice informed her that it was her
privilege to speak in person to the jury. Secure from question,
she arose and repeated the thirteen words in which her counsel
had coached her:

'I am innocent. I leave it to my counsel to speak for me.'

On the twelfth day of the trial Mr Robinson made the final
argument for his client. One gathers from reading it, that, like
his conduct of the case, it was marked by courtesy, and even
more by kindliness, and a manner of transparent honesty. The
advocate was held in respect everywhere in the State. He was
addressing a jury chiefly from the country, or from small towns
and villages, and he never failed to put himself in sympathy
with them. Although he had dwelt in the tents of wickedness
long enough to study at Harvard, to serve in the State Legislature in Boston, and for three years as Governor of the Commonwealth, and although he had even been in Washington for

number of years, as a Member of Congress, he never failed to drop a hint as to what he thought of city folks, or about the general superiority of men who lived on farms.

He described the murders as terrible and revolting beyond all imagination—so terrible that they could only be the work of a maniac, a fiend, a devil. Such acts were morally and physically impossible for the prisoner at the bar. In the days following the murders the police had been criticized for not catching somebody; they had perforce to go out and make an arrest. Once having done this, they easily persuaded themselves of the prisoner's guit. The prosecution had said that she was in the house on that morning. Well, that was a proper place for her to be. Did they wish her to be out on the street? It was where he would wish his daughter to be; at home. He made a strong argument against the contention that she necessarily would have seen the body of her stepmother from the hall at the head of the stairs, or from the stairs while descending. He said that *Bridget*, as well as Miss Borden, had been told by Mrs Borden about the note. Mr Robinson's words were:

'Both Bridget and Lizzie had learned from Mrs Borden that she had had a note. Mrs Borden had told Lizzie. Mrs Borden had told Bridget. She had given Bridget the work to do, washing the windows. She said to her: "I have got a note to go out and see someone that was sick." '

On this point, Professor Wigmore writes:

'The only blot upon an almost perfectly conducted trial was the attempt of the counsel for the defence in argument to show that the information as to the note emanated originally from Bridget, and that the accused merely repeated it. This was decidedly a breach of propriety, because it was not merely an argument suggesting the fair possibility of that explanation, but a distinct assertion that the testimony was of that purport, and therefore, in effect, a false quotation of the testimony. In truth, the accused's statement about the note was her own alone and was one of the points to be explained.'

Mr Robinson suggested that the note might have been a part of the scheme of the murderer to get Mrs Borden out of the house, or otherwise to entrap her. He made light of the supposed discomforts of the Borden home, and of the plain fare served at their table. He held the array of hatchets up to ridicule. In ending he asked for a prompt verdict of ' "not guilty" that she may go back and be Lizzie Andrew Borden of Fall River in that blood-stained and wrecked home, where she has passed her life so many years.'

Mr Knowlton, in closing for the Government, had a much harder problem. He was asking for the conviction of a woman, and a church member, who was supported and buttressed by friends, and by a press which had almost ceased to do anything except palpitate to the sentimentalism of the nosier section of the public. He was a thickset man, with a tenacious manner, easily exagerated by his detractors into the air of the inquisitor or the tyrant.

No prosecuting officer in Massachusetts ever had a less enviable task than his; none ever carried his work through with more ability or more courageous fulfillment of a public duty. His address was acknowledged, even in the hostile press, as far abler than that of his opponent. Mr Robinson talked down to the whims and prejudices of a country jury; Mr Knowlton talked straight to citizens whom he assumed had an eye to their duty. He argued that neither church membership nor the fact of being a woman were proof against guilt.

'With all sympathy for the woman, in which, believe me, I share with you; with all distrust of any evidence until it is brought home to your convictions, in which you will let me share with you, and all good and true men; with due regard, if you please, to the consequences of your action, yet let me remind you that you stand not only to deliver that woman but to deliver the community. It was a crime which may well challenge your most sober and sacred attention. That aged man, that aged woman, had gone by the noonday of their lives. They had borne the burden and heat of the day. They had accumulated a competency which they felt would carry them through the waning years of their lives, and hand in hand they expected to go down to the sunset of their days in quiet and happiness. But for that crime they would be enjoying the air of this day. But for that assassin, many years of their life, like yours, I hope, sir, would have been before them, when the cares of life are past, when the anxieties of their daily advocations had ceased to trouble them, and together they would have gone down the hill of life, serene in an old age which was happy because the happiness had been earned by a life of fidelity and toil.

'Over those bodies we stand, Mr Foreman. We sometimes forget the past. Over those bodies we stand, and we say to ourselves, is it possible that this crime cannot be discovered? You are standing as has been suggested, in the presence of death itself. It is not only what comes hereafter, but it is the double death that comes before. There is a place, it is the chamber of death, where all these personal animosities, passions, and prejudices, have no room, where all matters of sentiment are aside, where nothing but the truth, the naked truth, finds room and lodgment. In that spirit I adjure you to enter upon the trial of this case. It is the most solemn duty of your lives.'

Illustrations of circumstantial evidence have often been given in Court, from Thoreau's playful remark about a trout in the milk, to the more familiar one of footprints. Perhaps it has seldom been more effectively presented than in Mr Knowlton's speech:

'What is called sometimes circumstantial evidence is nothing in the world but that presentation of circumstances—it may be one or fifty—there isn't any chain about it—the word chain is a misnomer as applied to it; it is the presentation of circumstances from which one is irresistibly driven to the conclusion that crime has been committed. Talk about a chain of circumstances! When that solitary man had lived on his island for twenty years and believed that he was the only human being there, and that the cannibals and savages that lived around him had not found him, nor had not come to his island, he walked out one day on the beach, and there he saw the fresh print in the sand of a naked foot. He had no lawyer to tell him that that was nothing but a circumstance. He had no distinguished counsel to urge upon his fears that there was no chain about that thing which led him to a conclusion. His heart beat fast; his knees shook beneath him, he fell to the ground in fright, because Robinson Crusoe knew when he saw that circumstance that a man had been there that was not himself. It was *circumstantial evidence;* it was nothing but *circumstantial evidence*, but it satisfied *him*.'

The District Attorney emphasized the pre-decease of Mrs Borden as the key to the case, since the murderer of Mr Borden was also the murderer of Mrs Borden. No outsider could have planned it, nor lurked about the house to execute it. Mrs

Borden, he said, had no outside enemies. These men with a grudge against her husband had no grudge against her. He touched upon Mrs Gifford's testimony, and upon the prisoner's promptness in saying to the officer: 'She is not my mother.' He refused to withdraw, but re-affirmed Mr Moody's statement that the story about the note was a lie.

'No note came; no note was written; nobody brought a note; nobody was sick. . . . I will stake the case on your belief or disbelief in the truth or falsity of that proposition.'

He disputed Mr Robinson's claim that Bridget said she had heard about the note from Mrs Borden. Mr Knowlton met the argument that the prisoner had no quarrel with her father by asserting that when Mrs Borden had been killed, it became apparent to her that she must kill Mr Borden too, in order to save herself from his accusation. Her father was the one person who would be in no doubt who was guilty, as he knew who hated the stepmother. The prosecutor dwelt upon the absurdity of the stay in the barn loft on so hot a day. The defence, he said, could introduce evidence about dogs upsetting ash-barrels, why did they not explain what screen needed repair, and why did they not produce the fish-line for which sinkers were required? The prisoner's coolness was touched upon; she did not rush out of the house, nor send for police; she sent only for her friends; and public knowledge of the murders came by accident. On the difficulty of the blood stains upon her clothing, he reasoned that she had ample opportunity to remove the stains of the first murder. As for the second, he ackowledged the difficulty of the question.

'I cannot answer it. You cannot answer it.'

He did draw attention, however, to the roll of paper seen in the stove, which might have been used for protection; and to the murdered man's coat, not hanging on a hook, but folded at the head of the couch where he lay. That also might have been used as a shield. The question about the dresses was debated at great length by both counsel. The prosecution contended that, at all events, the one produced by the prisoner was not the one worn on that morning. It was silk; an unlikely material for morning housework.

The charge to the jury was given by Mr Justice Dewey. It

Lizzie Borden (left) and sister Emma at the trial.

became the subject of a great amount of discussion, and the mildest comment is that it was extremely favorable to the prisoner. Mr Howard, the newspaper correspondent, and by this time one of the warmest of Miss Borden's sympathizers, called it 'a plea for the innocent,' a description which could hardly have been enjoyed by the learned and supposedly impartial judge who delivered it.

At twenty-four minutes past three, on the afternoon of June 20, the thirteenth day of the trial, the jury went out. They stayed a little over an hour, or until about half-past four. At that time, they came in with the verdict.

'Not guilty.'

The *Boston Journal*, which was favorable to Miss Borden, said that two ballots were taken and that on the first ballot one juror voted for conviction. It is usually said, however, that they were agreed from the start, and that they stayed out an hour only to avoid suspicion of not having considered the Government's case.

The familiar scene was enacted—cheers, tears, congratulations; hand-shakings and thanks for each of the jurymen—all a matter of course as long ago as when Mark Twain and C.D. Warner wrote the court scene in *The Gilded Age*. Mr Howard had a few words of felicitation for the heroine, and received her thanks, as he modestly records in both his papers. It was a privilege to shake her hand. Mrs Livermore and Mrs Fessenden were in raptures; they wired congratulations, and spoke of the District Attorney and other officers of the Government in terms of severe condemnation. The impression given by the newspapers is that it was a popular outcome. The *Boston Journal* said that the verdict 'saves from deadly peril and vindicates from cruel suspicion a true, modest, and upright woman.' The same paper had published a poll of citizens of New England as to whether the case were 'proven' or 'not proven.' Persons were consulted in many of the larger towns, and there was a strong majority of 'not proven.'

The *Boston Globe* agreed with the verdict; The *Boston Herald* was neutral, and said that the evidence was insufficient. The *Boston Post* criticized the Government. The *Springfield Republican*, which in the early days of the case had taken a severe line with the police, was less outspoken, and intimated that many persons would still believe her guilty. Another paper of more than ordinary merit, the *Providence Journal*, said that many would find the verdict unsatisfactory. The *Fall River Globe*, which firmly supported the police and the case of the Government (and never ceased to do so) suggested that there were many in Fall River who would not agree with the jury—a sound prediction, and one which has not been falsified.

But if the press of New England were not absolutely unanimous in throwing their hats into the air, and cheering for the defendant, the newspapers of New York had no such hesitation. The *New York Herald* said: 'It will be the verdict of the great public.' The *Herald* held a poll of lawyers all over the country, and these almost unanimously voted the case of the State as 'not proven,' although here and there a lawyer said that he believed in the defendant's guilt, but did not expect a conviction. The *World* said: 'No other verdict could have been expected'; it had protested against the indictment; the trial was merely an instance of 'police blundering,' and in the meanwhile the real culprit had escaped. The *Tribune* remarked that: 'The New Bedford jury have done what they could to restore Lizzie Borden to her rightful place in a world of hope and happiness.' The advantage was all with the State in the final arguments; Knowlton's speech was much superior to Robinson's. 'We have no hesitation in pronouncing this a righteous verdict.' The cynical will say that it is a Scotch verdict of 'not proven,' but the *Tribune* cried out against such injustice.

It remained for the usually sober *New York Times* to reach the heights of ecstasy. The verdict, according to that paper, was 'a certain relief to every rightminded man and woman.' The *Times* spoke of 'this unfortunate and cruelly persecuted woman. . . .' 'There was never any serious reason to suppose that she was guilty.' The result was 'a condemnation of the police authorities of Fall River and of the legal officers who secured the indictment and have conducted the trial.' It had been 'a shame to Massachusetts.' The article, filling half a column on the editorial page, varies from severity towards the law officers, to touching sympathy for Miss Borden; it condemns the conduct of the former as 'outrageous'; they were 'guilty of a barbarous wrong to an innocent woman and a gross injury to the community.' It is a misfortune that she has not legal recourse against them and a means of bringing them to account. 'Her acquittal is only a partial atonement for the wrong that she has suffered.' The police force of Fall River is denounced as the 'usual inept and stupid and muddle-headed sort.' If the writer for the *Times* had never read a word of evidence in the case, and had turned for his information to an especially lachrymose sob-sister, who, like Miss Borden's friends in Court, held their hands over their ears when anything was uttered against her, this article might be explained.

It is not true that, on the case as it was presented to the jury, a verdict of 'guilty' was to be expected. Few lawyers have been willing to assert that the result was against the weight of evidence. The *New York Recorder*, for which Mr Howard wrote his letters, tried the case in its columns more frankly than any of the other papers, and actually organized a 'special jury' of more or less distinguished citizens, whose pictures were printed every day. They were furnished verbatim reports of each day's proceedings, and on the last day of all were asked to vote 'proven' or 'not proven.' This 'jury' included the Rev Dr Edward Everett Hale, William Sulzer, Samuel Gompers, George Fred Williams, DeLancey Nicoll, Lucy Stone, and Albert A. Pope, and these with the other five, all voted 'not proven.'

After the newspaper comments, it is instructive to read a few passages from two articles on the case both written by lawyers, who were, moreover, conversant with all the evidence. They are the only serious discussions which I have seen. Professor Wigmore, writing in the *American Law Review* for November, 1893, said:

'It is difficult to see how the assailant could have avoided receiving blood-marks during the assaults; it is also difficult to understand what arrangements of implements and clothing, and what combinations of opportunity, suffered to allow the accused, if she was the assailant, to remove the traces upon weapon and clothes after each assault. But, first, these are difficulties of ignorance; in other words, there is no proved fact which is inconsistent with the thing being so; we merely cannot find traces of the exact *modus operandi*; second, this difficulty is equally as great for any other person than the accused, and we may say greater; it is a difficulty that cannot change the balance of conviction. On the other hand, the conduct of the accused after the killing was such that no conceivable hypothesis except that of guilt, will explain the inconsistencies and improbabilities that were asserted by her. The statements about the purpose of the barn visit, and about the discovery of the father's death, are frightfully inconsistent; while the story of the note requires for its truth a combination of circumstances almost inconceivable. We may add to this the inevitable query, Why did the accused not take the stand to explain these things? Of course, it was her legal right to remain silent; but the rule against self-crimination is not one of logic or of relevancy; it is a rule of policy and fairness, based on broad considerations of average results desirable in the long run. It cannot prevent us as logical beings, from drawing our inferences; and if we weigh in this case the confounding inconsistencies and improbabilities of these statements and then place with these the opportunity and the refusal to explain them, we cannot help feeling that she failed to explain them because she could not; and one side of the balance sinks heavily.

This is not saying that the evidence justified a conviction. . . .'

On the rulings of the Court, Mr Wigmore almost invariably disagrees.

'It may be suggested . . . with all deference, that . . . most of what was excluded seems admissible.'

On the prussic acid evidence the Court decided that the evidence did not come up to the offer.

'As for the authorities . . . the clear result is for the admission of the evidence.'

On the question of admitting the inquest statement, Mr Wigmore adopts Mr Moody's argument; that there was no doubt that Mr Jennings informed his client of her rights, 'and that he allowed her to go on the stand because he deliberately concluded that it was the best policy for her, by so doing, to avoid all appearance of concealment or guilt. And yet the ruling of the Court allowed them to blow hot and cold—to go on the stand when there was something to gain and to remain silent when the testimony proved dangerous to use.'

The Court ruled against the defence when it proposed to prove the family custom of burning old dresses, and this, Mr Wigmore believes, would have over-turned the verdict if it had resulted in a conviction. He further said that the charge that the police showed a spirit of persecution was 'an unfounded accusation.'

Judge Charles G. Davis of Plymouth, wrote to the *Boston Advertiser*, letters afterwards published as 'The Conduct of the

Law in the Borden Case.' They contain the severest criticisms
of the rulings by the Court, and leave no manner of doubt that
the author thought that these decisions led to a grave error. The
ruling about the poison 'was received with almost universal
surprise by the bar.' On that which excluded the inquest
testimony he remarks:

'It is difficult to see how Miss Borden was under arrest when
she was not under arrest.'

Judge Davis's analysis of the evidence is an extremely interesting consideration of the laws of chance and of averages to
show the improbability or impossibility of the murders having
been committed by a person from outside the house.

'It is a rule of law that the possession of property recently
stolen and unaccounted for is sufficient for conviction . . . But
the same law . . . applies to capital crimes. Here was a person
who had in possession the bodies of two victims robbed of the
precious jewels of their lives. Does anybody think that if this
evidence had been applied to a case of robbery, or of mere
property, the law administered or the verdict would have been
the same?'

In the charge of the Court, writes Judge Davis, the justice
went beyond his legitimate function with respect to matters of
fact. On the charge and on the rulings, Judge Davis says in his
second letter:

'It was not the prisoner, but the Commonwealth which did
not have a fair trial.' Was Mr Justice Dewey's 'the tone of a
judge or of an advocate?' Here the author referred to such
words in the charge as this: 'Is it reasonable and credible that
she could have killed Mrs Borden at or about the time claimed
by the Government . . .?'

It is impracticable to quote more, but I am led to believe,
from conversations with lawyers, that the Superior Court of
Massachusetts has never been subjected to such criticism as
that resulting from the conduct of its justices in the Borden
case. And in this criticis, there was no hint or intimation of
corruption, but of a mental infirmity or bias resulting from an
unwillingness to believe that a woman could murder her father.

The sense of outrage felt by a considerable portion of the
community becomes apparent in the extraordinary series of

articles published annually, for many years, in the *Fall River Globe*. These were written by the city editor, the late James D. O'Neil. They always appeared about August 4, the anniversary of the murders, and were very pointed, to say the least. Thus, on August 4, 1904, an article one and a half columns long is headed: 'A Dozen Years Since the Bordens Were Brutally Butchered. Perhaps Murderers or Murderess May Be in the City. Who Can Tell?' It says that the police were abused, although they made up their minds correctly within forty-eight hours 'as to the dastard.' It jeers at the story of the 'Wild Eyed Man,' and the Portuguese farm laborer, and the man with the grudge against Andrew Borden, 'and Lubin-sky,' 'and me and Brownie,' 'and the sinkers in the barn loft and all the rest of the rot and nonsense that ran riot through the disordered imagination of a prejudiced and gullible public . . . Who knows, even now, that the vile minded murderer, may not be at large in the community, walking, stalking or driving obout in carriage or car . . .? Perhaps the good people of Fall River may be daily meeting him—or her—in hall, store, or railroad train . . .' The 'man—or woman' 'he—or she' 'him—or her' *motif* recurs throughout.

On August 4, 1905, a less indignant article had the caption: 'Great Wrong is Righted after 13 Years of Misrepresentation. No Murders were Committed On August 4, 1892. Despite the Belief that Andrew and Abby Borden Died in that Manner.' There follow nearly two columns of sarcasm, ending:

> There were No Borden Murders!
> Both the Victims of 13 Years Ago
> Died as the Result of Excessive Heat!

This persecution of the 'unfortunate girl' was probably resented by the Borden partisans in Fall River, but for some years nothing was done about it. It is one of the oddities of the case that once the acquittal was secured the Borden party began to melt and disintegrate. Finally, however, influential persons were induced to bring to bear a pressure which stopped the articles.

There is a persistent belief that the case has figured in fiction, and that more than one novelist has drawn upon it for a plot.

There is a noticeable fact about real crimes when they are put
into novels or stories; they appear in the fictitious form so
altered as to be almost unrecognizable. The writer has merely
borrowed a hint, if anything, from the supposed source. The
tale most frequently mentioned as based upon the Fall River
murders is Miss Mary Wilkins's story, 'The Long Arm,' but it
really contains hardly as much of the case as an analytical
chemist would call a 'trace.' A woman is accused of killing
somebody, but she is, of course, triumphantly innocent. Much
nearer to the real thing are a few sentences in *The Summit House
Mystery, or The Earthly Purgatory*, by Lily Dougall (1905). The
author, a native of Canada, but living in England, had
apparently slight acquaintance with the United States. She had
heard something about the Borden case. The scene of her story
is Georgia, and there is simply a brief reference to 'Mr Claxton
and his second wife' who were 'suddenly killed.' It appeared
that 'a large body of circumstantial evidence proved that
Hermione,' his daughter, 'was alone in the house with them.'
Hermione, needless to say, is quite innocent.

Miss Borden's name appeared again in the newspapers in
February 1897, about three and a half years after the acquittal.
On the 16th and 17th of that month, articles were printed in the
Providence Journal, the first being headed:

'Lizzie Borden Again. A Warrant for her Arrest issued from a
local Court. Two Paintings Missed from Tilden Thurber Co.'s
Store. Said to Have Been Traced to Miss Borden's Home in
Fall River.'

In the warrant, according to the second article, she was
charged with larceny of a painting on porcelain, called 'Love's
Dream.' 'It is known,' said the *Journal*, 'that the warrant was
issued. It was never served and it is said that the two paintings
are still in the possession of Miss Lizzie Borden.' The incident
attracted much attention in Fall River. The Tilden-Thurber
Corporation, a firm of silversmiths and jewelers in Providence,
write (1924):

'We have no records regarding the Lizzie Borden case but
our recollection of the situation is that the warrant for arrest
was based on shoplifting episodes which were finally adjusted.'

At a later date, Miss Nance O'Neil, the distinguished actress, was involved in financial difficulties and litigation with her managers and creditors. These took the form of hearings in the equity session at the Court in Boston. Miss Borden emerged from her retirement and became an almost daily spectator at the trial. Since she can hardly have been amused by the legal proceedings, it is supposed that the attraction lay in the interest she felt for Miss O'Neil as an artist, for the latter was a tragedienne of great ability.

The closing appeal in Mr Robinson's final address to the jury has not been fulfilled with precision. He asked that she might go back 'and be Lizzie Andrew Borden of Fall River' in her old home. In later years Miss Borden lived about a mile and a half from her old home, and her name appeared in the telephone director as Lizbeth A. Borden. She was not often seen in public. Her house was spacious enough for a family of ten; a gray building in modified Queen Anne type of architecture, by no means in bad taste. A touch of romance appeared in the name *Maplecroft*, in raised letters on one of the stone steps. The street was pleasant, and the houses were fairly large, with lawns and gardens. The window shades of *Maplecroft* were methodically drawn down to the middle-sash, while white curtains screened the panes. There was a large glass sun-porch, also well-curtained. The big garage, at the rear of the lawn, had an extravagant amount of plate glass set in its doors and windows. The garden accessories included a sundial on the lawn, while thoughtfulness for small creatures was manifested in a green bird-house in one of the trees. It was a generous bird-house; no mere box for a pair of wrens, but one capable of sheltering families of bluebirds, if they cared for it.

Miss Emma Borden did not remain long with her sister. They separated when the elder lady went first to Fairhaven—where she had been on that famous 4th of August—and then elsewhere, to live. On May 11, 1923, the newspapers recorded that Miss Lizzie Borden was engaged in litigation with her sister. There was a disagreement between them about the sale of the A.J. Borden building on South Main Street, owned jointly by the two. The younger desired to sell her share, but the elder objected. Hence a petition in probate, filed by Miss Lizzie, or Lizbeth, seeking an equal distribution of the property.

Miss Lizzie Borden died in Fall River on June 1, 1927; Miss Emma, in New Market, N.H., June 10, 1927. Few others of the participants in the trial survive. When Mr Jennings died, in 1923, there were no others of the justices or the counsel living. Perhaps, on a farm in Seekonk, or another of those little villages, lingers some member of the jury which for thirteen days endured all that examination of expert, and other, witnesses; and then when they had received the thanks of the lady they had freed, stayed not a moment, but (to the great delight of Julian Ralph) strode right across the market-place to the nearest hotel-bar, and (still acting in unison) drowned the dreadful thirst which had so long accumulated. I have read of one jury—I am not sure if it was this one—who were deprived, by some severe sheriff, of the consolation of tobacco, during their long confinement. Perhaps the idea was that by making men unhappy you enable them to arrive at the truth.

Those who remember the murders in 1892, and the trial in 1893, sometimes enjoy raking up the old embers, and recalling the days when families bickered about the case over the dinner table; when husbands and wives parted in wrath after breakfast, and met again at evening to take up the controversy once more. The fact that the plot of 'Edwin Drood' is never to be solved, makes the book exasperating to some readers, but highly fascinating to others.

There are, in the Borden mystery, a dozen unanswered questions to ponder. What was the meaning of the laugh from the head of the stairs, heard by Bridget Sullivan? What is the explanation of the burglary, in 1891? What caused the mysterious illness in the family? Assuming the theory of an assassin from outside, where did he go? What did he do with the weapon? What was his motive? Why did he kill Mrs Borden? Adopting the opinion of the prosecution, how could the departure of Bridget, to her own room, be counted upon? Or the time of Mr Morse's return? What was the truth about the poison story? Could anybody have made this attempt so openly? (The answer is that such things have often been done.) Were there any grounds for the suspicions entertained against two men, and at least one other woman, all of whom testified at the trial? (Suspicions, that is, of complicity.) Will the whole truth ever come out?

AFTERWORD

Will it, indeed? Edmund Pearson's piece on the Borden case was written in 1924, and for nearly 40 years it was regarded as more or less the last word on the subject. Pearson's status as a crime-writer was (and is) very high, and if he suggested that Lizzie Borden was guilty, most people went along with that. Lizzie was even portrayed in a stage musical, brandishing a hatchet and doing a spirited can-can around the courtroom while the jury sang 'Oh you can't chop your poppa up in Massachusetts'; the song became quite a hit in the 1950s. How guilty can you get?

Then in 1971 a journalist called Edward Radin launched a scathing attack not only on Pearson's views but on his very integrity as a writer; he 'presented such a biased version of the case that it might be considered a literary hoax', said Radin, and in his own book Lizzie Borden, the Untold Story *he set out to restore the balance, naming as the murderer the parlourmaid Bridget Sullivan. Radin did a splendid job in his re-presentation of the material, analyzing events, drawing up detailed timetables and bringing out inconsistencies that Pearson certainly did gloss over. He makes out quite a convincing case for Bridget as the murderer too, failing only to suggest a plausible motive for such drastic crimes from a mere maid. Nonetheless, many readers were at least half-persuaded by his arguments, and the criminological world was split into Pearson v. Radin factions. By this time Pearson himself was dead, but his widow sprang to his defense, and for some time the controversy raged on in the press. No doubt it sold a lot of books as well.*

Whether or not you believed Bridget to be guilty, the effect of all this was certainly to make you think again about Lizzie's role in the murders, and the case seemed incapable of resolution until the publication of yet another book, Victoria Lincoln's A Private Disgrace *(1967), which at last shed some new light on the matter. The author, a native of Fall River, brought both local knowledge and a sharp female insight to the case, and she offered a totally new and very plausible explanation: Lizzie suffered from periodic bouts of psychomotor epilepsy, a rare condition, knowledge of which was suppressed even within her family, but which could have produced short spells of temporary, violent insanity, with little recall afterwards. The book cannot be recommended too highly to anyone interested in the Borden case.*

And there the matter rests at present, with the ball firmly back in Lizzie's court. Has the whole truth now come out? It seems unlikely, at least as far as crime-writers are concerned.

JULIAN SYMONS

The Death of
Sir Harry Oakes

JULIAN SYMONS

The Death of Sir Harry Oakes

There was nothing unusual about the last day in the life of the Canadian millionaire, Sir Harry Oakes. He planted trees at Westbourne, his home near the Bahamas Country Club in Nassau. In the afternoon he played tennis at the Club with his friend Harold Christie, a local estate agent and a member of the Governor's Executive Council.

That evening there was a small dinner party at Westbourne, with Christie and two other friends of Oakes' as guests. The party broke up early but Christie stayed the night, as he often did. He told Sir Harry good night, went to his own room, which was separated from Sir Harry's by a bedroom and a bathroom, undressed, crawled under the mosquito net and went to sleep.

Christie woke after daybreak. He went to the screen door of Sir Harry's room on the northern porch and called 'Hi, Harry', but got no reply. He then went into the bedroom, and there saw the millionaire's body. Oakes was lying on the bed, his body burned in several places. Fire was still smouldering in the mattress. The mosquito net was burned. There were burns on the carpet and on the wardrobe, and a fine soot was lying about the room. Christie did not notice all these things at once, but he saw enough to call a doctor and the police. Sir Harry Oakes was dead. At some time during the night he had been attacked, and his skull fractured by a hard, blunt instrument. Death was caused by this fracture, by a brain haemorrhage, and by shock.

Sir Harry's sudden and violent death shocked the whole island. The Duke of Windsor, who was Governor-General, cancelled all his appointments so that he could take a hand in the enquiry. He telephone to Miami, and the Florida police arranged to fly out two experts at once. Sir Harry Oakes died on

275

the night of 7th July, 1943, and on the following day Captain
E.W. Melchen, homicide investigator, and Captain James O
Barker, fingerprint and identification expert, arrived. Sir Harry's body had been taken by plane to the United States for
burial. Now the plane was recalled for an autopsy. Melchen
and Barker moved swiftly. Three days after the death Sir
Harry's son-in-law, Marie Alfred Fouqueraux de Marigny,
was charged with murder.

So opened one of the most curious crime puzzles of this
century, a puzzle still unsolved. It is remarkable partly for the
characters of the participants, and partly because 'expert
evidence' of identification through fingerprints has seldom, if
ever, been so utterly destroyed in cross-examination.

Let us look at the people and their backgrounds. Sir Harry
Oakes was a remarkable man by the standards of any period.
He had tramped Canada in youth as a poor prospector. Kicked
out by a railway guard when he hitched a lift in a car travelling
north to Northern Ontario, he found the second richest gold-
field in the world on Lake Shore, one reputed to bring him an
income of a million pounds a year.

Oakes looked for the railway guard and had him pensioned.
His generosity was multifold, his influence international. He
gave £90,000 towards the rebuilding of St George's Hospital.
He had homes in Florida and Maine, a house in Kensington
Palace Gardens with separate flats for each of his five children
by the Australian girl he had married, an estate of 850 acres in
Sussex. When he decided to settle in the Bahamas, he financed
Bahamas Airways for inter-island communication, built Oakes
Airfield, and stocked a 1,000 acre sheep farm with sheep
specially imported from Cuba. In the early days of the war he
had made a gift of £5,000 to the Ministry of Aircraft Production
for a fighter plane, and more recently had given £10,000 to
provide two Spitfires, named Sir Harry and Lady Oakes.

The multi-millionaire, now in his late sixties, was a man of
simple and unpretentious tastes. In the Bahamas he wore often
the slouch hat, khaki shirt, corduroy breeches and top boots of a
prospector. Generous in the ordinary affairs of life, and indulgent to his children, he was not a man who took kindly to
having his wishes thwarted. He made no secret of his dis-

Top left: Sir Harry Oakes. Centre: Alfred de Marigny. Top right: Nancy Oakes de Marigny. Below: Sir Harry's body on the bed.

approval when, in 1942, his daughter Nancy secretly married Alfred de Marigny, two days after her eighteenth birthday. The marriage took place in New York, just after Nancy had left school. Sir Harry and his wife learned of it on the evening after the wedding. It is hardly surprising that they were displeased, and what they knew of the man generally called Count Alfred de Marigny cannot have reassured them.

He was not, as his name implied, a French nobleman, nor was his name Marigny. He had been born in Mauritius, and although his mother's name was de Marigny, his father's was merely Alfred Fouqueraux. The Count had blended the names and added the title, although his friends called him Freddie. He had come to the Bahamas in 1937 with his first wife, was active in yachting circles, bought and sold estates. He was a fast, fluent talker, a playboy devoted to all kinds of sport, lavishly hospitable. Where his money came from—whether, indeed, he had any money—was not known. In fact, he was in receipt of £100 a month from his first wife.

From the beginning Sir Harry disliked his son-in-law, and an incident a few months after the marriage widened the estrangement. Nancy became very ill with typhoid while travelling with her husband in Mexico, and her state of health on recovering from this was so bad that an operation was necessary to terminate her pregnancy. Marigny came into hospital at the same time for a tonsil operation, and occupied the room next to his wife's. Sir Harry told him to get out of this room, or he would kick him out. Marigny left the hospital. His feelings were not openly expressed at the time, but may be imagined.

On 10th February, Marigny went to see a lawyer named Foskett, who acted for the Oakes family, and asked Foskett to do his best to establish good relations with Sir Harry. He was a gentleman, Marigny said, and he was not treated as one. Foskett said that he disapproved of the way in which Marigny had pursued Nancy in New York, and had married her without the knowledge of her parents. He refused to give any help. Five days later Foskett prepared a new will for Sir Harry by which, although the body of the estate was to be divided among the five children, none of them obtained a share until they reached the age of thirty.

In the following month there was a furious scene. Sir Harry went to Marigny's house in Nassau where his eldest son, sixteen-year-old Sydney Oakes, was staying the night. He made Sydney get up, dress and leave. He was like a madman, said the foreman of Sir Harry's Nassau estate, as he called Marigny a sex maniac, said that he had better not write any more letters to Lady Oakes, and threatened to horsewhip him if he did not leave the Oakes family alone. After this Nancy wrote a letter in which she said that the Marignys were cutting themselves off from the Oakes family until they had confidence in Alfred.

So much for the background. How had Marigny spent the evening of 7th July? With his wife Nancy away in the United States, Marigny, in the company of his friend and fellow Mauritian the Marquis Georges de Visdelou Guimbeau, had entertained the wives of two R.A.F. officers to dinner. Mrs Dorothy Clark and Mrs Jean Ainslie testified that Marigny drove them home at 1:30 in the morning. This, however, did not provide him with an alibi, since the time of death was placed between half past two and five o'clock. Marigny said that he had gone straight home, and his friend the Marquis de Visdelou was prepared to support that statement.

A neighbour had seen a light on in Marigny's room between 12.30 and 4 a.m. and on the vital night. On the following morning, very early, he had come in to the local police station, with bulging mouth and wild eyes, to make some routine enquiry about a car.

Slowly the prosecution accumulated evidence. Fingerprint expert Barker found the print of Marigny's little finger on a screen drawn across Oakes's bed. He also carried out a heat test and found that Marigny's beard, and the hair on his hand, forearm and head all showed signs of scorching under a microscope.

Homicide investigator Melchen found smudge marks in the hall. He reconstructed the case to show that Sir Harry had staggered into the hall, pyjamas aflame, had gripped the stair railing and tottered against the wall. Then he had been dragged back to his room, and the bed set on fire.

Melchen said Marigny had told him: 'Oakes hated me for

marrying his daughter, Nancy. I hated him because he was a stupid old fool who could not be reasoned with.'

The prosecution suggested that Marigny, tired of attempting to reason with Sir Harry, had planned and executed his murder, and then attempted to burn the body. The strong points of their case were the expert evidence relating to finger-prints and scorched hair. It was essential to the prosecution to prove these beyond question in court.

Into the small court room at Nassau people crowded every day to watch the case, bringing sandwiches and ice cream sodas, often sitting two to a seat. The preliminary investigation in the Magistrates' Court had opened a week after Marigny's arrest. It was adjourned more than once, dragged on through August. The trial itself finally opened on 18th October in the Supreme Court, before Sir Oscar Daly, Chief Justice of the Bahamas. The Attorney-General, the Honourable Eric Halli-nan, led for the Crown, with one of the colony's leading lawyers, the Honourable A.F. Adderley, to assist him. The Honourable Godfrey Higgs led for the defence.

The trial lasted more than three weeks, with preliminary challenging for many jurors by both sides, and several others providing medical certificates to say that they were unfit to serve. During those three weeks the prosecution saw the case steadily slipping away from them, because of the inefficiency of many of the police officials who worked on it.

Consider that vivid reconstruction of the case made by Captain Melchen, when he said that Sir Harry had staggered into the hall, tottered against the wall and been dragged back to his room. In face of positive medical evidence that Sir Harry never got out of the bed in which he was found, Melchen retracted this evidence. He admitted that no analysis had been made of the material used to light the fire in the bedroom. Certain hand marks on the wall of Sir Harry's room had not been measured.

There followed the curious story of the bloodstained towels. Major Herbert Pemberton, head of the C.I.D. in the colony, had removed a bloodstained towel from Sir Harry's bed. He had also found a towel with what appeared to be bloodstains on it in Christie's bedroom.

While giving evidence in the Magistrates' Court Pemberton had forgotten all about these towels, and indeed denied seeing them. He was tired, he explained, and didn't recollect the matter. As a matter of fact the towel in Sir Harry's room had been in his possession for some weeks, and he had forgotten all about it. As for the towel in Christie's bedroom, why, it had just been left there. He had not made a note of finding the towels, Pemberton told an astonished court room, and did not think they were important.

How had bloodstains got on to Christie's towel? The estate agent explained that when he found Sir Harry's body he poured water in his mouth, wet a towel and wiped his face with it. He believed that the towel came from his own bedroom. There were certain bloodstains on the glass door and screen door of Christie's bedroom, and he said that these were probably from his own hands, after he had found Sir Harry.

A strange story was told by Captain Sears, the Assistant Superintendent of Police. Driving in Nassau on the fatal night Captain Sears had seen a station wagon with Christie sitting in the front seat, and somebody else driving. Sears, however, must have been mistaken, for Christie said positively that he did not leave Westbourne on that night.

The severest blow struck at the prosecution came with the evidence of Captain James Barker. It was evidence which at times turned the tragedy into something like a farce. It was also evidence of historical importance about the methods of obtaining fingerprints.

The first step in taking fingerprint evidence is usually to photograph the prints. This fingerprint expert, however, had left his fingerprint camera behind. Perhaps Pemberton might have one? Well, yes, he had, but it was out of commission.

Without bothering to make any further enquiries about cameras or to send for his own camera. Barker proceeded to take prints by 'lifting' them on to Scotch tape. This is a recognized method. When he ran out of tape he 'lifted' them on to rubber, a procedure which has the effect of destroying the original print. Having done this, he forgot all about the print on the screen for ten days when, he said, he examined it and found that it was Marigny's.

Judge Daly called Barker's conduct 'quite incomprehensible', and his forgetfulness was really extraordinary. In court he identified the place on the screen where the print had been found—and it turned out to be the wrong place. He said that certain lines on the screen were not made by him—and they turned out to be marked with his initials. Looking at the lifted print, this expert was unable even to say which way the finger was pointing.

There was worse to come. It was obvious that, for the fingerprint evidence to be effective, Marigny must have had no possible access to the screen before it was fingerprinted. Now, Marigny had been taken upstairs at Westbourne to be interviewed on the day Barker took the prints. Had he gone before or after the work was done? In the Magistrates' Court all the police officers agreed that it was after.

Pemberton said the screen was under constant police guard. Two other police witnesses said that Marigny, on strict instructions, had not gone upstairs in the morning, while the screen was being finger-rinted. Melchen confirmed that he had taken Marigny upstairs between 3 and 4 in the afternoon.

At the trial, however, Mrs Clark and Mrs Ainslie said that they had been summoned to Westbourne that morning, and that Marigny had been taken upstairs between eleven o'clock and noon. Now, quite suddenly, the prosecution evidence on this point collapsed. The police guards admitted that they had been mistaken about the time, and so did Melchen. It was just a mistake, he said.

'What a mistake,' defence counsel commented ironically. 'What a coincidence that you and the constables should make the same mistake.'

In his final speech for the defence Higgs plainly accused these witnesses of perjury. While Melchen was examining Marigny upstairs Barker had come to the door and asked if everything was O.K. The defence suggested that Marigny had been taken upstairs deliberately, to get his print on to the screen.

By the time that Marigny went into the witness box, the incompetence or corruption of the police had made his acquittal almost inevitable. He explained that the burnt hair on his

beard and forearms had been caused when he lit a cigar over a
candle in a hurricane shade. He was a confident witness,
laughing, joking occasionally, winking at his wife.

The jury voted 9 to 3 for acquittal. They unanimously
recommended Marigny's deportation.

Talking to reporters afterwards Marigny told them to keep
out of prison. 'It's a hard life,' he said. 'I could see that I had a
good foreman to guide the jury. By the way, did you notice that
he was the only one who was awake all the time?' Asked if he
would try to solve the mystery he said, 'I'll leave that to Erle
Stanley Gardner.'

Echoes of the case can be heard occasionally through the
years. In 1950 a Finnish seaman said he had been told the name
of the Oakes murderer by an American landscape artist, and a
search was made for a blonde model named Betty Roberts, who
gave evidence in the case. When found, Miss Roberts, now
happily married, proved to have nothing to say. In this same
year Betty Ellen Renner, who came to the Bahamas to investi-
gate the case, was murdered and put into a well. At this time,
also, Marigny was heard of, working as a part-time French
translator in New York. His marriage to Nancy Oakes had
been annulled. In 1953 Barker was shot dead by his son, after a
quarrel. But these are mere sidelights on some of the characters. Neither Erle Stanley Gardner (who was there as a reporter) nor anyone else has ever solved the problem: who killed Sir
Harry Oakes?

Any investigation of the Oakes case is bound to leave one
with the feeling that much less than the whole truth has been
told. But in the welter of contradictory evidence, and the
evasions of police officials (the jury expressed their regret that
no evidence had been obtained from Lieutenant-Colonel
Erskine-Lindop, Commissioner of Bahamas Police, who left to
take up another appointment between the Magistrates' hearing
and the trial), some questions stand out. They are questions
that seem, strangely enough, never to have been asked:

(1) Oakes was killed in his bedroom, as the result of a blow with a heavy
instrument. The night of the murder was stormy, but still, there must have
been considerable noise. Why was it not heard?

(2) Where did the inflammable material come from that was used to set
the fire?

(3) And why, having decided to burn the body, did the murderer make such a bad job of it, when he had apparently all night at his disposal? Was he disturbed? Or was the body-burning an elaborate pretence to lead suspicion away from the real murderer?

There are other questions too, which it is not possible to ask publicly, even fifteen years after Marigny's trial. But the Oakes case is one on which the file is not completely closed. It is possible, at least, that one day an answer will be provided to one of the most remarkable murder mysteries of the twentieth century.

AFTERWORD

Plenty of people have tried to provide the answer, notably James Leasor in his book Who Killed Sir Harry Oakes? *(1983). The argument proposed is a complex one, which is not helped by its quasi-fictional form of presentation, but it goes roughly like this. The Mafia were determined to build and run hotels and casinos on Nassau, and if they were allowed to do so they would return the favour by facilitating the Allied landing in Sicily. The only real opposition to this scheme came from Sir Harry Oakes.*

He therefore had to be 'persuaded', and to this end he was lured onto a yacht where a struggle developed and he was (accidentally?) hit on the head by an engineer, unnamed in the book. In panic, Sir Harry was moved back to his house, soaked with flykiller and set alight. Captain Barker was sent over from Miami to organize a cover-up (hence the messy investigation), the Allies landed safely in Sicily, and Nassau became the gambling-place that everybody except Sir Harry wanted.

Pleasing though this may be, one must add that there is not a shred of evidence for any of it.

Postscript

We should never dismiss a murder as 'unsolved' for, as we have seen, there is always a possibility that new evidence will be found, new explanations suggested, and a solution eventually reached. Admittedly, not much progress has been made in the Starr Faithfull, Elwell and Kiss murders, but that is not to say that it never will. Other cases are far from closed and, as we have seen, there is a real possibility that the Wallace case might yet be solved, while there is still much fruitful speculation about Jack the Ripper, Lizzie Borden and Florence Bravo which, even if it does not bring solutions as such, might at least lead to some sort of consensus about what really happened.

We now know much more—though still not enough—about people who commit crimes like those of Jack the Ripper. In the 1880's the solutions proposed were highly *logical* ones based on clear-cut motives such as revenge: the sort of neat answer that Sherlock Holmes (a contemporary of the Ripper) might have found at the end of one of his cases. But crimes like those have happened more and more frequently in our own century, and they have taught us that the 'motive' is much more likely to be one of psychopathic sexual gratification than anything so obvious as vengeance or monetary gain: the sort of explanation that simply could not have been discussed at the time, and which probably would not have been understood even if it had been. Then, madmen were wild-eyed maniacs. Now we know that a psychopath can live a very normal, anonymous life and still commit atrocities.

In the Bravo and Borden cases too, the most plausible explanations come not from detective-story solutions but from our greater understanding of the sort of sexual and emotional problems that might have prompted these women to do such seemingly uncharacteristic things. In each case the 'motive' for the crimes can only be understood in terms of domestic pressures concerned with money and petty jealousies, but to understand why they should have boiled over into murder is less a matter for strict logic than of understanding the extremes of human personality and behaviour. To view these cases as mere puzzles is condescending and probably misleading. Perhaps if we knew more about the muddled motivation of someone like poor Starr Faithfull we would be able to make much shrewder guesses about the precise manner of her death.

The tragic thing is that none of this helps where help really is needed: to clear the innocent or to help the victims. In both Britain and the USA very little effort is made to increase our understanding of convicted murderers, and what we *have* learned generally proves to be of pathetically little help when the police are actually faced with the task of catching a killer or preventing further murders. Neither is there any very obvious solution. We can only hope that eventually a more enlightened attitude will prevail, and that in time we shall be able to learn something useful from those who violate the rules of behaviour.

Perhaps cases like the ones in this book, particularly when they are analyzed by such excellent writers, can help to increase our understanding a little.

While every effort has been made to trace authors and copyright holders, in a few cases this has proved impossible; the publishers would be glad to hear from any such parties so that these omissions can be rectified in future editions of the book.

Thanks are due to the following for permission to reproduce the photographs and illustrations on the following pages:

Mail Newspapers plc 19 t + b; UPI/Bettmann Newsphotos 36, 110, 162, 277 tl, tc, tr, + b; Popperfoto 52, 78; BBC Hulton Picture Library 99; The Mansell Collection 123, 140; John Topham Picture Library 168, 198 t + b.